CHOMSKY, PROUTY
AND ME

Michael David Morrissey

CONTENTS

PREFACE

This is a collection of the letters I wrote to Noam Chomsky and L. Fletcher Prouty, and a few others, over a period of six years (1989-1995), along with some essays that derive from this correspondence. Obviously, it would be better if I could publish their letters to me as well, as I was able to do with my *Correspondence with Vincent Salandria* (2007), but I cannot do so without their permission. Furthermore, Noam Chomsky and Fletcher Prouty were both prolific writers, and most of what they wrote to me can be found in *Rethinking Camelot* (South End, 1993) and *JFK: The CIA, Vietnam, and the Plot to Assassinate John F. Kennedy (Birch Lane, 1992)*. In the text I refer to my other books, *Looking for the Enemy* (Kindle Direct Publishing 1993-2015) and *The Transparent Conspiracy* (Kindle Direct Publishing, 2010-2015), and to my articles in this book, arranged chronologically by date of publication (or composition, if not previously published) in this form: year.month.day.

There is a lot of redundancy here, which I suppose would make the book unacceptable for a commercial publisher, but for which I do not apologize. The letters to Chomsky are all included as an addendum to *Looking for the Enemy*, as are the letters to Newman and Parenti, but the others (to Prouty and Weisberg) are published here for the first time. Since this is meant as a kind of memoir, I wanted all the letters to appear together and in chronological order to show how my ideas changed over time and in interaction with my interlocutors. The redundancy itself shows how preoccupied I was with certain issues — primarily the question of whether President Kennedy was assassinated because he had decided to withdraw from Vietnam. Opinion is still divided on this question, and it is still important. Chomsky is certainly the primary advocate of one point of view, and I know of no one who has challenged him on it to the extent that I have. Nor have any of my arguments, as far as I know, found their way into any of the published literature, and I think they deserve the full (even if repetitious!) exposition presented here.

1989.04 REVIEW OF THE MEN WHO KILLED KENNEDY

[*The Men Who Killed Kennedy* is a British (ITV) documentary film directed by Nigel Turner. I wrote this shortly after I interviewed Turner in London in March 1989. Turner's film was finally broadcast in the US in September 1991 on A&E cable, just a couple of months before Stone's JFK opened. I sent a copy of this review to Noam Chomsky, L. Fletcher Prouty, and Oliver Stone. All three replied. Stone said he was working on three films and could not pursue the matter. Chomsky's and Prouty's replies began a correspondence with both that lasted almost six years.]

In view of the lukewarm reception given to several television documentaries last November on the assassination of President Kennedy, it is astonishing that the best film on the subject has not been shown in the United States. *The Men Who Killed Kennedy*, produced by Nigel Turner for British Central Independent Television, was broadcast in England on October 25, 1988, and subsequently in thirty other countries by Christmas–but not in the United States.

What this film, nominated for best documentary by the British Association of Film and Television Arts, reveals about the Kennedy assassination and its aftermath is so spectacular that it is unconscionable to ignore it. It presents key evidence and testimony made public for the first time in 25 years, including an eyewitness who was standing on the grassy knoll, probably a few feet away from the gunman who fired the fatal head shot. The most spectacular revelation, based on the research of American writer Steve Rivele, is nothing less than the names of the probable gunmen (none of whom was Lee Harvey Oswald).

These findings are the result of years of painstaking research, presented soberly and without melodrama. If it smacks of sensationalism, it is only because anything hinting at the truth in this case must sound sensational. If the government has colluded with the press for over 25 years in propagating a fictitious account of what happened in Dallas, which unfortunately seems to be the case, how could the truth sound anything other than sensational?

If the press has not been participating in the cover-up, why do almost all reports on the subject continue to flout the evidence, referring disparagingly to those who do not accept the now thoroughly discredited Warren Commission Report as "conspiratorialists"? The evidence that the assassination was a conspiracy is overwhelming, and has been in for a long time. The majority of the American people believed it in 1966, according to a Louis Harris poll of that year, and even the House Assassinations Committee was finally forced to conclude in 1979 that there had to have been more than one gunman (i.e., a conspiracy).

How is it possible, then, in 1988, for otherwise respectable journalists to mouth such pablum as "the single-bullet theory, though implausible, remains intact" (Walter Goodman, paraphrasing Walter Cronkite, in the *New York Times*, Nov. 15, 1988)? How is it possible that the Abraham Zapruder film of the shooting, which clearly shows Kennedy's head jerked back by a bullet fired from the front, has been kept secret for 25 years, although Time-Life has been in possession of it all this time? How is it possible that Gordon Arnold, the eyewitness on the grassy knoll, who offered to testify years ago, has been totally ignored not only by investigating agencies but also by the press? Above all, why has this superb documentary, which presents this evidence and testimony, and more, for the first time, been denied an American audience?

I talked about this in London with Turner and his associate producer, Susan Winter. The major American networks have seen the film, of course, and it is being shown privately in the U.S. A well-placed friend of Turner's who had seen the film explained the American networks' curious disinterest this way: "Nigel," he said, "you're shaking the leaves on the trees." No one can see this film without being shaken, but Turner's friend was referring to foliage of monstrous proportions. Two witnesses in the film give us an idea of just how large and pernicious a growth we are dealing with:

Dr. Cyril Wecht, forensic pathologist:

> I think it's extremely important for the American people to know that there can be the overthrow of a government, and that there can be a coup d'état, in America, that that in fact did happen through the assassination of President Kennedy.

Col. Fletcher Prouty, Chief of Special Operations of the Joint Chiefs of Staff during Kennedy's presidency:

> I think without any question it's what we called the use of hired gunmen. And this isn't new. In fact, this little manual here, which is called "the assassination manual for Latin America" [*Clandestine Operations Manual for Central America*, a CIA publication] says that, talking about Latin America, 'if possible, professional criminals will be hired to carry out specific, selective "jobs"'–"jobs" in quotes, which means murders. Well, if this manual for Latin America, printed within the last few years, and a government manual, says that, there's

no question but what the application of the same techniques was dated back in Kennedy's time–in fact I know that from my own experience, you know, I was in that business in those days. So, with that knowledge, you begin to realize hired criminals, the way this book says, can be hired by anybody in power with sufficient money to pay them, but, more importantly, with sufficient power to operate the cover-up ever after.

Because you see it's one thing to kill somebody; it's another thing to cover up the fact that you did it or that you hired someone to do it. That's more difficult. So they used the device of the Warren Commission to cover up their hired killers. Now, who would hire the killers? And who has the power to put that Warren Commission report out over the top of the whole story? You see, you're dealing with a very high echelon of power. It doesn't necessarily reside in any government. It doesn't necessarily reside in any single corporate institution. But it seems to reside in a blend of the two. Otherwise, how could you have gotten people like the Chief Justice of the Supreme Court to participate in the cover-up, the police in Dallas to participate in the cover-up, etc.–and the media, all the media, not just one or two newspapers, but none of them will print the story that other than Oswald killed the President with three bullets–something that's absolutely untrue.

It must be remembered that the first hints at Mafia involvement in the assassination came from Europe. French journalists had suggested a Mob conspiracy as early as December, 1963, a suggestion which was reiterated by Thomas Buchanan in the 1964 British edition of his *Who Killed Kennedy?* But as David Scheim points out in *Contract on America: The Mafia Murder of President John F. Kennedy* (sold in England under the title *The Mafia Killed President Kennedy*), the American edition of Buchanan's book was censored to remove all references to organized crime. The fact that Turner's team was able to get witnesses to speak out who had kept silent for 25 years has a lot to do with their being British. Money, at least, was not a factor; no fees were paid for the interviews, and some witnesses had refused lucrative offers from American journalists.

To understand this, we must remember that these eyewitnesses know the truth. More to the point, they know that the truth has been systematically suppressed by their own governmental agencies and the press. It is not only the fear, as one comments in the film, of becoming one of those witnesses who committed "suicide" by shooting themselves in the back. They have been profoundly and tragically isolated, knowing from first-hand experience that the government and the press cannot be trusted. The fact that Turner was offering them a chance to be heard *outside* the United States is what gave them the courage to finally speak out. These are not kooks or publicity hounds, but ordinary Americans who have been caught and almost lost in a web of violence and duplicity so finely meshed that they have had nowhere to turn. Their testimony under these circumstances is an act of both physical and moral courage.

Turner, a free-lancer, was still at Oxford when Kennedy was killed. He came to the assignment to do a documentary for the 25th anniversary of the assassination four years ago, with no reason to doubt the Warren Report. Three years of research, including a year in Dallas, and over 300 interviews changed that.

I had the impression that this scholarly-looking Englishman, with sensitive features and an unassuming manner, who admires much about the United States (there are still some Europeans who do), had stumbled onto an America which he had not set out to find, and which saddened him profoundly. As an American, I am also sad, but more than that, I am angry.

Who cannot be incensed, for example, when we learn from eyewitness accounts, after 25 years, that the casket Kennedy's body left Dallas in was not the same one that was opened for the autopsy in Washington, and that although the physicians in Dallas found only 25% of the brain tissue missing due to the wound, there was no brain matter at all in the skull when it was examined again in Washington? This means that essential information about the bullet and its trajectory disappeared forever. How can we swallow the fact that key evidence confiscated by the FBI simply disappeared? There was physical evidence of a missed shot that hit a curbstone and slightly injured a bystander, but the supposedly inconclusive spectrographic analysis of the stone was destroyed for lack of space–1/32 inch in one of the largest archives in the world! There was an amateur film taken by a bystander as the motorcade passed between her and the grassy knoll: if anyone had fired from the knoll, as this woman and more than fifty other eyewitnesses testified, the gunmen would be visible in the film. This film was dutifully handed over to the FBI immediately after the assassination–and never heard of again.

We also see in *The Men Who Killed Kennedy*, astonishingly enough, also for the first time, not only the Zapruder footage, showing the impact of a bullet fired from the front, but also the official autopsy photos. These photos show a tiny entrance wound in the back of the skull, in exactly the position where the examining physicians in Dallas describe a massive exit wound. It is obvious, as Robert Groden points out, why the Warren Commission refused even to look at the photos, and why the House Assassinations Committee, though it looked at them, refused to show them to the Dallas doctors: they had been faked. What's more, it would have become obvious that they were faked by someone in the United States Government, because no one else had access to them.

At the end of the film, we are told the names of the probable hit men, the men behind the contract, and the underworld sources of this information. All of the principals, according to Steve Rivele, who spent five years investigating the case, had

CIA connections at some point in their careers. Rivele believes that the CIA felt so "compromised" by these circumstances that the cover-up became necessary. This is a relatively innocuous explanation of the CIA's role in the affair.

Of the three men Rivele claims were the assassins, two are still alive. One of these is at large on outstanding drug charges; the other lives in Marseille. Not surprisingly, all three have alibis for the time of the assassination. It would be much more surprising if anyone involved in a conspiracy on this scale did not have a good alibi. What is surprising is the willingness of the authorities and the press to dismiss Rivele's allegations so easily. The FBI has long since been informed, but no one has been apprehended, even for questioning. The reaction of the press, in this case the European press, since the film has not even been shown in the U.S., is typified by Pierre Salinger, writing in the *International Herald Tribune* (Nov. 2, 1988):

> We now know that two of them were nowhere near the scene of the crime. One was aboard a French minesweeper in the harbor of Toulon (as verified by the Defense Ministry in Paris). The second was in prison in Marseille (as the Justice Ministry confirmed). The third man, a French newspaper has established, was on sick leave from his job in Marseille as a docker, having lost an eye. Is it possible to believe that such a man was recruited to kill the American president?

A more interesting question is: Is it possible to believe the former press secretary to President Kennedy is so naive? Can such a man sincerely believe that a newspaper report "establishes" anything, that the statement of the one of the accused or medical certificates produced by the daughter of another of the accused are credible, that 25-year-old government records cannot be manipulated, in a case where the official autopsy photos of the President of the United States were probably faked?

The strangest thing about Salinger's article is what it doesn't say. He mentions nothing about the evidence in the film of a cover-up, which is much more important than the question of who fired the shots. Is it possible that a man as close to Kennedy as Salinger was is not affected by the news (if it is news) that the president's corpse was manipulated and the autopsy photos faked? Is it possible that a journalist has no curiosity as to why Time-Life kept the Zapruder film under lock and key for 25 years? Is it possible that the former Kennedy press secretary is unaffected by the suggestion of the former Kennedy Chief of Special Operations (Col. Prouty) that the assassination and cover-up were both part of an egregious conspiracy that continues today?

Because of Salinger's special position in this history, as one close both to Kennedy and to the establishment press, it is particularly interesting to note that he, too, continues to make light of "conspiracy theories," in spite of the evidence. The title of his article is "The Conspiracy Theories Come–and Go." His resumé:

> But over the years, and with the plot mentality that grew out of the Watergate affair and the congressional investigations of the CIA in the 1970s, some Americans moved to the European view–yes, there was a conspiracy.

This is a distortion of even the officially acknowledged view, as stated ten years ago in the House Assassinations Committee Report (p. 95):

> The committee believes, on the basis of the evidence available to it, that President John F. Kennedy was probably assassinated as a result of a conspiracy.

Yes, there was a conspiracy. Why does the press seem determined to make us believe otherwise?

Another interesting press reaction to The Men Who Killed

Kennedy was a widely quoted statement by another American, G. Robert Blakey, who was chief counsel to the House Assassinations Committee:

> The central part of this thesis, that is to say that the president was hit from the front right, is just simply medically not true.

This is a very curious statement. One wonders what medical evidence Blakey can be relying on, since we are told in the film that Kennedy's brain was removed before the autopsy and the autopsy photos faked. Dr. Wecht also tells us that no forensic examination of the few bullet fragments that remained were ever made, which might have proved (or not) that they were fired from the same gun. The point is that the "medical evidence" was either missing or had been falsified, a point which Blakey's remark misses entirely. One cannot help wondering if he saw the film at all, or if was quoted correctly. Things become even more confused when, for example, the *Birmingham Post* (Oct. 27) continues as follows:

> He [Blakey] said medical evidence presented by the Select House of Representatives Committee on Assassination in 1979 showed President Kennedy was hit only by bullets fired from behind by Lee Harvey Oswald.

We now have the clear impression that both Blakey and the Committee do not believe there was a conspiracy–an impression which is absolutely false. Can this be the Blakey who said, in a *Newsweek* interview in 1979 (July 30, p. 38):

> I am now firmly of the opinion that the Mob did it. It is a historical truth.

Can this be the same Committee which said on page 1 of their report:

> Scientific acoustical evidence establishes a high degree of probability that two gunmen fired at President John F. Kennedy.

Whether this kind of distortion is intended or not, it is very convenient for those who would still have us believe the fairy tale of the Warren Commission Report, which, in the words of Dr. Wecht, "should be taken from the non-fiction shelves of all the libraries and placed with Huckleberry Finn, Tom Sawyer, and Gulliver's Travels." Whether in that case even poetic justice would be done is questionable.

Against this background, the authentic news footage we see again in *The Men Who Killed Kennedy* of Oswald and Ruby themselves takes on a different hue. Oswald shows genuine surprise when he is told by a reporter that he has been charged with shooting the president, which is quite understandable, if he was a patsy. Ruby, in a BBC television interview, says:

> Everything pertaining to what's happening has never come to the surface. The world will never know the true facts of what occurred, my motives.

In response to the question, "Do you think it'll ever come out," he answers:

> No, because unfortunately the people [who] had so much to gain, and had such an ulterior motive to put me in the position I'm in, will never let the true facts come aboveboard to the world.

And in response to the question, "Are these people in very high positions," the answer is:

> Yes.

It is easy to question Ruby's credibility, but everything points to the truth of these statements. He is saying essentially the same thing that Wecht and Prouty say in the film, and these are very credible men who know from experience what they are talking about. The blend of power that Prouty refers to in the earlier quote would not be simply a matter of a few Mafia chieftains and a corrupt official or two. It would be a blend of criminal, political, and corporate interests amounting to a conspiracy of mammoth proportions, which did not end with the murder of John Kennedy. If these forces are diabolical and powerful enough to assassinate a president and get away with it, many more questions about the course of political events since 1963 must be answered. John Kennedy's assassination is not the only one which has been inadequately investigated (to say the least), and as David Scheim argues in *Contract on America*, the web of interests linking organized crime–which by now is often indistinguishable from "legitimate" capitalist greed–with anti-communism, with the CIA, with ghetto politics, with drugs and the munitions industry, with Cuba and Latin America, with Vietnam and God knows what else, is one that reaches right up to the White House of today.

We tend to forget, and we are not often reminded, that Kennedy's foreign and domestic policy initiatives were inimical not only to organized crime but to big money in general and a number of other interests. He alienated the CIA and the Mafia (for whom pre-Castro Cuba was a major source of income from gambling and prostitution) by refusing air support for the Bay of Pigs invasion and subsequently discouraging further anti-Castro activities. General recollection has it that Kennedy "stood tall" before the Russians in the Cuban missile crisis, but the fact is that he averted war by agreeing not to invade Cuba if Russia removed the missiles. He alienated a broad spectrum of right-wing extremists by pioneering civil rights and acknowledging the leadership of Martin Luther King. He alienated the arms industry by proposing, in agreement with Khrushchev, major long-range cuts in defense spending, and the oil industry by demanding cuts in the oil depletion allowance. General recollection also has it that Kennedy got us involved in Vietnam, but in fact he had already ordered the first withdrawal of troops when he was killed, and had planned major withdrawals by 1965.

If we look at the course of events since 1963 with what Salinger might call a "plot mentality," a number of things begin to make horrible sense. First of all, there were the assassinations of Robert Kennedy, Martin Luther King, and Malcolm X, none of which have been properly investigated. For example, thousands of documents pertaining to the RFK case were kept secret by the state of California for twenty years, despite numerous appeals for their release. When the files were finally released, in April, 1988, it was learned that 2,410 police photographs had been burned in 1968, and that the Los Angeles police had also destroyed important physical evidence (The New York Times, April 21, 1988). If we look beyond the quagmire that surrounds all four assassinations (not to mention the murders of numerous witnesses and investigators), what binds them together is that they effectively decapitated the civil rights movement. In the 1960s, civil rights activism, coupled with the powerful religious leadership of King and Malcolm X, represented a virulent threat to the life blood of those who profit from the crime that is bred by poverty and social injustice. The Mafia needs the ghetto and the slum, where their "businesses" (drugs, prostitution, gambling) flourish and where they recruit their soldiers. Making good Christians (or Black Muslims) out of poor people means draining the bank accounts of the crooks.

Secondly, Kennedy's developing foreign policy of accommodation with communism was reversed. Cuba was already a lost cause, but at the same time a perfect excuse for continuing the holy wars against the red peril in virtually every country in Latin America and in southeast Asia. Anti-communism is the ideological banner under which these wars are fought–whether directly or by proxy or covert action–but the non-ideological and unscrupulous force of greed plays a greater role than most of us know. It is a fact that wars make certain people richer in a hurry. In addition to the "legitimate" spur to certain sectors of the economy that any war provides, fighting communism–however sincerely people may believe in this–also protects the interests of organized crime. It is a fact that southeast Asia and Latin America are the world's major sources of opium. And it is a fact that communist countries do not cooperate in international drug-trafficking.

The third way that things have changed since 1963 is in the character and spirit of presidential leadership itself. The question is whether this dearth of inspiration, not to mention charisma, in the White House is accidental. America is full of people with brilliant leadership potential: why don't they get near the White House? The Kennedys were hardly perfect, but they did move people in a way that none of our politicians have since. If there has been a conspiracy to *suppress* exactly this kind of leadership, it has been eminently served, wittingly or not, by Kennedy's successors. Johnson and Nixon pursued the Vietnam War until it brought the country to the verge of revolution, as the anti-war movement began to include large numbers of veterans and others who could no longer be dismissed as radicals, "effete intellectual snobs" (as Spiro Agnew infamously put it), or tools of the international communist conspiracy. Drug-trafficking and the arms industry have flourished, channeling billions of dollars into areas of the economy of dubious value to the welfare of the nation. There has been no continuation of John and Robert Kennedy's campaign against organized crime. We had a Warren Commission of questionable integrity, and a former member of that commission (Ford) who, on becoming president, pardoned his former boss (Nixon), whose integrity was so questionable that he was run out of office. We have had eight years of a president (Reagan) who seemed a mere caricature of leadership–the very image of a puppet.

And now, another aspect of Kennedy's presidency has been reversed. We have gone from a president antagonistic to the CIA to one who directed it (1976-1977). We know that the CIA has covertly and violently manipulated political events around the world, and there is reason to suspect that it was involved in the events of the 1960s which radically changed the political course of our own country. Given what we know, and what we further suspect, about the CIA, is it not curious that the former head of this agency turns up in the White House? We do not wonder when the head of the KGB (Andropov) accedes to the highest office in the Soviet Union; after all, that is not a free country. But how can we not wonder when the analogous situation occurs here as the result of a supposedly democratic electoral process? If we assume the worst, that the assassination of Kennedy was a coup d'état engineered by the CIA (in conjunction with even more anonymous forces), as Dr. Wecht and Col. Prouty suggest, everything that has happened since then also makes sense, up to and including the fact that the former boss of the CIA, Kennedy's anathema, is now sitting in the oval office. If this is nonsense, and I hope it is, no one is in a better position to clarify matters than George Bush. And why should we not expect him to do so? National security? Just how much secrecy can a country tolerate, in the name of national security or anything else, and still call itself free?

On Nov. 25, three days after the assassination and the day after Ruby silenced Oswald, Deputy Attorney General Nicholas Katzenbach wrote the following memo to Bill Moyers:

> The world must be satisfied that Oswald was the as-
> sassin; that he did not have confederates who are still
> at large; and that the evidence was such that he would
> have been convicted at trial.

One must conclude that the government and the media have done their best to adhere to this line for the past 25 years, and that the non-appearance of *The Men Who Killed Kennedy* on any American television station, after enthralling audiences in 30 other countries, is just another example of the cover-up. It may be true, as Walter Goodman writes about the documentaries that were shown on American television, that the Kennedy case "will continue to produce inconclusive exposés for at least another quarter-century" (*New York Times*, Nov. 1, 1988). Not a bad estimate, since by 2013 most of the principals will be dead. (Salinger predicts another 100 years.) But the Turner film is anything but "inconclusive"; it is a strong yank at what looks like a hideous web of lies and murder at the highest levels of power, and if the American people get hold of it, it might just come unraveled. If they don't, the idea that the United States is a free country with a free press and a public with a right to know will someday be revealed as the biggest lie of all.

1989.05.26 TO CHOMSKY

May 26, 1989

Dear Prof. Chomsky,

Thank you so much for writing. It was quite a thrill to get your letter, and to know that you found my review of interest is enormously satisfying. I've sent it off to *Covert Action*,[1] which I am also glad to know about.

When I finally get hold of *Manufacturing Consent* (*Necessary Illusions* also on order — I have to order new books from England, one of the drawbacks of living here), I would like to review it, and I hope to do a better job than Lemann. I had not read the *New Republic* for many years until recently, when a friend started passing on his copies, and I was surprised (though I guess I shouldn't have been) to see the degree of convergence between it and *Time*, that one of *Time's* essayists (Michael Kinsley) is also the editor of NR, that people like Krauthammer regularly write for both, etc.

I've spent most of the last two days re-reading *Language and Responsibility*, and it struck me too that Warner Brothers, which suppressed your book *Counter-Revolutionary Violence* (which I will try to get hold of), is now the same corporation as Time-Life and many other enterprises. I suppose these corporate affiliations would explain a lot if they could be fully revealed.

I am very interested in your structural analysis of what I suppose we can call the capitalist ideology, particularly the role of the media, because it is the only way to explain how the forces of evil (for lack of a better term) work in a relatively free society. I am not paranoid by nature, but I am afraid the idea of conspiracy at the very top is plausible enough to be taken very seriously. It is quite plausible that these forces of evil are individuals powerful enough to make things happen on a grand scale with virtually no one knowing about it. The function of politics, from this point of view, is to obscure what is really going on. The Kennedy assassination seems the most obvious example of this. Another possible example is AIDS. I don't know if this is being discussed in the States, but there has been some discussion here of the possibility that the virus originated in germ warfare research laboratories. Whether this is true or not, and whether it was accidental or not, remains to be seen (perhaps), but it does seem likely that the African monkey theory has been propagated mainly to divert attention from this at least equally plausible hypothesis. After all, these laboratories exist for the expressed purpose of developing just such viruses, and they would seem to be the most logical place to look first. I believe the monkey theory appeared around 1984, just about the time there apparently was some speculation about an artificial origin. If people are moved to believe that AIDS is God's doing, it is certainly rational to suspect that it is rather the doing of certain people playing God. I do not find it inconceivable at all that human beings, given the means, might take it upon themselves to eradicate homosexuals and drug addicts, even if that also meant sacrificing a few "innocent" victims in addition. Hatred of communists and homosexuals also fits the ultra-conservative mind-set: they are all sinners. Few would doubt that Khomeini might be tempted to use a virus, if he had one, that would kill off large numbers of people he considers satanic. If the virus affected only or primarily blacks, like a more virulent form of sickle cell anemia, I suppose it would be even more suspicious.

I know this sounds (to most people) even crazier than the Kennedy conspiracy "theories" (though these, despite popular belief, are no longer theories but established fact), but who would have believed, in 1939, that in the next decade 6 million Jews would be exterminated? Prof. Jakob Segal, a biologist at Humboldt University in East Berlin and to my knowledge the most qualified supporter of the artificial origin thesis. is also a survivor of Auschwitz, which perhaps gives him a more realistic view of how such things can happen.

I am sorry you can't make it to Duisburg, but maybe I'll get a chance to meet you some other time. I'm wondering if there is any interesting way to look at etymology and the history of word meanings from a theoretical point of view. Lakoff's work on metaphor seems relevant, and Eve Sweetser seems to be working along these lines, but I don't see anything really coherent — not that I am competent to judge. I suppose it boils down to the old question of what relation, if any, historical analysis has to synchronic analysis. This seems to me a crucial difference between linguistics and physics. There can be a history of both as sciences, but there is no counterpart to the historical dimension of language in physics. The historical dimension of language is most clearly represented in polysemy, which can be seen from an idealized standpoint as a partial history of the word, a segment of its etymology. I have tried to think of this historical sense of the integrity of the word, and of the etymological relationships among different words, as "genetic" — but I have no idea at this point how such notions might be fit into a theoretical framework, or whether it's even worth thinking about.

Sincerely,
Michael Morrissey

1989.09 IS AIDS MAN-MADE?

[I sent this to Chomsky and I think also to Prouty. I included it in *Looking for the Enemy*, Ch. 4.1.]

The theory that AIDS originated in the laboratory has been circulating in Europe, particularly in West Germany, since late 1986.

The theory hinges on the claim that the AIDS virus (HIV) is virtually identical to two other viruses: Visna, which causes a fatal disease in sheep but does not infect humans, and HTLV-I (Human T-Cell Leukemia Virus), which infects humans but is seldom fatal.

Prof. Jakob Segal, the author of the theory, says that structural analysis using genome mapping proves that HIV is more similar to Visna than to any other retrovirus. The portion (about three percent) of the HIV genome which does not correspond structurally to Visna corresponds exactly to part of the HTLV-I genome.

This similarity, says Segal, cannot be explained by a natural process of evolution and mutation. It can only have resulted from an artificial combination of the two viruses.

He notes that the symptoms of AIDS are consistent with the complementary effects of two different viruses. AIDS patients who do not die of the consequences of immune deficiency show the same damage to the brain, lungs, intestines, and kidneys that occurs in sheep affected with Visna. Combining Visna with HTLV-I would allow the virus to enter not only the macrophages of the inner organs but also the T4 lymphocytes and thus cause immune deficiency, which is exactly what AIDS does.

As further evidence that HIV is a construct of Visna and HTLV-I, Segal cites studies which show that the reverse transcription process in HIV has two discrete points of peak activity which correspond, respectively, to those of Visna and HTLV-I.

AIDS is thus, according to Segal, essentially a variety of Visna. This has important implications for research, since a cure or vaccine might be found sooner by studying Visna in sheep than by concentrating, as at present, on monkeys.

The theory of the African origin of AIDS, that it developed in African monkeys and was transferred to man, has been abandoned by most researchers. All of the known varieties of SIV (Simian Immunodeficiency Virus) are structurally so dissimilar to HIV (much less similar than HIV and Visna) that a common origin is out of the question. Furthermore, even if such a development by natural mutation were possible, it would not explain the sudden outbreak of AIDS in the early 1980s, since monkeys and men have been living together in Africa since the beginning of human history.

The "Africa Legend," as it is called in a 1988 West German (Westdeutscher Rundfunk) television documentary, is further debunked by the epidemiological history of AIDS. There is no solid evidence of AIDS in Africa before 1983. The earliest documented cases of AIDS date from 1979 in New York.

In addition to the WDR documentary and occasional mention in magazines like *Stern* and *Spiegel*, Segal's work has been published in West Germany (*AIDS-Erreger aus dem Gen-Labor?*

[AIDS-Virus from the Gene Laboratory?], Kuno Kruse, ed., Simon & Leutner, 1987) and India (with Lilli Segal, *The Origin of AIDS*, Kerala Sastra Sahitya Parishad, 1989). He has also been conducting lecture tours in West Germany.

Scientific journals, Segal says, have refused to publish or discuss his theory. This is difficult to understand. If he is wrong, he should certainly be refuted. The cornerstone of the theory is that HIV is a combination of Visna and HTLV-I. Segal claims that any trained laboratory technician could produce AIDS from these components, today, in less than two weeks. If this is true, it should be demonstrable by experiment.

The next question is, if it is possible to produce HIV from Visna and HTLV-I now, was it also possible in 1977, when Segal claims the AIDS virus was created? He says it was, by use of the less precise "shotgun" method of gene manipulation available then, though it would have taken longer — about six months. If this is true, it should also be demonstrable.

The final question would be: Was it produced in a laboratory? Segal believes he has shown that it was, but he goes further than that. He also believes he knows who produced it and why. Segal quotes from a document presented by a Pentagon official named Donald MacArthur on June 9, 1969, to a Congressional committee, in which $10 million is requested to develop, over the next 5 to 10 years, a new, contagious micro- organism which would destroy the human immune system.

Whether such research is categorized as "offensive" or "defensive" is immaterial: in order to defend oneself against a possible new virus, so the reasoning goes, one must first develop the virus.

Since the Visna virus was already well known, Segal continues, the problem was to find a human retrovirus that would enable it to infect humans. Scrutiny of the technical literature, Segal says, reveals that Dr. Robert Gallo isolated such a virus, HTLV-I, by 1975, though it was not given this name until later.

1975 was also the year the virus section of Fort Detrick (the US Army's center for biological warfare research in Frederick, Maryland) was renamed the Frederick Cancer Research Facilities and placed under the supervision of the National Cancer Institute, Gallo's employer.

It was there, in the P4 (high-security) laboratory at Fort Detrick, according to Segal, where the AIDS virus was actually created, between the fall of 1977 and spring of 1978. Six months is precisely the time it would have taken, using the techniques available then, to create the AIDS virus from Visna and HTLV-I.

Segal claims that the new virus was then tested on convicts who volunteered for the experiment in return for their release from prison. Failing to show any early symptoms of disease, the prisoners were released after six months. Some were homosexual, and went to New York, where the disease was first attested in 1979.

The researchers had not counted on creating a disease with such a long incubation period. (One year is relatively short for AIDS, but would not be unusual if the infection was induced by high- dosage injections.) If the researchers had kept their human guinea pigs under observation for a longer time, they would have detected the disease and been able to contain it.

In other words, Segal claims that AIDS is the result of a germ warfare research experiment gone awry.

In an interview on April 18, 1987, published in the Dutch newspaper *De Volkskrant*, Dr. Gallo describes Segal's theory as KGB propaganda.

Segal, who is Russian (Lithuanian Jewish) but has been a professor of biology (now emeritus) at Humboldt University in East Berlin since 1953, is a bit old (78) to be starting a career as a propagandist. Soviet and East German officials, for their part, have maintained a discreet silence on the matter, for reasons of realpolitik, Segal believes.

The question of whether AIDS is man-made or not cannot be answered by dismissing it as propaganda.

Segal believes he has answered the question. We do not have to believe him, but we do have to believe that the following questions are answerable:

1) Can HIV be produced by combining Visna and HTLV-I in the laboratory now?

2) Can it be produced using the techniques available in 1977?

3) What *did* go on at Ft. Detrick between 1969 and 1978? What were the results of the $10 million Pentagon research project announced on June 9, 1969?

1989.09.14 TO CHOMSKY

14 Sept. 1989

Dear Prof. Chomsky,

Thank you very much for your letter and kind offer to help me get hold of the books, but I will persist with Heffers. I finally heard from them about *Manufacturing Consent;* the original order, they said, had been "lost by publisher"! They have re-ordered it, and I've asked them to try again to locate *Necessary Illusions.*

I am currently reading *The Washington Connection and Third World Fascism.* The war in Columbia is another case, no doubt, thinly disguised as a "drug war," but even *Time* can't help mentioning that many left-wing and reformist elements are getting purged with the Mafiosi. How convenient.

Prof. Segal[2] gave a talk here a few days ago, and we had a little chat afterwards. He is an extremely alert, clear-thinking, and articulate 78. I told him I had sent you the material. If Gallo thinks he is a KGB agent, his opinion of Gallo is even worse: he calls him "ein ganz großer Gangster." For Segal, Gallo is not only responsible for creating the virus but also for the disinformation campaign afterwards, and even for deliberately falsifying evidence to get credit for having isolated it first (before Montagner). This seems illogical, if he created it in the first place, but I suppose money and megalomania would explain it. Segal told us a little story about a visit they got from the US embassy (CIA) in 1986: Frau Segal asked them if they didn't think Gallo was a Mafioso, and instead of reacting indignantly, they just said, "You know, there are millions of dollars involved in this." They invited Segal to Atlanta, but he didn't want to go anywhere on the invitation of the CIA. I told him, naively I guess, that even if he went at their expense he wouldn't have to say what they wanted him to, but he has a different idea about that. I asked him if he would go to the US if invited by someone other than the CIA, and he said he probably would, provided he could get a visa. Britain has apparently barred him, and France has made it difficult; the only western country he has been able to move freely in is West Germany.

I've sent the enclosed report[3] to a few newspapers and magazines (including the *Boston Globe*, NYT, CAIB, etc.), without much hope of getting it published, but at least I'll feel I did something.

Sincerely,
Michael

1989.10.13 TO PROUTY

Oct. 13, 1989

Dear Col. Prouty,

I was tremendously pleased to receive your letter — it was much more than I had hoped for! It left me speechless for a couple of days. Reading it, I had the same feeling as when I saw the film, and when I read your book — that I was hearing the truth for the first time. At some point, one must choose whom to believe, and I can't help it, I believe every word you say! This is no doubt partly due to personal reasons, since I come from a military family, and though I am the renegade, I still feel a certain kinship with people from this milieu. My father and brother are West Pointers, two uncles went to Annapolis and one to the Coast Guard Academy. I was a protester and a draft dodger. When my brother was about to ship out to Vietnam in 1967 and I was still at Johns Hopkins, I wrote and told him not to go, because he wasn't saving anybody's ass and might get his own blown off in the process. He wrote back, very pragmatic-ally, that he had no illusions about fighting communism but that he had chosen the military as a career and therefore had to go. Fortunately, he came back unscathed. We've never talked about it since. A few years ago, after seeing the PBS history on TV, my father, who is 3 years older than you are and was in North Africa and Korea, mentioned in a letter that I had been "right to stay out of all that." In 1968, when the draft started breathing heavily down my neck, his advice had been to enlist — I could type, and would surely end up in a Quonset hut at a safe distance from the action. I said it was also a matter of principle, and he said that in that case he would act on principle too, and hung up on me. We've never really talked about it since, either. There are so many things unsaid, so much missing dialogue, not just in my family but in the country and the world (but especially in America).

It would be fantastic if you could come over here. I have talked with colleagues in several different departments about it, and they feel the same way. German universities are state-controlled, so there is money, but getting the bureaucracy moving is always difficult. I'll do my best, you can be sure of that. One thing they will want is a formal curriculum vitae with list of publications, teaching experience, etc.

Your Oral History idea is very appealing. I would certainly like to be helpful in that in any way I can. How about making it a biography? All of the history, and your interpretations, much of which you've already written, could be worked in, and I think the personal side would be very interesting and important. How does a man go from where you were, as a member of the ST, to where you are now? I don't know of many such stories — in fact, I don't know of any. How does one wake up? How does one become aware of the spider in the web (which strikes me as an appropriately sinister metaphor for the ST, or the High Cabal, or whatever else one might call it)?

In my case, I guess you could say it was pure happenstance: I saw a film on TV, and the whole world changed, at least my view of it. But even such a mundane event as that is interesting, precisely because it is mundane, and yet so important. In retrospect, I don't think it was happenstance. I can't explain it, but I'll put it this way: I think there was a little bug buried deep within my brain for 25 years that finally decided to surface and take over a good deal of my conscious thoughts! I had no particular interest in the assassination until last November, had never read a single book about it, so why did I notice that particular film in the TV guide, on a channel we don't even receive, and arrange to have it recorded at the university media center — something I had not done in the 11 years I have been teaching here?

That may be a little metaphysical, but one thing my own experience has made clear is how extraordinarily powerful television can be. One tends to forget this, amidst all the mindless trivia that is normally offered, but it shows that one TV film can do more than any number of books and that the Spider's obvious fear of the film is justified (even if it doesn't quite hit the mark). I am a perfect example of how an average educated adult American, even a "liberal," can remain unaffected by any number of books (including yours), sitting in the libraries and (to a much lesser extent) in the bookstores, waiting to be read. I can't even say that the books would have affected me the way the film did. Seeing and hearing people is different from reading.

I think what you call the "bewildering innocence of American citizens" is the heart of the problem — and that is the right expression, because it is more a problem of the heart than of the mind. We just don't want to see that Spider. It is frightening and depressing. We are caught in the web, fully in the grasp of academic-business-media propaganda, and we like it that way. Even now, I have only to open up Time magazine, and I am tempted to feel again that all is right with the world, after all. America is benevolent, we are benevolent — there is no Spider. I have much more understanding now of the Germans who managed to stay "innocent" in the Third Reich. The willingness — the willfulness — Not to Know is very strong. The Germans under Hitler had a much better excuse for Not Knowing than we do. If we can still blame them for their "innocence," how much more must people in the Third World blame us for ours! How should they, suffering and dying by the thousands as the direct or indirect result of actions (or inactions) by the US government, understand that we do not see this, that we are more ignorant and in a sense less free than they are, that we live in relative freedom, but also under the illusion of freedom? After My Lai, Watergate, Irangate, etc., the American public is convinced that the press is fulfilling its adversarial function, that they will get the truth handed to them on a silver platter, on the 6 o'clock news or in the NYT — which is not true at all. We get a lot of the truth, but what we get also serves to convince us that we are getting all of it, which is not true. The truth may be in the library, but it is not on TV or in the (big) newspapers. But how must this sound to people living in really totalitarian countries? It's hard not to feel guilty, and not only bewildered but angry at our own "innocence."

I've written to Sue Winter about getting hold of the tapes/transcripts of your work with them, but I don't have very high hopes. I don't know why Turner decided to emphasize the Mafia aspect. When I talked with him in London last April, he seemed quite aware of the big picture (the first inklings of which were just dawning on me) — without being very specific. I will always be grateful to him and everybody involved in that film, though, because for me it was a turning point.

What about the tapes/transcripts of your broadcasts in Los Angeles and with the BBC, and the ones you are doing now?

I had planned to photocopy *The Secret Team* anyway, but after hearing the story I did so immediately! Why didn't they just censor it, as in the case of Marchetti? I read recently that according to an official estimate in 1983 by the General Accounting Office, 225,000 people had agreed to lifelong censorship. All the more important to pursue the Oral History idea (and for you come here!), since there may be things that you could communicate this way which you can't write, perhaps not even in a letter.

The articles from "Saigon Solution" are fascinating, and I

would very much like to read more. It should certainly be published as a book. I suppose the Spider is particularly afraid of people like you (and Agee, Marchetti, etc.) because of your credibility. It does make a big difference who says something. When you tell me Segal is right, or even that he may be right, it has more weight than if 100 molecular biologists tell me he's wrong. Have you tried Pantheon, South End, Sheridan Square, Noontide, Black Rose, Claremont, Amana, Beacon? (The first two publish Chomsky, who has difficulty publishing his political stuff, although he is without doubt the most famous living linguistic scientist.) How about Lyle Stuart (*Dirty Work*), Shapolsky (*Contract on America*), or Zed Books (Blum's *The CIA*) or Pluto Press (last two are British)?

I've ordered Livingstone, Honneger, and Garrison, and will try to get hold of Wriston. I couldn't find anything on *Farewell America*, though. In general, what you say seems to confirm what the Marxists (that horrible word!) have been saying all along, but their arguments are so programmatic and diffused with ideology that they are too easily dismissed. Your critique, based on personal experience and concrete examples, is far more effective, and because of your background, it is difficult to dismiss your arguments with the usual ploy of accusing you of Marxist/communist/subversive motives (though I'm sure some would try and probably have tried).

As for the assassination literature, perhaps Garrison and Livingstone/Groden say it more clearly, but it seems to me that what has been missing (except for Canfield) is a clear statement, as opposed to innuendoes about "sinister implications." Someone needs to say, loud and clear, J'accuse: the CIA did it (etc.). It need not be "proved" and no doubt cannot be, since the government has control of the evidence; that is like asking the judge to prosecute himself. What is needed is not proof but a coherent, comprehensive explanation, and I think you have that.

Your article about Barney Troy is charming testimony to the power of the individual to make a mark in a quiet way. A drop in the bucket is better than a lot of splashing around. Better to wake one person up than put a million to sleep. How much do all those fine journalists and academics contribute to the progress of civilization, to our slow walk out of the jungle? All we have to do is look at the Warren Report to see the relationship between prestige and quantity of effort, on the one hand, to truth and humanity, on the other: zero.

What you say about the 60s counter-culture movement and the rest is mind-boggling, but it makes sense. Were the protesters, hippies, and yippies the scapegoats for pulling out of Vietnam, just as Defense, State, and the White House were the scapegoats for getting us in (re your analysis of the Pentagon Papers)?

Speaking of yippies, recently *Time* reported that Abbie Hoffman had been found dead, fully clothed, in his bed, and that the autopsy was "inconclusive." Another victim?

Interesting that you should mention Burt. I became suspicious a few weeks ago, when I read that he was the NYT "journalist" that broke the "yellow rain" (bee shit) story (in 1979, I think), so you confirm my suspicions. Carlucci fits the pattern — Ambassador to Portugal after his "service" in the Congo (getting rid of Lumumba). Quite a change from Kennedy's time, when (as either you or David Wise said) the Ambassador was still supposed to be over the Chief of Station (as the President is supposed to be over the DCI, as the DCI is supposed to be over the DD Operations...?). Now the whole world looks like one big Station.

If it was MONGOOSE (is this your theory/knowledge, or from another source?) then we can attach names, can't we (Helms, Harvey, etc.)? I was thinking McGeorge Bundy and McCone, since they were the top constant element in the transition JFK-Johnson. If I read you correctly, the strings come together at the DD for Operations. But who pulls his strings? I cannot get away from the idea that individuals must be behind these things, that somewhere, certain people must get together and make certain decisions. If the Rockefellers, the Hunts, the Hughes, the Murchisons, and the rest of the billionaires are the ultimate string-pullers — which I do not doubt — they must have some kind of organization.

Even a cybernetic machine, the analogy you used in *The Secret Team*, has to have its buttons pressed by somebody, doesn't it?

It's hard to understand how things actually go from Mammon to the shots in Dealey Plaza and all the rest. The hardest thing of all is to understand how so many people can be involved, who must know the truth or part of it, or suspect it, and still keep quiet or be kept quiet. You can imagine individuals being intimidated or bribed, but it's hard to imagine hundreds or thousands of people being controlled in this way. (I guess we need only look at Nazi Germany again, though, to see another clear example.) The first question students and friends I show the Turner film to is "Why has Jackie kept quiet?" I remember what she said when she married Onassis: "I like everything green." Was she trying to tell us something? Still, I don't understand that either, and whatever the explanation might be in her case, there are so many others who must know but haven't talked — or have we just not heard them?

The super scenario — was that the Iron Mountain Report? Very frightening, but it makes a lot of sense. AIDS fits in perfectly, too. Segal (who gave a lecture here a few weeks ago) doesn't think it was deliberate, because — he answered in a typically pragmatic way — it is decimating the potential military manpower pool of the US. I said I didn't think manpower was as important militarily today as it used to be, that homosexuals might not be considered good military material anyway. A lot of Americans think fags and whores and drug addicts are sinners, and some of these fanatics are among the richest and most powerful people in the world and no doubt part of the High Cabal, so if overpopulation is a problem which can be ameliorated by war, why shouldn't they develop and use a disease for the same purpose? AIDS is even better, because the perpetrators are totally anonymous (so far), and the people who are dying, this time, are sinners anyway, so there is even a vague feeling that it is right, even that God may be behind it.

The effect will be to reduce the population drastically in Africa and the Third World (poor hygiene and medical services) and among undesirables in our own exalted paradise (gays, addicts, prostitutes, the promiscuous — also the homeless, for the same reasons as in the Third World), and, of course, the disease has already generated billions for research. Many billions more will come when a vaccine is discovered and implemented; I wouldn't be surprised if they already have a vaccine and are just waiting for the financially propitious moment. Who would doubt that Hitler would have used a virus against the Jews if he had had one? Sure, a lot of innocents are sacrificed, but far fewer than in a war! If AIDS attacked primarily blacks, they wouldn't get away with it, because blacks are attuned to racism and would rebel. As it is, disproportionate numbers of blacks are in fact being affected (as in Vietnam), but the suspicions have been kept under control (again — so far). If "decent" people can think that God is behind AIDS, it is certainly rational to suspect that people are behind it who are playing God. It wouldn't be the first time. If necessary, they could even see their brilliant strategy in the fully Orwellian sense as being in the cause of science and humanity, since the AIDS research will contribute to general progress in genetic engineering, with all its promises (and further threats).

I suggested to Segal that the Spider might have suspected potential danger in the gay liberation movement, but he didn't go for that, either. He said the gays he knew were rather conservative, more concerned with being accepted into the mainstream than with changing society. I'm not so sure about that.

What about Harvey Milk and San Francisco in 1978? It's quite obvious that as soon as there is danger of grass roots rebellion or change, the leaders are simply knocked off (Martin Luther King, Malcolm X, even RFK), a strategy which unfortunately seems to work.

Segal is being muffled quite effectively, apparently. How did you find out? What other materials do you have? Since I wrote the article I have received a copy of the English publication (*The Origin of Aids*), which includes the protocol of the House Subcommittee meeting on DOD Appropriations for 1970, which includes the statement:

> Within the next 5 to 10 years, it would probably be possible to make a new infective microorganism which could differ in certain important aspects from any known disease-causing organisms. Most important of these is that it might be refractory to the immuno-logical and therapeutic processes upon which we depend to maintain our relative freedom from infectious disease.

> A research program to explore the feasibility of this could be completed in approximately 5 years at a total cost of $10 million.

Another appendix in the book is Jeremy Rifkin's petition to Carlucci of Feb. 10, 1988 for information about what happened to this project. I don't know if it was answered. I sent a copy of my article to Rifkin, but I haven't gotten an answer. In fact, the only answers I've gotten so far are from you and a couple of other individuals (like Chomsky, who didn't know about it). Dr. Antonio DiAngelo, whom I used to know as a teenager, now a renowned virologist (and a consultant at Ft. Detrick!) wrote back (almost in Gallo's same words) that AIDS is not man-made, we cannot make a virus, and if we could we would be able to destroy it. I wrote back that I didn't understand this, because although we cannot make a horse or a donkey, we can put them together and "make" a mule; and if that mule runs wild, why should we be able to catch it more easily than any other wild animal? When I was 13, I thought Tony was one of the coolest kids around. Now I'm wondering if he might be one of the guys that made the damn thing! I wish we could tell all these guys, "Ok, ok, nobody will be prosecuted. General amnesty for all. But just tell us the TRUTH, for Christ's sake!"

How tragic and ironic that the Segals, these two brilliant and brave souls, having survived the Nazi terror and now in their late seventies, working from a country (DDR) which is outside what we call "the free world," are virtually the only people, East or West, with guts and awareness and humanity enough to spread the word. If Segal were wrong, I don't think the Russians and East Germans would let him travel around lecturing and publishing even in the modest way he is doing. Certainly, the US experts would prove him wrong if they could. (They have tried, and failed, with the Africa and green monkey theories.)

So much for scientific objectivity. As soon as important political questions are involved, scientists clam up and play dumb or lie just like everyone else. So many current issues come down to questions of science and technology, but if we can't rely on our scientists to tell the truth, where does that leave us? Many people hide behind science as a kind of cocoon, where truth can be pursued beyond the reach of politics. The effectiveness of the coverup of Segal's work within the scientific community should banish that illusion forever. Even if he is completely wrong, the failure of scientists to respond reasonably or adequately is a damning indictment not only of so-called scientific "objectivity" but also of the "Search for Truth" which most scientists pretend to be dedicated to.

Perhaps you are right that a depression would do us good. That would be better than a nuclear holocaust, in any case, which would also be an eye-opener — if there were any eyes left to open. We think we are the pinnacle of civilization, but in fact we are only halfway out of the jungle, and we might take a "giant leap for mankind" back into it at any moment.

I guess we just have to go on doing our little bit, and take inspiration from people like you, who do more.

Sincerely,
Michael

1989.11 REVIEW OF MANUFACTURING CONSENT AND NECESSARY ILLUSIONS

[This was never published, though I sent a copy to Chomsky with my next letter to Chomsky (1989.11.29). A shorter version was published in *Looking for the Enemy* Ch. 3.6.]

Review of Edward S. Herman and Noam Chomsky, *Manufacturing Consent: The Political Economy of the Mass Media.* Pantheon, 1988, and Chomsky, Noam, *Necessary Illusions: Thought Control in Democratic Societies,* Pluto Press, 1989.

Noam Chomsky is the most famous linguist in the world and generally acknowledged as one of the greatest minds of the century. He has also been writing, voluminously and with an indefatigable commitment to rational and humane discussion, about American foreign policy for more than two decades. Still, his political writings are better known in Europe than in the United States, where they are ignored, with few exceptions, by the mainstream press. This is the fate of all dissident opinion in America that goes beyond the tolerable limits of debate and challenges certain fundamental assumptions, the "necessary illusions" one must at least pay lip service to in order to gain access to the mass media.

Chomsky and Herman (Professor of Finance at the Wharton School of the University of Pennsylvania) follow in the courageous, unpopular tradition of men who dare to serve the state with their consciences as well as their heads, as Thoreau put it:

> A very few, as heroes, patriots, martyrs, reformers in the great sense, and men, serve the State with their consciences also, and so necessarily resist it for the most part; and they are commonly treated by it as enemies ("Civil Disobedience").

For those who serve the state with their bodies and their heads alone ("as most legislators, politicians, lawyers, ministers, and office-holders" — and, we may add, journalists and scholars), "patriotism" means nothing more than subservience to the established political order, by which definition Joseph Goebbels, Adolf Eichmann, and Klaus Barbie were great patriots. Thus critics like Chomsky, regardless of the magnitude of their contribution in other areas (Bertrand Russell was another example), who dared from the beginning to judge American intervention in Vietnam by the same criteria as Soviet intervention in Afghanistan is judged today, were eliminated from the discussion as "wild men in the wings," as McGeorge Bundy referred to them in 1967. Even today, it is not permissible in the mainstream press to characterize the Vietnam War as anything other than a "tragic mistake," i.e. a well-intentioned failure, quite unlike the Soviet invasion of Afghanistan — the truth being, of course, that the situations were exactly analogous.

Herman and Chomsky present a number of meticulously documented examples of such media bias. With a devastating use of paired examples, they offer incontrovertible statistical evidence of how prestigious news organs such as the New York Times, Time, Newsweek, and CBS News systematically suppress or diminish the importance of state-sponsored atrocities in murderous regimes supported by the United States (like El Salvador and Guatemala), and greatly magnify the far fewer instances of government abuse in countries like Poland and Nicaragua. The reason for this bias is simply that the press conforms to the point of view of the US government.

The authors' comparison of press coverage of the Vietnam War before and after the Tet offensive in 1968 is a very insightful illustration of media conformism. Until 1968, there was virtually no criticism of American involvement in the war in the mainstream press, despite widespread popular opposition. After the Tet offensive, which convinced Johnson's advisors (most importantly, his intellectual henchmen such as Bundy, McNamara, and Rostow) that a military victory was not possible, the "anti-war" press suddenly appeared in full force, to the extent that right-wing institutions like Freedom House accused the media of having "lost the war." The image of a cantankerous adversary, of course, is precisely what the press likes to think it is, and what the government wants us to think it is. All is well, because we have a watchdog press, the "guardian of freedom," in Horace Greeley's phrase. The fact that these fearless watchdogs emerged only after the government had decided on disengagement is forgotten, if it was ever known. The truth is that the watchdog is more a performing dog, and will even play the role of scapegoat if called upon. When the people needed him, before 1968, he was docile; when the government needed him, after the change in policy in 1968, he dutifully bared his teeth. It would hardly have done to admit that the US had been defeated by one of the weakest nations on earth, that the government had driven the American people to the limits of tolerance and the verge of revolution. Far better to blame our "tragic failure" on the ferocious anti-war press, which in fact behaved exactly as the government wanted it to.

The fundamental premises and necessary illusions are bipartisan. The illusion of an adversarial press, for example, is greatly strengthened by inter-party rivalries and scandals such as Watergate and Irangate, which may (in Nixon's case) or may not (in Reagan and Bush's case) result in the sacrifice of individual politicians. Occasionally these partisan rivalries will touch on important issues, as in the case of military aid to the Contras, but basic questions, such as why we support a murderous regime in El Salvador and oppose a relatively humane regime in Nicaragua, are simply never asked. If someone did ask, the answer, from Democrats and Republicans alike, would be that we are "defending freedom." This is the necessary illusion that the (our) government is benevolent. It can make mistakes, even tragic ones, as in Vietnam, but it is always well-intentioned. It is not acceptable in the mainstream press to point out, as Chomsky does (and as Thoreau did), that good intentions "are not properties of states, and that the United States, like every other state past and present, pursues policies that reflect the interests of those who control the state by virtue of their domestic power" (NI, 9).

Those who control the state are not necessarily or primarily politicians. American foreign policy is formed in the oak-paneled board rooms of the giant corporations, banks, and other financial institutions, which are not even necessarily American, but multinational. R. Buckminster Fuller refers to this primum mobile as "Grunch" (Gross Universal Cash Heist). We are not defending any freedom except that of Grunch to pursue its sole interest: profit. The mechanics of exploitation are well known in principle, but complicated in detail, and any attempt to elucidate them is silenced with hysterical warnings of the Red Peril. The necessary illusion here is that "what is good for business is good for America." The man in the street knows that what this really means is "what is good for Grunch is good for Grunch," and that Grunch does not include him, that he is not part of the corporate and intellectual elite who run the country, and that our electoral system has devolved into an elite game of musical chairs in which he is only a spectator.

That is why barely 50% of the eligible population bothered to vote in the last presidential election; it is not apathy, but despair. Where is the candidate who will point out that the $85 million in military aid given to El Salvador "aids" no one except that corrupt puppet government (to murder their own people) and, most of all, the corporate manufacturers of the weapons and other goods which are bought with this money? The money does not disappear. It is simply transferred from the pockets of American taxpayers to the bank accounts of weapons merchants and other corporations which are thus provided with a government subsidy at our expense — and, of course, at the expense of the people of El Salvador, who pay in blood. Where is the presidential candidate who will tell the truth about the Vietnam War, this "tragic mistake" in which we "defended" the people of South Vietnam by killing a million of them and making a moonscape of their country? This noble enterprise, so passionately encouraged by our journalistic and scholarly elite ("the best and the brightest"), at least until 1968, cost the American people 58,000 lives and $220 billion dollars. This money did not disappear either. It ended up in the hands of government contractors. Where is the presidential candidate who will erect an anti-war memorial, listing the names of the corporations that profited so much from this war, alongside the names of the 58,000 Americans who died?

The media are as much a part of Grunch as any other corporate entities. Herman and Chomsky point out that in 1986 there were 1,500 daily newspapers, 11,000 magazines, 9,000 radio and 1,500 TV stations, 2,400 book publishers, and seven movie studios in the United States. This would seem to indicate a basis for pluralism and independence, but the appearance is deceiving — another necessary illusion. Less than thirty giant corporations account for more than half of the newspapers and most of the sales and audiences in magazines, broadcasting, books, and movies. This is only the tip of the iceberg, and even that is not obvious. NBC does not advertise the fact that it is owned by General Electric. Underneath the hierarchy of formal ownership relations, however, is a gigantic web of interlocking directorships and shared stockholders (who are in many cases banks or other corporations), in which the only control or influence is wielded by relatively few people — namely those with the most assets. Media professionals are just as subject to pressure to conform within this corporate system as anyone else:

> ...those who do not display the requisite values and perspectives will be regarded as "irresponsible," "ideological," or otherwise aberrant, and will tend to fall by the wayside. While there may be a small number of exceptions, the pattern is pervasive, and expected. Those who adapt, perhaps quite honestly, will then be free to express themselves with little managerial control, and they will be able to assert, accurately, that they perceive no pressures to conform (MC, 304).

Conformity is not the same as censorship, which is crucial for understanding how "manufacturing consent" is possible in a relatively open society like the United States:

> ...the U.S. media do not function in the manner of the propaganda system of a totalitarian state. Rather, they permit — indeed, encourage — spirited debate, criticism, and dissent, as long as these remain faithfully within the system of presuppositions and principles that constitute an elite consensus, a system so powerful as to be internalized largely without awareness (MC, p. 302).

The authors also take pains to point out that theirs is not a "conspiracy theory":

> Institutional critiques such as we present in this book are commonly dismissed by establishment commentators as 'conspiracy theories,' but this is just an evasion. We do not use any kind of "conspiracy" hypothesis to

explain mass-media performance. In fact, our treatment is much closer to a "free market" analysis, with the results largely an outcome of the workings of market forces. Most biased choices in the media arise from the preselection of right-thinking people, internalized preconceptions, and the adaptation of personnel to the constraints of ownership, organization, market, and political power. Censorship is largely self-censorship, by reporters and commentators who adjust to the realities of source and media organizational requirements and by people at higher levels within media organizations who are chosen to implement, and have usually internalized, the constraints imposed by proprietary and other market and governmental centers of power (xii).

As if determined to prove the accuracy of this prediction, establishment commentator Nicholas Lemann, the national correspondent for the *Atlantic Monthly*, responds in the New Republic (Jan. 9/16, 1989):

This sounds reassuring, but it's misleading: *Manufacturing Consent* really is a conspiracy theory.

Chomsky himself comments in NI on several other gross distortions in Lemann's review, but this one also deserves special attention. After all, Lemann is representative of the journalistic elite which Chomsky and Herman are criticizing, and if this is what we can expect of the *New Republic*, once cringes to think how less "liberal" journals might react (though the usual reaction is silence).

It requires some Orwellian flips to follow this, but first we must note that it is Lemann who has the conspiracy theory. His theory is that Herman and Chomsky have a conspiracy theory, though he doesn't say what the theory is. If we examine his language a little more closely, we discover that he really thinks that Herman and Chomsky do not have a conspiracy theory — they are the conspiracy. This turns out to be none other than our old friend, the Red Peril: the International Communist Conspiracy. When Herman and Chomsky say that the press fairly openly serves the interests of government and corporate centers of power, Lemann renders this as "the press fairly openly serves the interests of its capitalist masters" (my italics). When they give examples of the press printing falsehoods and suppressing inconvenient truths, the better to maintain the government propaganda line, Lemann transforms this into "the better to maintain the party line." No amount of Orwellian acrobatics will make sense of this, since "capitalist masters" and "the party line" just don't jive, but the point is simply to raise the specter of the Red Peril and associate it by hook or crook with the antagonist — here the dastardly Herman and Chomsky.

Lemann demonstrates a few lines later how the conspiracy chimera is used as an evasive tactic, just as Herman and Chomsky predict. He summarizes two chapters of *Manufacturing Consent* (occupying 105 pages and 229 footnotes in the book) as follows:

> When Nicaragua abrogates civil liberties, it's big news, but the much more serious abuses in Guatemala and El Salvador get much less attention here. Genocide in Cambodia by the Khmer Rouge [from April 1975 through 1978] is covered more than genocide in Cambodia by the United States and its allies [bombing from 1969 through April 1975]. Guess why?

The sardonic "Guess why?" might as well have been "So what?"

That the US committed genocide and the American press failed to report it adequately elicit not so much as a whimper of protest from this conscientious patriot. Presumably, genocide is ok, as long as we do it, and the press should feel perfectly "free" to look the other way. Rather than address the issue, with "Guess why?" Lemann sends the reader off on a witch hunt, in search of the elusive conspiracy theory, which exists only in Lemann's mind — and quite nebulously at that.

In a final paroxysm of distortion, Lemann accuses Herman and Chomsky of advocating "more state control" in order "to move the press further to the left," though it is quite clear that the authors are calling for more public control:

> Grass-roots and public-interest organizations need to recognize and try to avail themselves of these media (and organizational) opportunities [cable and satellite communications]. Local nonprofit radio and television stations also provide an opportunity for direct media access that has been underutilized in the United States...Public radio and television, despite having suffered serious damage during the Reagan years, also represent an alternative media channel whose resuscitation and improvement should be of serious concern to those interested in contesting the propaganda system. The steady commercialization of the publicly owned air waves should be vigorously opposed. In the long run, a democratic political order requires far wider control of and access to the media. Serious discussion of how this can be done, and the incorporation of fundamental media reform into political programs, should be high on progressive agendas.

Lemann interprets as follows:

> This assumes that the political order that controls the press won't be a conservative one, which is a stretch, but there are certainly plenty of examples around the world of a press controlled by a left-wing political order...But the temptation to view the mainstream press as a potential locus for liberalism outside the electoral system should be stoutly resisted. Not only is the prospect of a politicized press a little frightening, because the press is so powerful, and so much

less accountable than government; it's also probably unattainable. For a variety of reasons, the mainstream press almost always responds to, rather than creates, the political mood.

The only person here suggesting that any "political order" should control the press is Nicholas Lemann. If he finds a "politicized press," one which is a locus for all political views, "frightening" and "unattainable," he has not only misunderstood Herman and Chomsky but also the First Amendment. A press which is "free" only to respond to the "political mood" is not free.

I wonder why Lemann finds the authors' disavowal of a conspiracy theory "reassuring." Is it reassuring to know that press conformity is structural rather than "conspiratorial"? Herman and Chomsky's "free market" analysis suggests that what amounts to the colossal failure of the press to do its job is a more or less natural development of our socio-economic system. I find this unsettling enough. Chomsky really doesn't have a conspiracy theory. As he wrote to me:

> I don't doubt that people in power consciously plan in their own interests, sometimes with others, hence technically a conspiracy. But my own feeling is that the major things that happen depend upon institutional structures and arrangements, and involve individual planning largely within these constraints. Thus, the board of managers of General Motors surely plans to maximize profit and market share, but it would be misleading to call this a conspiracy; it is an institutional imperative, and if they didn't do it, they would no longer be the board of managers. Our work on the media is far from a conspiracy theory. We in fact begin by drawing plausible conclusions from a guided free market model that is relatively uncontroversial, and then argue that the media behave much as should be

expected on these assumptions.

I would add, however, that such a structural analysis does not exclude a conspiracy theory. Lemann will be glad to know that conspiracy theories much more plausible and concrete than the one he is playing with are alive and well, both in the United States and in Europe. It is quite possible to fit Herman and Chomsky's propaganda model within a conspiracy theory; in fact, it would be necessary in order to explain how a conspiracy of any magnitude could operate.

Censorship, for example, may be "largely self-censorship," as Herman and Chomsky say, but this does not mean there is no overt censorship. It is well known that the CIA requires its employees to submit to lifelong prepublication review. Reagan extended this practice to a wide range of government and industry personnel who have access to classified information. By the end of 1983, according to the US General Accounting Office, 225,000 people had agreed to lifelong censorship. This means that any of these free Americans who decide to tell the truth are liable to prosecution. Any book which threatens to tell the truth about the CIA faces serious difficulties, as the publication history of Marchetti and Marks' The CIA and the Cult of Intelligence, McCoy's The Politics of Heroin in Southeast Asia, Wise and Ross's The Invisible Government, and Agee's Inside the Company will show.

Even after a book is published, attempts may be made to keep it from reaching a wide audience, or from being distributed at all. Herman and Chomsky don't mention it here, but their earlier joint work, later published in expanded form as *The Political Economy of Human Rights* (South End, 1979), was kept from being advertised or distributed by the conglomerate (Warner Brothers) that owned the original publisher. Another technique to prevent circulation of a book is to buy up all the copies. L. Fletcher Prouty has told me that his book *The Secret Team* (Prentice-Hall, 1973), to my mind the best book ever published on the CIA, began to disappear when Prentice-Hall was going into its third printing and Ballantine had already distributed 100,000 copies of the paperback edition. Prouty learned later that the entire 3,500 copies that arrived in Australia were bought by an "Australian Army Colonel," and that a publishing executive secretly working for the CIA had ordered the demise of the book. The responsible editors at Prentice-Hall and Ballantine were fired, and despite continuing interest, all further inquiries about re-publishing the book have eventually been stifled. (Fortunately, the book is still to be found in libraries.)

We need not look very far to find the infrastructure of a conspiracy theory that will accommodate Herman and Chomsky's propaganda model — and much more. The CIA is a conspiracy, and we do not need a theory to know that it exists. Its Directorate of Operations ("covert action") would fit anyone's definition of the word. The CIA is the most powerful secret police force in the history of mankind, and as far removed from the ideals of individual freedom and democracy as one can get. It is above the law, since "national security" is the ultimate priority, and by law there is only one man who can overrule the decision of the Director of Central Intelligence as to what constitutes a breach of national security: the President. Anyone looking for a conspiracy need look no farther than this. This is not the place to go into detail, but suffice it to say the following (none of which we will hear about in the New York Times or on any of the television networks): there is substantial evidence linking the CIA to the assassination of President Kennedy; Kennedy was antagonistic to the CIA; Kennedy wanted to withdraw from Vietnam, where the CIA had been waging secret war (as well as in the rest of Indochina) for a decade, and had already ordered the first troop withdrawals (a decision that was secretly reversed by Johnson); an ex-Director of the CIA (Dulles) was on the Warren Commission; and — skipping up to the present — another ex-CIA Director (Bush) is now sitting in the oval office. This is only the barest outline of a conspiracy theory, but it's enough.

Not even the slightest adumbration of the significance of these observations will be discernible in the American mass media. The rest of the "free world" is less constrained — and more informed. In November 1988, on the occasion of the 25th anniversary of the assassination of President Kennedy, the American public was treated to a number of sanitized television histories, none of which even hinted at the possibility that Kennedy's murder was a coup d'état engineered by the CIA (in collusion with the Mafia). A British Central Independent Television documentary which did, and was shown in 30 countries, has to this day not been televised in the United States. There are a number of excellent books which point to similar conclusions (most recently Robert Groden and Harrison Livingstone's *High Treason*, and Jim Garrison's *On the Trail of the Assassins*), but this is a numbers game: how many people will read the books, and how many people would see the film? We have a "free press," but the freedom one has to reach a politically significant mass audience is a quite different question.

Herman and Chomsky have shown — definitively, for all who will listen — that the mainstream press is not doing its job, that it is fully entangled in the web of illusions that are necessary for the maintenance of state and corporate power. Beyond that, we may well ask — though the answer will be long in coming — if there is a spider in the web.

1989.11.29 TO CHOMSKY

Nov. 29, 1989

Dear Noam,

I finally received the books, as you can see, and enclose another probably unpublishable review[4] — but I'll give it a try. On the off chance that someone might publish it, is it ok to use the quote from your letter on p. 6? (I haven't sent it off yet.)

Enclosed also are the pages of the Hearings[5] Segal refers to and which are included as an appendix in the English edition of his book (published this year in India), which will come out in a slightly expanded version in German here early next year. I believe the original source of the document is Jeremy Rifkin, whose letter of Feb. 10, 1988 to Carlucci requesting information about what happened to this project is also appended to Segal's book (*The Origin of Aids*, Jakob and Lilli Segal, Kerala Sastra Sahitya Parishad, Parishad Bhavan, Trichur-680 002, India, 1989). I've written to Rifkin a couple of times but he doesn't answer. The silence in general about AIDS, at least here, is deafening. Segal seems to be totally isolated, though he cites people who agree with him incognito. The only reaction I've had to my little article is a number of letters from a guy I knew as a kid who is now a well-known virologist (and has been a consultant at Ft. Detrick!) — the latest one is enclosed. Segal says the opposite on each point: 60% homology between Visna and HIV-1 in 1986, with the latter mutating at 10% every 2 years, would point to near identity in 1978, which Segal says is not only significant but cannot possibly be explained unless HIV-1 was made from Visna (by adding a small piece of HTLV-1). Segal says Gallo published his discovery of HTLV-1 in 1975 but called it something else and has tried to cover up this fact ever since. Visna does not infect human cells, which is why HTLV-1, which does attack T cells, was added. The exact definition of the genetic codes of the viruses (I'm not sure how exact they are now) would not have been necessary to do the splicing in 1978, when the less precise and more time-consuming (Segal says 6 weeks instead of 2 days today) "shotgun" method was well known. The "evidence" attesting to the existence of HIV-1 before 1981 is very inconclusive. The question about the experiment is the same one I asked Segal (and in my article), but apparently it's not so simple to get hold of the viruses, find a laboratory which has the requisite security clearance and is willing to do the experiment, and (as one biologist told me) find out if the virus produced actually causes AIDS, since that would require a human guinea pig.

Obviously, I can't make a scientific judgment about any of this, since I'm not a microbiologist, but one microbiologist I talked to said not even microbiologists working in genetic engineering can judge the matter: you have to be one of the microbiologists doing AIDS research (and Segal says none of them are working with Visna). As a layman, one is so easily put down and made to feel not only that understanding is impossible but that you have no business even trying. If this is what science becomes when it has political consequences (i.e., ceases to be science), it is very discouraging. You have often referred to the standards of natural science vs. social "science," and I agree, at least I would like to, which is why this bothers me so much (quite apart from the AIDS question per se). The idea of 99% of the microbiologists in the world playing dumb or lying about questions of <u>science</u> is very hard to stomach. Necessary illusions about microbiology among microbiologists? Science and

Nature operating within a scientific propaganda model that falsifies, if need be, or simply ignores our understanding of the physical world?

You are much more of a scientist than I am, and perhaps you won't mind if I ask you straight out what you think. Is it possible to find out if Segal is right or wrong?

Sorry to make this so long. You are very kind to write to me at all, and please be sure that I appreciate it very much.

Sincerely,
Michael

[Chomsky replied to this on Dec. 28, 1989 thanking me for writing the review and allowing me to use the quote. His comment on the material from the Hearings was: "Sends a chill up the spine." But it was far from his field and he found it hard to believe that "one can't obtain a scientific judgment from some knowledgeable and unprejudiced source," given the number of people involved in AIDS research.]

1989.12.30 TO PROUTY

Dec. 30, 1989

Dear Fletch,

Thanks so much for your marvelous letter. I'll need time to digest it all. Remember, I'm a guy who just pulled his head out of the sand.

I want to get this off to you with the Herrhausen speech. I also have the German version, if you want it.

By now, the story has all but disappeared from the media, but no one here seems to doubt that the RAF (Rote Armee Fraktion) did it, although there is no hard evidence (just a letter found at the scene, which could have been planted). What you say makes sense, and I'll be very interested to hear your thoughts on the speech.

Maybe his ideas about debt reduction (p. 7) and setting up in-country development banks (p. 8) are the key. What, by the way, is the "Paris Club"? I am completely ignorant of these things.

An accompanying article in *Die Zeit*, where the speech appeared in German, said DB just bought Morgan-Grenfell and was the first big German bank to put a foreigner (John Craven) on its board. Is this significant?

I've just re-read Chapters 16 and 17 of your Saigon Solution[6] and am wondering how the changes in Europe fall into the changed scenario. All the commentators are saying that neither Russia nor the US is in control of these "popular movements towards democracy," but it all seems extremely well orchestrated to me (except for the snags in maverick Rumania). I'm trying to put this together with your analysis of the import-export, border control, etc.

In those chapters you also talk about Marcos and Aquino. I wonder who is behind the anti-Aquino forces now? Has she gotten too independent? If the CIA is secretly fighting against her (just a guess), then why the double game of official US support?

The Columbian "anti-drug" war sounds a lot like the 1986 Bolivian campaign you talk about on p. 132. Noriega is a clear further example of CIA dictators hoisted and dropped. You say the reason they are dropped is they get too greedy, but you'd think they would have learned when to draw the line. Bush seems to have made a deal by letting him sneak into the Vatican embassy — to keep him from talking? Why don't they just shoot him?

On p. 22 of Chap. 14 you mention the "grand strategy planner of the High Cabal." That sounds pretty specific. I guess you don't mean McGeorge Bundy or Maxwell Taylor, do you?

You ask who had the power to order the Cabinet to Honolulu at the time of the assassination, who controlled the Secret Service...these are just rhetorical questions, aren't they? Who was behind these things?

Also, that Special Study Group's report on the Lewin book (p. 122, 133). Who was in that Group? Is that report (which you quote from) still secret?

Is the speech JFK intended to give on Nov. 22 printed somewhere?

I finally received (and read) *High Treason* - -fascinating. I'm gratified to see that Groden and Livingstone think as much of your opinions as I do, and also of the Turner film. Shows my instincts were right, which is at least something, when just about everything else seems wrong.

I wonder what those names are that are whispered among retired intelligence officers (p. 367). G/L seem to know — too bad they can't find a way to say it.

You say in your letter that you have been close enough to Nelson Rockefeller and others to know they get instructions. I keep trying to imagine how this works in concrete terms. It's hard enough to imagine anything about the lives of these biggies, either in government or in business, and the connection with the High Cabal is extremely difficult — which I guess is why it works so well. Still — any hints?

I am pursuing all the books you mention, and thanks for the address of Tom Davis. I hope I get Garrison before it's stopped. There should be an underground circulation of stopped books. G/L mention another one with a chapter entitled "How Close We Came" (to Naziism), by Liddy I think, but I can't find the reference now.

I can't quite latch onto the religion aspect. I would like to hear more of your thoughts on Darwinism, too. I remember reading a review a number of years ago of a book by either Watson (now heading up the huge HUGO gene-mapping project) or Crick that played with the idea that life on earth may have been seeded extra-terrestrially. I don't know how seriously they meant that.

I've read in Ranelagh's (highly sanitized) history (*The Agency*) that James Schlesinger coined the term "Knights Templar" to refer to CIA top brass, which brings to mind P-2 (which you mentioned in your first letter) with its Masonic connections. Is the High Cabal "P-1"?

About coming here, it isn't complicated at all as far as I'm concerned, if we omit the financial question. You can stay with us.

I haven't heard from either Sue or Nigel. I sent Sue my article about Segal, thinking they might do a film on that, but Segal says the Brits won't even let him in the country, so I guess a film would be out of the question. This guy Peter Duesberg, who questions whether AIDS is caused by HIV at all, gets talked about all over the place — why not Segal? His theory is much more plausible. I have just received two back issues of CAIB on AIDS, which are good but even Lederer gives Segal short shrift and diffuses the issue, I think. He doesn't mention the House Hearings document. Is this supposed to be still secret?

I wholly agree that TV can do great things, but mostly what it does is mind control. We just got cable here, and in the morning one channel (World Net) ties in for a few hours to C-Span, which of course is squeaky clean (even sounds like a detergent!). I think it's all USIA, isn't it? More interesting than most stuff, though. One international caller during a discussion about Panama managed to squeeze in "You fucking terrorists!" before they cut him off. At least it's a way to keep in touch.

The trouble is, for people (like me until recently) who are in the grip of US propaganda, it entangles them still more. This constant parade of super-informed, intelligent, articulate — and thoroughly indoctrinated — journalists and scholars is enough to drive any notion of dissent from your head before it even has a chance. I got free (I think) at the age of 42 and had the advantage of relative non-exposure by living abroad for 12 years, but I know from my own gut experience how difficult and significant that process of change is. That's why I was wondering if you too had gone through a similarly sudden "radicalization," which apparently you didn't. (But the truth about the JFK assassination must have hit you at some point.) You are right, of course. There is no reason to wonder why anyone is oblivious, no matter how brilliant or informed they are. The propaganda is just too powerful.

I have always particularly hated, or at least remembered hating, McGeorge Bundy, because he seemed to be the incarnation of intellectual dishonesty and perfidy, although rationally I was never clear about it. That was my problem: how could such a smart guy (and by extension the whole government) be so stupid re Vietnam? Now it's clear, and I am glad to see, reading you, that my gut feeling about Bundy, especially, was exactly on target.

I would love to see that BBC show you did on the Pentagon Papers. Also the MLK show, which didn't play here, I don't think. Trouble with audio/video is that it disappears. Books are less effective in getting messages across but are still the only reasonably permanent sources. If they ever seriously start transferring them to computer storage we'll be lost.

Something that has struck me while reading G/L and your letters — if the conspiracy is this big, why didn't they do a better job of it? They surely could have done it any number of ways (a pin-prick, a drop in cup of coffee, etc.) and left no traces and no questions. Even a bomb, as with Herrhausen, leaves only the slightest trace, which, if you are right, is false — but the case is already virtually closed. They could have done the same thing with JFK and the others, even afterwards, finding plausible scapegoats and settling the dust. The point is, I wonder if the "carelessness" is deliberate? Do they want us to suspect the worst, and at the same time, want us to know that they can get away with it? What could be a better, and more intimidating, demonstration of absolute power and control?

When you say you all (in McNamara's office) knew that war was a Malthusian necessity, how did such sentiments make themselves known?

The "Energy Crisis" scenario staged by the Center for Strategic and International Studies at Georgetown — is there anything available on that?

I would of course be interested in whatever material you have on "the AIDS cycle" (and, obviously, so would Segal).

I've met Segal a couple of times and corresponded with him and his wife. He is 78 but apparently in good health and continues to make lecture tours in West Germany. Britain won't let him in, he says, and France makes it difficult. He has been to our house and invited us to visit him in East Berlin, which shouldn't be difficult nowadays. I'm quite certain he would be extremely glad to meet and talk with you.

About the Korean Airlines 747 — wasn't there somebody on there that had something to do with the JFK case?

Back to Herrhausen, why is his death a blow to Germany and the world? Do you mean reunited Germany? What is the cui bono fact here?

There is a lot more I want to ask about, but I'll get to it one step at a time. I'm reading and re-reading everything. I have a lot to learn — I've had my head in the sand for a long time.

Thanks so much again for your extraordinary letters. They are invaluable. I'll try to do them justice, but mostly I'll just have questions, which as I say I will put to you as I digest things. And thanks too for the compliments on my own little articles. Even if they are ignored by everybody else, recognition from the people I respect means a lot.

I'm planning a short trip to the US in late Feb., including a stop in Washington. I was born there in 1946 (a year before the CIA!) but didn't spend any time in the area until my father was sent to Fort Meade (he was Public Information Officer, I think they call it — nothing to do with NSA). I did my last year of high school there (Gambrills, Md.) and went on to Johns Hopkins — in 1963, the pivotal year. It's not for sentimental reasons though — I'll visit first with my parents in Pensacola, and then I would just like to get a feel of Washington, from the point of view I have now, maybe meet some people who — how should I put it — share our ideas. You, of course, primarily.

Will you be there around Feb. 26 or so? Maybe we could have a chat. At least, I should be able to pick up some books there that I won't find in Pensacola or Atlanta (my other planned stops). Recommend any stores?

Got to get this off. I may have already missed the last pickup before New Year, but I'll try.

All the best,
Michael

1990.03.24 TO PROUTY

March. 24, 1990

Dear Fletch,

This won't be a long one but if I don't do it now I won't get to it for another couple of weeks, and I do want to thank you again for taking time out to see me. I hope you're feeling better.

I've been through all of Saigon Solution now — you must get that published. You have said that *Critical Path* is an important book, but it pales in comparison to your work, and I'm not saying that to flatter you. There can be no question about the importance of what you say. The only question can be: How true is it? This is exactly the same situation as the Segal thing. Both of you, for different reasons (you because you were there, he because of his scientific expertise), make exceedingly plausible arguments that can only be effectively combated by being ignored as much as possible.

Tomorrow I'm going to Duisburg for three days to co-host a conference on "Language History and Cognition," something I proposed several years ago when I was living in a different world. I don't know how I'm going to get through it — I'm not interested in linguistics any more. It should be about "History and Cognition," i.e., about how little we know or even suspect about what really goes on in the world and becomes "history." All those brilliant minds — just think what they could come up with if they could or would dedicate their scholarship to things that really matter. As you said in one of your letters, it does seem as if the High Cabal has done its best to keep the best minds out of politics and business and the things that matter, kept them in their Ivory Towers where they can delude themselves into thinking they are doing "important work." Meanwhile, people have been dying — at the very least, living lives of complete obliviousness (including the scholars themselves). They chalk this up to "politics," and pretend to be above it all, but in fact they are below it. They've been duped like all the rest of us. I guess things have always been this way, but I can't help but feel the medieval serf, the most wretched slave on the plantation, at least knew he was being screwed. If someone had told them, "You know, your ignorant asses are being had," they would probably have laughed at the naivety of anyone assuming they did not know this. I don't think what is called the "Vietnam syndrome" has anything to do with the horrors of combat. I think a lot of people just realized, without necessarily being able to verbalize it, that they were getting screwed. I doubt that any Vietnamese (on the other side) had any such syndromes, because they knew what they were fighting for.

I have also been able to read *The End of Economic Man* and a couple of other books you have put me onto. I still have a whole shelf to go through — I spent most of my time in Washington in bookstores. Everything he says about the end of Marxism would of course sound even more appropriate today, but I wonder if he would say the same about capitalism? Maybe he wouldn't say it, but giving him credit, maybe he would say that capitalism is indeed long since dead, in the same sense as Marxism is dead, both having failed (as he said) to prove themselves as true harbingers of freedom and equality. Maybe he would add that fascism also failed (I hope), but what do we have now and what are we heading toward? Certainly free enterprise is a thing of the past. He didn't mention this in his 1969 preface, but seemed to be worried that the youth rebellious of that time was essentially negative and had the seed of totalitarianism within it. That surprises me, since he says nothing about the reasons for the rebellion, namely the war, the civil rights movement, and attendant offshoots. Could Drucker have been naive enough about a war to fight communism, after all that he had seen, that all he felt moved to say about the domestic turmoil in 1969 was that it was dangerous?

I know that you feel much of the anti-war movement was staged, and I would like to hear/read more about this. I have just finished John Marks' *The Search for the 'Manchurian Candidate'*, where he describes how MKULTRA was "ironically" behind LSD coming out in the universities and then the general population. And this reminds me of the current "drug war," where the "enemy" seems to get stronger, the more we fight it. I simply do not believe that the US government could not control the problem if they wanted to, and without draconian measures. As you said, this does give them a perfect excuse to increase domestic secret surveillance — and this is happening in Germany too. Now we can invade countries, kill civilians, and kidnap heads of state — all with 80% approval of our own citizenry and without a single reference to Communism! I could hardly believe it when I read a few weeks ago that now it is legal, by our laws, to search homes in foreign countries without a warrant. Nothing could be better evidence of what you have been saying all along — that national sovereignty is dead.

Speaking of national sovereignty, on the plane coming back I read an article by Richard Helms in the *Intern. Herald Tribune* (Feb. 2), in which he voices his fears of a neutral united Germany:

Internationalization of development efforts in Eastern Europe also makes sense, rather than leaving the task to the new German superpower. For example, Washington might sponsor a joint development bank to support the East Europeans; this would allow America, Germany, Japan, France and other countries to share responsibility for rebuilding Eastern Europe — and to share whatever influence came with it.

This doesn't sound like he [Helms] would have been too enthusiastic about Alfred Herrhausen's initiatives to put the Deutsche Bank at the center of Eastern developments, and to establish in-country development banks (e.g., in Poland).

I also recently read Turner and Christian, *The Assassination of Robert F. Kennedy.* It is obvious that Sirhan didn't do it, that he was a patsy, just like Oswald, maybe hypnotized to fire a few blanks and then forget it all. Well, what other multi-billion-dollar legal secret organizations were actively involved in research and experimentation to develop capabilities such as this? the LAPD also put officers with CIA backgrounds in key positions on the investigation team. Etc. etc. One of the most interesting things in the book, though, was the bit about Hilder and Steinbacher and their Illuminati conspiracy theory. These guys were (are?) obviously right-wingers (John Birch Society), but the funny thing is, what they say makes sense — if you leave out certain elements. It sounds like your High Cabal, if you add the CIA and omit the racist and anti-Semitic elements. Even there, the racist element fits, but in reverse (Vietnam and AIDS victims being disproportionately black, for example). What do you think of this? I guess this is why Bill Vornberger at CAIB thought of Lyndon LaRouche, who apparently has similar views, when I told him briefly about your High Cabal theory. It is curious that LaRouche was one of the first to come up with a version of the Segal theory — but again in reverse, saying it was a KGB lab product. And of course in the Kennedy murders, the first accusations out of the mouths of "responsible" officials were to the effect that they were communist conspiracies. We also know that these kinds of smokescreens are effective intelligence maneuvers to conceal the truth: the lie is very close to the truth, but so outrageous that no version of it will subsequently be made to appear plausible

— "Yeah, sure, the CIA did it...ha, ha. That's an old one, just like the one about the KGB."

I've read *October Surprise* now too, and I'm wondering how she [Honegger] got away with it. Bush an "honorary member" of P-2? Kissinger and Haig in the Monte Carlo Committee? Where did she get this, and how did Tudor Publishing Company (ever heard of them?) get the nerve and wherewithal to publish it? The implications are mind-boggling, though she doesn't spell them all out. Even Casey a victim — and Abbie Hoffman, all the others in her list at the back? What do you think? Could this be another smokescreen — exaggeration to make the only somewhat less enormous truth henceforth inaccessible? I just wonder how she got it out — I even found a copy in a Dalton's (nary a trace of Garrison's book, by comparison).

Well, I said this would be short, so let me stop before I think of something else. I'm going to go back over *Saigon Solution* and *Secret Team* in the new few weeks to make detailed notes to use in my course, so I'll be feeding you questions.

Best regards also to your wife and daughter.

Sincerely,
Michael

1990.05.10 TO PROUTY

May 10, 1990

Dear Fletch,

I am wondering about your health. How are you?

Did your piece on Herrhausen ever come out? I sent something on it to *Lies of Our Times*, a new magazine published by Ellen Ray and William Schaap of *Covert Action Information Bulletin*, but I haven't heard from them.

What do you think of the Lafontaine case? Another Manchurian Candidate — like Sirhan? If she's a crazy, as they say, why HIM? I just don't believe in coincidence anymore.

I'm 3 weeks into my "History of the CIA" course — with Saigon Solution and *Secret Team* constantly on my desk.

I'm reading Lansdale's *In the Midst of Wars* and a biography by Cecil Currey called *The Unquiet American*. You're mentioned a couple of times in the latter, unflatteringly, of course.

Re Lansdale, can he be identified in other photographs?

I finally have gotten hold of *Farewell America*, though a German translation. Do you have any idea who Hepburn really is/ was? He must have been FBI or Secret Service, or talked with someone who was, since he reports things that only an insider could know. For example, he says that when JFK told the Secret Service in Tampa that he didn't want them on the rear bumper anymore, this was communicated immediately to the organizer in Miami. At another point, he mentions, quite mysteriously, without further explanation, as if we are meant to read beyond the lines, the name Morgan Davis. Is that name significant? Just about everything he says seems right, and all back in 1968!

Is it possible that the CIA (and the High Cabal) wanted Cuba to be Vietnam, that JFK screwed it up — by not committing US forces — and paid the price?

You said Bundy called off the crucial (3rd) air strike while JFK was asleep. Surely this would have been the rudest awakening for JFK. If he could fire Dulles and Bissell, why not Bundy? This seems crucial. Are you the only one who has said this — that it was Bundy sabotage?

They certainly had JFK, literally, by the balls, at least from March 1962 when Hoover told him he knew about Judith Exner and her ties to Rosselli and Giancana — and no doubt he also knew about their contract with the CIA to kill Castro. Maybe that was all just a setup. How much did JFK really know about Mongoose? Did he know that the CIA contract on Castro was still out?

In any case, with that skeleton in his closet (sleeping with the girlfriend of mobsters he had hired — as the public would assume — through the CIA to murder another head of state!), he was certainly helpless. Still, he must have thought he could get out of it. Why else would they have had to kill him?

Speaking of binds, I read recently that Robert Owen, Ollie North's cohort, had two Indiana connections — John Hull and (then Senator) Dan Quayle. Owen was Quayle's secretary. That would seem to explain why he was picked as VP. He's wrapped up tight, too.

I'm reading a biography of LaRouche by Dennis King. LaRouche is enough to discredit any conspiracy theory, and I wonder if that is not his real function, i.e., a smokescreen. He was the one (or one of the ones) who first cried "KGB!" as soon as the questions started appearing, around 1986, I think. This is effective. If one conspiracy theory looks crazy, it's much easier to dismiss them all as crazy.

This word "conspiracy" has been so propagandized that it has lost its meaning. The definition is "a secret plan by more than one person, usually to do something bad or illegal." This is a perfectly adequate description of the Directorate of Operations, isn't it?

Did you read *Time's* recent article on the CIA? The only "news" value of that seemed to be that the CIA wants more money. I would have been much more interested to know how they "estimated" the overall intelligence budget at $30 billion. I figure it more like $70 billion, and about $8.4 billion for the CIA — extrapolating from Marchetti's 1973 figures — and not including proprietaries, transfers from other government agencies, etc.

Any news on Saigon Solution? The very fact that people like LaRouche seem to have no trouble publishing their stuff, and you (and others) do, makes it pretty clear that LaRouche and his ilk are part of the general conspiracy to suppress the truth, don't you think?

I'd like to know if you know if anyone else has written about the following:

1) the arming of Ho Chi Minh and Syngman Rhee in 1945

2) China's participation in the Tehran conference

3) Bundy's sabotaging of the Bay of Pigs air strike

4) the sabotaging of the plan to evacuate Diem

5) the significance of the various NSAMs

6) JFK's Cabinet's mysterious trip to Japan on Nov. 22

7) EGL

8) the real purpose of the Pentagon Papers

By the way, Canfield and Weberman back in 1972 identified two of the tramps as Howard Hunt and Frank Sturgis. Do you agree?

Is Lucien Conein still alive? Do you know him? He runs through the whole thing, doesn't he, from 1945 with Ho to Diem to his appointment as head of Nixon's task force (hit squad?) on drugs in 1972. According to Jim Hougan (*Spooks*), Nixon got him to suggest to the press the JFK knew about the plan (i.e., that it was his plan) to assassinate Diem. This could hardly have been true, since there was a plan to evacuate him and Nhu.

The connection between Conein and the Corsicans in Saigon and Marseilles (including Guerini, mentioned in the Turner film) is also interesting. I've been reading Alfred McCoy's *Politics of Heroin in SE Asia* — is he still around? Seems like you and he would have a lot to talk about.

Speaking of talking, are you on-line yet? That's one network I'd like to get in on. Can you send details?

And how about your oral-history idea? How would that work? If you could give me an idea of what it would entail, maybe I could interest someone here, e.g., the JFK Institute for North American Studies in Berlin.

We drove to visit some people in Heiligenstadt, DDR, on May 1. It might be free now, but it's still depressing. I don't think they really realize that they're free yet — their heads are still drooping. Lafontaine was (is?) the one politician who might slow down the unification process, which is why I wonder about the stabbing.

All the best,
Michael

1990.06.09 TO WEISBERG

[Harold Weisberg was an assassination researcher and author of several books.[7]]

9 June 1990

Dear Mr. Weisberg,

I hope this reaches you. I have the address from Groden and Livinstone's *High Treason* (p. 413).

I would like to read your *Case for Conspiracy with the CIA*. I have read Garrison's *On the Trail*, which seems to make the same case, but perhaps you have more.

I saw the ITV documentary *The Men Who Killed Kennedy* here in Dec. 1988, in which you appear. This really turned my head around. Since then I have been obsessed with what I guess we can only call the secret history of our country and the world.

I have a few questions and would be very grateful if you could respond. I'll list them for convenience.

1) Have you written anything lately on these topics? I know you have also worked extensively on the MLK case. I have just read Melanson's *The Murkin Conspiracy*.

2) Do you know Tom Davis' excellent catalogue (Tom Davis

Books, PO Box 1107, Aptos, CA 95001 - 1107)? If you have it, I wonder if you would be kind enough to give me some hints about what to read. I am interested in all of the topics, but it's hard to know where to start and I can't buy everything, and otherwise I have to work through interlibrary loan here, which takes forever. Let me tell you what I have read: re assassinations, Groden and Livingstone's *High Treason*, Garrison's *On the Trail of the Assassins*, Scheim's *Contract on America*, Lifton's *Best Evidence*, Marrs' *Crossfire*, Melanson's *Murkin Conspiracy*, Turner and Christian's *The Assassination of RFK*. Davis lists a number of works by Joesten and others as "mss." which look particularly intriguing since one might assume that what is not published or easily available is more likely to be the truth: Ted Gandolfo, *The HSCA Cover-Up* 1987, Roger Craig *When They Kill a President* 1971. Do you know these? The works by Sutton on *The Order*?

4) [sic][8] Do you know Carmichael et al., *JFK: The Mystery Unraveled*, published by Liberty Library? I believe this is the LaRouche organization. What do you think of LaRouche? Some people think he is right about some things, despite the anti-Semitism. 5) I have just read Hepburn's *Farewell America* in German translation. He seems to have gotten everything right — in 1968! Some think he was/is French intelligence, but whoever he is he must have either been in on the assassination plan or talked with someone who was. Or else a brilliant liar. At one point he mentions, quite mysteriously, the name Morgan Davis. What do you think? Do you have any idea who he is/was? Do you know anything of the history of the book? It's the only publication I know of which seems to have been written by someone on the inside (and telling the truth). But why doesn't he mention the war?

1990.06.17 TO PROUTY

June 17, 1990

Dear Fletch,

I was glad to hear that you are ok and recovering well.

Yes, thanks, I wouldn't mind having the Joesten book. He is listed a number of times in the Tom Davis catalogue. Do you know him or any of his other work? Might be interesting to see what he said in 1958 — before the coup.

I hope the letter I sent to Cavin does some good. (Too late, I noticed a couple of typos.) Let me know if there's anything else I can do.

I understand well how frustrated you must be as far as publishing is concerned. You deserve tremendous credit for staying power — lesser men would have given up long ago. As you point out, though, you are not alone.

If it's any comfort, you can be sure that what you write to me will go further, one way or another. My students hear it, and I'll keep trying to publish too.

Do you know Walter Marchetti, John Marks, John Stockwell, Ralph McGehee, or other (more or less) renegade ex-CIA people who have gone into print? Do you read *Covert Action Information Bulletin*? I remember what you said about Agee. I was told he now has all his writing cleared by CIA, which sounds suspicious, but it may well have been some sort of legal compromise to allow him to get his passport back or avoid further prosecution.

I am aware of the "wilderness of mirrors" problem, but I have to agree with Bill Vornberger of CAIB, who said the only way to really judge a person is by what he actually says and writes. What Agee and CAIB write seems accurate and is certainly anti-CIA, so why not take them at face value, barring evidence to the contrary?

Stockwell is apparently active on the lecture circuit and was even on C-Span some time ago, though I didn't see it. Marchetti seems to have disappeared from the scene. I'm trying to get an idea of what currents of thought may exist below the media surface and who and how many people might be involved. I wish I were in the States to explore this first hand, because I suspect that even — or especially — among ordinary people, perceptions vary widely.

For example, I don't think poor blacks would have nearly as much difficulty accepting your ideas as middle-class blacks or whites. Blacks are used to being screwed. Same goes for the Third World in general. It's no coincidence that Segal, for instance, is widely published and known in Africa and India, whereas the "well-informed" American public is totally ignorant of him.

And then there are the journalists. Very interesting, what you say about Hersh. Readers Digest — my God! (CAIB did an excellent exposure of their CIA connections.) What about Bob Woodward? I haven't read *Veil* yet, but I can imagine it's superficial. The question is, what do such people really know and think? What about George Lardner, Jr., the last person to see David Ferrie alive?

Jack Anderson was on "World Net's Dialogue" the other day, which is USIA, of course, and I know he is a funny guy, but he does seem unable to resist a good story. Would he go for the

Segal thing, I wonder? You could provide him with a number of "scoops" — which would be great advertisement for Saigon Solution, or whatever the title ends up as.

The head of USIA was also on World Net not long ago, somebody named Gelb. Could that be the same Gelb (Leslie) that did the Pentagon Papers?

I still think your biography would be a good idea. If handled the right way, it could be the best way to get exposure. By putting the focus on you as a person, your ideas could be presented from a certain distance, which might make them more palatable for a publisher. The important thing is that what you have to say gets said, and you certainly have been personally involved in enough situations and enough people to make for a readable story. I could make an attempt at this already, just on the basis of your books and letters, but to do it right I would need more material.

Even Bill Moyers (*The Secret Government*) seems to have an idea of what is going on. Henry Steele Commager wrote the introduction to Moyer's book, and in his own *Pocket Hist. of the US*, 1981 ed., he says: "One such [US/SV intelligence and commando] raid produced the Tonkin Gulf Resolution providing the Tonkin Gulf incident of August 24, 1964, which in turn was used, fraudulently as we now know, to obtain the historic Tonkin Gulf Resolution..." (p. 566). This is the merest hint, and he completely ignores JFK's withdrawal plan, but still, the seeds of doubt are there, perhaps more widespread than we think. Makes me wonder what such established types like Moyers and Commager think privately.

I'm so far away I can only guess, but there may be an entire class of people, an underground, of people with similar feelings, although they keep them to themselves because they do not have a forum to articulate them.

In an issue of *The Nation* I just received there is a full-page ad sponsored by what must be a couple hundred Pantheon authors protesting the firing of certain editors who have made that press relatively independent. That frightens me that things have come that far. At the same time, it gives me some hope, because it shows that there are others who are deeply concerned.

The problem is communication. Your idea of an electronic mail network, the more I think about it, might be the best thing. I suppose nothing would be easier to censure, but it would be difficult to do so without it being obvious. There are a number of networks already being used world-wide — my father uses one (CompuServe) to correspond with people all around the country and in Europe. I haven't gotten into it because I haven't seen the need, but if people like you were involved it would be different.

If we rely only on private correspondence or traditional publishing, spreading the word will continue to be difficult. You have so many contacts — maybe you know someone who could help us get this started. All you really need is a number of people who want to do it. The technology is there, not very complicated or expensive. Computers and modems are cheap these days.

Another idea re communications. Going back to your oral history idea, why don't you just do it? Suppose you sent me cassette tapes instead of letters? After a while, you would have the oral history. I could help by keeping a running index, and also try to find an institutional purchaser over here, while you worked that end. Seems like that would be easier for you and you could get more material in, plus you already have some recorded material. You could just respond to my questions, or structure it (or not) however you like. You mentioned commenting on the Pentagon Papers in detail — that would be one thing you could do. Or just start with the day you were born.

The advantage for you would be that you wouldn't have to bother structuring and formulating it carefully as you would in writing, since even a letter requires much more effort than just speaking. Plus, you would be assured that there would be a permanent body of material which would be of general interest. So are your letters (which I keep and reread from time to time), but as oral history it would probably have more value, not the least simply because there would be more of it.

If this appeals to you, the mechanics would be simple. Mailing cassettes is not expensive, and if you didn't want to bother making copies I could do that for you and return the originals. You wouldn't have to worry about me stealing any material, because, first of all, I wouldn't, and second, as far as I know the copyright laws automatically cover (even without registering, though you could do that too) oral as well as written material. If there were any question about that I would be happy to sign whatever would be necessary to protect your rights.

That's not to say I wouldn't want to use what you tell me — I do that already! But I could hardly try to pass off what you say as my own; coming from me, it would be valueless. I can imagine, though, that I might at some point want to do a biography and/ or analysis of your work, in which I would need as much detail as I could get, so tapes would be ideal for that, as a kind of protracted interview-at-a-distance, but of course I would only do that with your permission and cooperation, and if something like that worked into a publishing contract we would work that out together.

Segal is coming here again June 23. I'm trying to get somebody competent to argue against him — he would like nothing better — but it's difficult. No one will take him on, much less in public. My brother-in-law is a doctor, and after hearing about Segal (and other things) from me he asked a colleague, who confirmed what he was determined to believe anyway — that the monkey business is God's truth. He hadn't even read the book! Even if he does read it, he won't believe it. He saw the Turner film, but his reaction was nebulous. "Depressing," he said, and that was it.

Something short-circuits the reaction, I guess simply because we don't want to allow ourselves to recognize the full unpleasant truth. It is frightening, and it does change you, but it's possible to live with it. That's an important message, too. I'm convinced that it is largely just this fear which actually prevents people from thinking rationally and, equally important, allowing themselves to react emotionally.

I also think there are some people who know the truth and are convinced it is better to keep it secret, because "ordinary" people just wouldn't be able to take it. That, of course, is a totally unjustifiable attitude, from any point of view, but in addition, I think it is wrong. I think people can take the truth. After all, "ordinary people," i.e., 99% of the population, have always lived with the knowledge that they are more or less the slaves of an elite few, whose knowledge, power, and privileges far exceed their own. What's different about our recent age is that we have been led to believe that we are somehow different, that there is no more elite that secretly controls our fate, that knowledge really is equally available to everyone. I think most people are afraid of recognizing that this is an illusion: yes, we are not that different than the serfs in the Middle Ages, as far removed from the world of the nobles whose land we work as in those days. Much better off, in many cases, but still ignorant.

Ironically, this illusion of being knowledgeable prevents us from becoming knowledgeable, even when we are informed. That is why you and others can speak and write and be heard, but the impact is minimal. There is no explosion, even though the pot is boiling, because they keep taking the lid off, just a little — or a lot, when necessary — but it always goes back on.

What do you think of Watergate? Wasn't that Nixon's Dealey Plaza? As you say, cui bono? Nixon lost, and the CIA came out unscathed, if not the better for it. Jim Hougan (know him?) wrote that employment applications for the CIA increased significantly after Watergate. I guess the idea that CIA was not involved accrued to their benefit, just as the Pentagon Papers portrayed the CIA as Dr. Jekyll, with nary a word of Mr. Hyde. Later, in the Church and Rockefeller hearings, the limited hangout went far enough to purge them almost completely. The very worst was out. Now we could relax, satisfied with the confessions, without changing anything that would prevent the same things from happening again and without the full truth even having surfaced.

I suspect Watergate played its part in this scenario. The HC needed a scapegoat for Vietnam. The CIA wouldn't do, because they are essential to the way things really work. In Iran-Contra, though, it seems they have tried to use the NSC the same way the CIA has been used. Now that Bush is President, Walters in Bonn, John Lilley in China, Gregg in S. Korea, etc., I suppose the entire government is now fully in position to do their bidding, with the hard core in CIA there as backup, though now they can afford to be less directly involved than in the past.

Nixon had to be the scapegoat, because the pot was boiling over. After the war, if he had not served to take the blame (along with the anonymous Pentagon), things could have gotten out of control, as they did in 1968. They had Nixon primed to create an overt police state, and I suppose there were elements in the anti-war movement (as you say) that played their roles as agents provocateurs to encourage this.

They saw, though, that knocking off RFK and MLK was carried out without full-scale rebellion and it proved possible to control things without letting Nixon pull out all the stops. That would have been a last resort, of course, since an overt police state is harder to control than a covert one like the US today. By 1971 Nixon had outlived his usefulness, except for the scapegoat role he then was called upon to fill, or perhaps tricked into filling.

In any case, Jim Hougan points out that the CIA probably

had much more to do with Watergate than the record shows, and I suspect they were behind the whole thing. The break-in was purposely bungled, Nixon was pilloried, and the nation was purged of their Evil Leader who killed 58,000 of his own people. When Nixon dies he may well take the blame for the assassinations too, when the point comes when that has to come out too. For the moment he is allowed to live out his life as Elder Statesman, helped along by *Time* and other organs of the HC.

A further result of Watergate was to re-establish the press as the indefatigable watchdog of freedom, which stops at nothing to expose the truth. "What about Watergate?" is the first thing people say when you try to tell them about control of the press.

Cui bono? After the Bay of Pigs, the assassinations, Vietnam, Watergate, the Congressional exposures — in all of which the CIA has not only been implicated but proved to have played a central role — who has come out on top? William Webster is on top of the world, just like Bush.

I wish I were in the US to be able to research how books like Honegger, Garrison, Groden/Livingstone, Marrs, are advertised and reviewed. As you said in the Turner film, it's one thing to kill somebody and quite another to get away with it, and it's also one thing to publish a book, and quite another to get people to read it.

Do you know any books on P-2, the Monte Carlo Committee, or the East India Company-Thomas Malthus-Yale connection?

In the current issue of CAIB there is an article about Skull and Bones. John Kerry of Mass. is also an alumnus. What has become of his brave investigation of the CIA-Contra-drug connection? As far as I know nothing has been published. Wm. Sloane Coffin is also an alumnus.

Speaking of drugs, since you were air force, you probably have a good idea of what was going on with Nugan Hand.

Several books mention Santos Trafficante's mysterious trip to Saigon, Hong Kong, and Singapore in 1968. How about this explanation: He knew that after Tet the US would pull out, so he arranged for heroin labs in Thailand and Laos (closer than Hong Kong and Marseille) that could supply pure heroin more efficiently to S. Vietnam, thus creating the GI heroin epidemic starting in 1969/70, which of course spilled over into the US. He used the last few years of the war to bleed the GIs while they were still there, create an addict population that would return to the States, and probably also arranged for the post-war transport routes that would by-pass soon-to-be Communist Vietnam and Laos.

Trafficante is also reported as having known about the JFK assassination beforehand.

Can you really recognize Lansdale from the back in that photo in the Garrison book?

Sprague does not fare too well in Groden/Livingstone. I see in the Davis catalogue that he wrote a book in 1976 called *The Taking of America 1 2 3* (if it's the same Sprague), but it's listed as a "mss." Read it?

I've ordered the Carmichael book and will try to get hold of the others you mention (as always!) by interlibrary loan.

I can't get over *Farewell America*. He pretty clearly says that H.L. Hunt was one of those behind it, also Johnson, Gen. Walker, and the Minutemen (with members in the Dallas police and FBI/CIA). (The fact that there are two Howard Hunts, and another H.H. — Howard Hughes, all with intimate CIA connections, seems strange too, come to think of it.) Some other names are mentioned: Michel Halbouty, Ray Hubbard, R.E. Smith, Algur H. Meadows, Jake Hamon, Kay Kimbell, O.C. Harper, C.V. Lyman, J.P. Gibbins, Ted Wiener, Thomas W. Blake, John W. Mecom, Billy Byars, Morgan Davis. Any of these names familiar? Hoover was well-informed and did nothing.

Hepburn says the Committee (HC?) decided on the assassination in Spring, 1963, and chose Dallas after considering several alternatives. He must have been directly involved in the planning or privy to someone who was. Do you know anything about the history of the book? It's hard to believe that it could have been written and published at all, or that Hepburn's identity could still be secret after so long. If you get a chance to re-read it, I would be very interested to hear what you think. He seems to have gotten everything right — in 1968!

For example, in one footnote he says the CIA budget was $2 billion in 1963, and $4 billion in 1967. This is much higher than Marchetti's figure of $750 million in 1973, but maybe he meant the overall intelligence community. By Marchetti's figures that would have been $6.228 billion in 1973, and by my reckoning $69.767 billion now ($8.4 billion for CIA) now (not $30 billion, as *Time* estimates). What's your guess? Anybody who could say that, without even saying it is a guess, must have been a high-level CIA officer, talked to one — or be a consummate liar, which is unlikely, since he says too many other things which have been corroborated since.

The one thing he doesn't go into is the war — I wonder why.

Honegger refers to the Association of Retired Intelligence Officers and another group of former OSS people, which apparently form a secret elite which actually run the CIA. At another point she says Kissinger is a member of the Monte Carlo Committee, which is associated with P-2, of which Bush is an honorary member.

Too much of this secret society business is not only frustrating but may be counterproductive. In the end, the only thing that really matters is how the government works — or doesn't work. We can't prevent people from forming secret societies or conspiring. What we can and should do is try to prevent the government from doing these things.

Strictly speaking, it may be true that it is the HC, not the CIA, that runs things, but the crucial difference is that we know about the CIA, and not about the HC. Therefore, the place to start is with the CIA. The simple fact that its budget is secret and non-accountable is enough to qualify it as Enemy No. 1. On top of that, the facts that have been revealed are much more than enough to nullify all reasonable arguments to justify its existence. If we want to do anything about the situation, we need an enemy, and the CIA seems to be the only identifiable element of the HC above the President which can be attacked with more than adequate justification.

Of course, it is a cliche to blame the CIA, but that doesn't make it less justifiable or necessary. If the HC is made up of Wall Street lawyers and bankers, the likes and successors of H.L. Hunt, Howard Hughes, T.V. Soong, etc., what practical good is it to try to identify them? They are way beyond our clutches. The institutions of government, like the CIA, may by now be equally invulnerable, but what else can we do?

Re Bundy. The question remains, why did he do it? I believe he would have done so without JFK's ok, but I don't believe he would have done so on his own, certainly not out of stupidity. Surely he had his orders, if not from the CIA, then from the HC directly.

My guess is that the Bay of Pigs, like Watergate, was a planned failure — maybe not from the beginning, but at least from the moment the HC realized that JFK would not commit US troops. The whole thing was set up, at least from that moment, as a prelude to Vietnam. The invasion would fail, JFK embarrassed, and Cuba would serve forever after as the best example of what not to do, and of the necessity for direct, massive intervention. Did we want the same thing to happen in Vietnam that happened in Cuba? Hopefully, JFK would have learned his lesson, and would make the commitment in Vietnam.

Maybe Dulles was out of the way in Puerto Rico so that Cabell and Bissell would take the blame alone. Maybe Cabell and Bissel weren't in on it all the way, i.e., thought it was really supposed to succeed. Maybe Dulles was away to add to the general impression afterward that everyone was confused and it was a general fuckup, when in fact what happened was precisely what was supposed to happen.

Cui bono? Would Vietnam have been possible if the Bay of Pigs had succeeded? Without the rationale and threat of Communist Cuba as a bad example? When JFK refused to go along, they got rid of him.

Is Krulak still alive? Other people you worked with in his office? Some of them must have similar feelings and insights as yours. Did McNamara and Taylor know what would be in the Krulak/RFK report they were given in Honolulu as "theirs"? They must have choked when they read it.

I just read Peter Scott's article in PP Vol. 5; I haven't got hold of the other volumes yet. From this it seems that what happened in Saigon in Nov. 63 was a replay of what had happened the previous year in Laos. After the Geneva agreement in July 62 forming a coalition, JFK recalled COS Gordon Jorgensen to signal withdrawal of support for Phoumi Nosavan, just as he recalled Richardson from Saigon in Oct. 63. Do you think JFK knew about and condoned the breaking of the cease-fire after the Geneva agreement?

Are you the only one who can confirm that Diem and his brother were actually taken to the airport, and got on the plane, before they were called back? That's important, because it shows that there was a plan to evacuate him.

Paul Kattenburg and Roger Hilsman resigned in Jan. 64, and Frederick Flott (JFK's replacement for Richardson as COS Saigon) was replaced by Peer de Silva. What about people like that? They must know a lot about what really happened.

I will reserve judgement on LaRouche until I can read something original, but if what King says about him is true, he has totally discredited himself, genius or no. Why do you think he is one, by the way?

Re Oscar Lafontaine. Like you, I no longer believe in coincidence in such matters. Why should this supposedly crazy lady pick him out to stab — the ONLY important politician in Germany to take a strong stand against reunification? Sirhan was clearly a Manchurian candidate. Who knows anything about this woman? She is declared crazy and that's the end of it. That's even better than the "terrorist" cover. "False sponsors" I think they call it. The guy is stabbed, and the next thing we know is he has accepted the "majority" SPD stand on unification after all. Ha.

I don't understand your point about "pinning" the "Great Society" on Johnson. His social programs are supposed to be his greatest (only) achievement. I will read the McNeil book when I can get it.

You mention the World Council of Churches. When I was in Wash. I talked with Andrew Kimbrell, a lawyer for the Rifkin organization, and he said he was also a consultant for them. I didn't like him. For one thing, he went around opening — and closing — a lot of files mumbling about giving me some documentation re the thing I was trying to pursue, namely Rifkin's petition to Carlucci asking for information about the disposition of the 1969 Pentagon "AIDS" project. But in the end I walked out of the office with nothing but a *Washington Times* article which said, in effect, watch out doing AIDS research with rats — that might lead to an airborne form of the virus. I got a very funny feeling talking with him. If they were really interested in exposing the issue, they would have seen to it that that paragraph from the 1969 Hearings got published somewhere. It's a matter of public record, but nobody knows about it.

You mention the Far East clan as the East India Company, once removed. You've lost me there. Peter Scott went into the China Lobby thing a little in his *War Conspiracy* — Tommy Corcoran and the Sullivan-Cromwell law firm are other names I remember — but Scott is so full of minutiae that it's hard to follow, much less retain and see the big picture. Was he the first to publicize the JFK withdrawal plan? Do you keep in touch with him?

You say Carter had no chance after Dallas. In an earlier letter you referred to him as David Rockefeller's boy. Here again I'm lost.

You say the Diem's died because of their inability to handle an important action. Do you mean their evacuation? All they had to do was stay on the plane! The only people who could have gotten them off, people they would have trusted at that point, must have been CIA.

Do you mean that someone other than JFK ordered the Cabinet to Honolulu? There simply was no one who could have done that, and after all he was still alive when they were ordered there. They were there for a full-scale review of Vietnam policy, and (according to Scott's article) issued a press release on Nov. 21 confirming the 1,000-man withdrawal plan and a $33 million Accelerated Withdrawal reduction plan for fiscal 1965.

Never heard of Project EAGLE. Lansdale is such a legend that virtually any anecdote about him would make a great story.

Ken O'Donnell? Hepburn exonerates him as a bungler, and the Secret Service as well, but films show that Bill Greer, the driver, still had his foot on the brake when the head shot came. Nobody could be that much out of practice. Surely O'Donnell hasn't told what he knows yet.

I get McNeil-Lehrer here, one day late. Pepsico is the sponsor. They were Nixon's hosts in Dallas the day of JFK's assassination, and are now the biggest investor in Russia. One of Hoover's top men, I forget the name, went to Pepsico. According to McCoy Ky's heroin lab in Laos was disguised as a Pepsi-Cola bottling plant.

I note that the explosives expert for B.R. Fox Co. which Conein worked with on the Nixon task force was Michael Morrissey!

I've just finished Melanson's *Murkin Conspiracy*. Anyone who has read about JFK and RFK would be a fool not to think the same about MLK. And Allard Lowenstein. They're just getting better and better, and they vary their technique. Here a crazy, there a terrorist.

I've got to get this off. Think about the cassette/oral history thing, also the computer. Either or both would increase your audience. I especially like the oral history idea, from a selfish point of view, because I would hear more from you. Your letters are very generous and fascinating, but I wish I could hear even more. Tapes might be the answer.

Sincerely,
Michael

1990.07 ALFRED HERRHAUSEN — TERRORIST VICTIM?

[As I mentioned in my letters to Prouty and Chomsky, this was published in July 1990 in *Lies of Our Times* 1.7, 4-5 and is included in *Looking for the Enemy*, Ch. 3.3.]

The murder of Alfred Herrhausen, chairman of the Deutsche Bank, on Nov. 30, 1989, has been treated from the beginning as an open-and-shut case by the media on both sides of the Atlantic: the RAF (Rote Armee Fraktion) did it. Everyone knows the RAF did it, but if you ask them how they know, all they can say is they read it in the paper or heard it on TV. The fact is that there is next to no evidence whatsoever for this contention, in the papers or anywhere else.

The first problem in questioning this foregone conclusion is that one can be easily accused of defending a terrorist group which has been German Public Enemy No. 1 for the past 16 years. This is like appearing to defend Saddam Hussein if you're against the Gulf War.

Nevertheless, the evidence is thin. The only witness who claimed to have direct knowledge of RAF involvement turned out to be a government informer whose testimony was totally discredited. Otherwise, there is a letter of confession found at the scene of the bombing, and another a letter written in October 1989 by Helmut Pohl (not to be confused with the German chief of state), an imprisoned RAF leader, and intercepted by German authorities. In the letter, according to *Der Spiegel* (Dec. 4, 1989), Pohl says "We must orient ourselves to a new phase of the struggle" and "strike at the mechanism which makes everything work."

As head of the biggest German bank, Herrhausen was certainly a key figure in the "mechanism," and after the opening of the border on Nov. 9, and of Eastern Europe in general, he was in a particularly powerful position to influence these massive changes. Shortly before his death he announced Deutsche Bank's purchase of the British investment bank Morgan Grenfell for 2.7 billion marks, which *Spiegel* calls "the most important strategic decision of the Deutsche Bank since World War II," giving them a bridgehead in London, still the most important European center for international banking.

But Herrhausen was controversial as well as powerful. Buried on p. 9 of the 10-page *Spiegel* article is a brief explanation of why:

> Some of the things Herrhausen said and did do not fit in the simple leftist image of the ugly capitalist enemy. For example, he was the first prominent Western banker to propose publicly, two years ago, that the debt crisis in the Third World could not be solved without a partial waiver of claims by the Western creditor banks. This was also clear at the time to most other heads of banks, but they would have preferred to keep it to themselves a while longer.

No one thought to ask if this might be the key to his murder. Herrhausen supported the strategy of debt reduction, as opposed to re-financing ("fresh money"), strongly and consistently. His detailed proposal was published in the German financial newspaper *Handelsblatt* on June 6, 1989, and repeated in a presentation to the annual meeting of the World

Bank and International Monetary Fund in Washington on Sept. 25, 1989. In the latter he remarked: "Mr. Reed, speaking for Citibank, has said they are a 'new money' bank. I can tell you that the Deutsche Bank is a 'debt reduction' bank." In the same speech, he pointed out that a major obstacle to his proposed debt reduction strategy is that Japanese and American banks would find it more difficult than their European counterparts to partially compensate for their losses through tax adjustments.

The *New York Times* of Dec. 8, 1989, printed portions of a speech which Herrhausen was to give in New York on Dec. 4 at the American Council on Germany. The entire speech was published in German on the same day in *Die Zeit*. The comparison is revealing.

The original manuscript is in English (which I obtained from the public relations office of Deutsche Bank), and the title is "New Horizons in Europe." The *Times* excerpt, about half the length of the original, is entitled "Toward a Unified Germany." This is already a gross misrepresentation. It is clear, even in what the *Times* printed, that Herrhausen is not pleading for unification. In fact, he is refreshingly cautious on this point, in contrast to the increasingly strident media campaign Germans East and West had been subjected to in the preceding months. He says that if the East Germans decide to join the West, fine, but

> At this point, the question is still very much an open question. [This sentence was omitted in the *Times*.] Secondly, such an endeavour would be a difficult and certainly a long process in view of the large economic and social differences that exist today.

Henry Kissinger appeared on German television at around the same time predicting unification within 5 years. Herrhausen was figuring on at least 10 years. The reader of the NYT cannot know this, however, because the following paragraph was excised from the middle of the portion of the speech printed by the *Times*:

> Of course, the process [of transforming a socialist society into a capitalistic one] could and should be managed in stages and it should be closely coordinated with price and currency reform. Price, currency and property reform would mean profound changes throughout society in Eastern Germany. Many people in the East, including some of the leaders of the present opposition groups, are already worried about the social costs of such adjustment. The rewards would certainly not accrue instantaneously. However, I am convinced that, given an adequate economic environment in the East and pertinent support by the West, the East German as well as the other Eastern economies could achieve impressive growth. I believe the GDR in particular could then catch up on the Western standard of living in about ten years or so.

More importantly, the *Times* excerpt also omits Herrhausen's discussion of the same proposals for debt reduction and in-country development banks which he had made to the World Bank and the IMF in September. These proposals, coming from a man in his position, are surely the most newsworthy items in the speech. Why did the *Times* find them unfit to print? Herrhausen refers here to Poland, but the same could apply to other highly indebted countries:

> In the past, the banks have agreed to regular reschedulings, but now the onus is on government lenders assembled in the Paris Club [a committee representing creditor nations that meets in Paris to deal with debt problems of individual countries] to come up with a helpful contribution. They account for roughly two-thirds of the country's external debt. If

there is to be a permanent solution, this will require enlarging the strategies hitherto adopted to include a reduction of debt or debt service.

As an alternative to the European Development Bank proposed by France, Herrhausen proposes

> ... the establishment of a development bank on the spot, that is in Warsaw. Its job would be to bundle incoming aid and deploy it in accordance with strict efficiency criteria. I could well imagine that such an institution might be set up along the lines of the German Kreditanstalt für Wiederaufbau, the Reconstruction Loan Corporation, whose origin goes back to the Marshall plan.

> Representatives of the creditor countries should hold the majority in the management board of this new institution. Such a Polish "Institute for Economic Renewal" (IER), as it could be called would have two functions: it should help and monitor. Since both these functions can only be exercised in close cooperation with the Polish authorities and with Polish trade and industry, genuine involvement on the part of the Institute in the Polish economy and the country's development process would be absolutely essential. It could be set up "until further notice" or come under Polish control after a transitional period. By channeling Western "help towards self-help" in the right directions, the Institute could play a constructive role in economic reform. Similar institutions could of course be established for other countries.

These are eminently sensible ideas, but it is not difficult to imagine that they would encounter powerful opposition, much more powerful than the likes of Helmut Pohl. No matter how you put it, for the creditors, debt reduction means giving away money. And of course it is sensible to put the lending bank "on the spot," since this would keep the repaid capital and interest in the country where it is needed, but this is not the way the big international banks make money.

Herrhausen may have been a terrorist victim. The question is: Who are the terrorists?

1990.07.23 TO PROUTY

July 23, 1990

Dear Fletch,

Thanks very much indeed for the books. I'm especially pleased to have a bound copy of *The Secret Team* — honored in fact, because you probably only have a few. Now I can donate my xeroxed copy to the library.

Have you heard from Cavin/St. Martins yet? You might also try Black Rose Books, 3981 Boulevard St-Laurent, #444, Montreal, H2W 1Y5, Quebec, Canada (also a NY office, 340 Nagel Dr., Cheektowaga, NY 14225).

They've published among other things a book I'm reading now called *Language and Politics*, ed. Carlos Otero, which is a collection of interviews with Noam Chomsky. If you have time to read it, I'd be very interested to know what you think. It's interesting because they're interviews and he ranges over a lot of topics, and because he loosens up from his usual style, which is pretty tight and dry and hard to read over a long period.

To be honest, you and Chomsky are the two writers I respect most, simply because I think I've learned more about the world from you two guys than anyone else. The difference is that he does not see a conspiracy. He goes about as far as you can go with what I would call a structural analysis, explaining everything as a more or less natural consequence of capitalism. He calls himself, if anything, an anarchist, which doesn't mean chaos but simply that the ideal form of government is no government, which I agree with. In fact, that is true conservatism. He doesn't propose, though, he criticizes, which is I guess in the tradition of Adorno and the Frankfurt School (Marcuse came out of that), so you don't have all this pie-in-the-sky stuff about revolution and the rise of the proletariat and naive (and false) evaluations of so-called Marxist regimes. He stops at conspiracy, though. The only assassination I know of him writing about is that of Fred Hampton, the Black Panther leader, who was apparently simply gunned down by the FBI.

I suppose in a way it all amounts to the same thing, whether you actually see a High Cabal, with (unknown) faces and names, or not. Chomsky would say that it is the system which reigns, not individuals, though obviously individuals have to get together to perform specific things — like shooting a president. Such things, though not predictable in any specific way, are inevitable consequences of a system which is structured to serve the interests of big business. People who get in the way too much are knocked off more or less the same way competition is eliminated by capitalism, by violence when necessary, hence not only individual assassinations but by wars and proxy wars, which of course also serve to create markets.

The trouble is, for people like I guess us, who seem to have concentrated more on the individual acts, it's hard to just chalk it up to the system, hard to see it as an abstraction. On the other hand, Chomsky would probably say that it is dangerous to try to identify specific groups as responsible for what is wrong with society, because it leads to scapegoating, with the wrong groups getting the blame, like Jews, blacks, communists, Catholics, or whatever. He says the US is ripe for such a fascist movement now, and that the level of religious fanaticism is a sign of that, comparable with Iran, except we are the only highly industrialized society with this level of fanaticism. Reagan has reduced the US to a Third World country as far as the majority of the population is concerned, and Chomsky does say that this is deliberate, but he means that is the way the system works and is supposed to work. That applies to the media and everything else. There is no reason for them to care about the freedom and well-being of people in general, since they serve and therefore reflect the interests of corporations, which are interested only in profit. We are not surprised to hear that General Motors does everything it can get away with to increase profit, so why should we not expect institutions like the press which are also corporations, or a government which serves the interests of corporations, to act differently.

I agree with all this, but I cannot also help thinking, like you, about the individuals who obviously must take part, knowingly, in specific acts. The problem is identifying and exposing them. Chomsky would probably say that is not so important, because as long as the system works as it does, there will always be individuals to serve whatever specific purpose comes along. When you get so many assassinations, though, connect them to Vietnam, and then to AIDS, it's very difficult not to see it as a conspiracy. That's why I was curious to see what Chomsky would say about Segal. I would also like to see what he would say about your work. Why don't you send him a copy of Saigon Solution (Prof. Noam Chomsky, Dept. of Linguistics and Philosophy, 20-D-219, MIT, Cambridge, MA 02139)? I think it would be worth it. I'm sure he would read it and write back to you.

By the way, he writes regularly for a new magazine called *Lies of Our Times*, put out by Ellen Ray and Bill Schaap of *Covert Action Information Bulletin*.

They're publishing a little article I wrote about the Herrhausen thing in the July issue, I think, and I'll send you a copy when I get the printed version.

I have to admit I'm feeling a little guilty for not mentioning you in the article, since you sent me the NYT article and it was your idea in the first place. I know you don't need it, and it wouldn't have served any real purpose, but still I hope it wasn't a faux pas on my part.

Do you read CAIB? For my money, that, *The Nation*, and *Mother Jones* are the only journals worth reading. I can't decide whether to let my subscription to *Time* lapse, simply because it is useful I guess to know what the current lies are. For example, recently they had a cover story on the so-called rise of neo-Naziism in Europe. I think this was a lie, intended to create public "concern" about a united Germany, especially a united neutral Germany. Result: Germany will stay in NATO. Anybody with a few bucks can get some hoodlums to desecrate a cemetery, and if the cemetery is Jewish and you are *Time*, you can create "the rise of neo-Naziism in Europe."

Similarly, the last issue with the long article on AIDS in Africa. They've hardly written anything on AIDS in the last couple of years. Buried in the article is the aside that "some think AIDS comes from Central Africa," though I guess even they don't dare to propagate the monkey theory in detail any more. Then you have a lot of stuff about how sexually promiscuous Africans are, with things like "ritual cleansing," i.e., sleeping with the nearest relative of a deceased spouse. Hardly a word about sanitation conditions or other factors that contribute to the spread of the virus. In fact, they say the problem of contaminated blood supplies is under control. I doubt that. On the other hand, they say educating the people about safe sex is almost impossible because of cultural prohibitions about discussing such matters. What is the result? The reader is forced to conclude that if AIDS kills millions of Africans, as predicted, it's their own damn fault, because 1) they fuck like bunnies, and 2) they're so primitive you can't get them to do anything about it.

That is pure propaganda, racist propaganda. Mere assertions, with no documentation, no attempt to back up what they say, no (apparent) recognition of the political consequences. At the same time, somebody like Segal presents just the opposite kind of argument, consistently over a period of years, clear, scientific, logical, documented, and is totally ignored. Can you imagine *Time* or any other publication mentioning, as an aside, that "some people" think that Robert Gallo created AIDS and set it loose on the world, presumably by accident?

I know I'm wasting too many words on a magazine that's not even worth wiping your ass with, but it's even more important as a propaganda organ over here. Most foreigners or Americans living abroad will pick up either *Time* or *Newsweek* or the *International Herald Tribune* if they want "news" (ha!) in English, simply because nothing else is readily available. At least in the US you have some choice. You can't buy *The Nation*, much less CAIB, at any newsstand, outside the US. You have to subscribe, and in any case you always get it several weeks late.

I'm happy to finally get something in print (about politics), but I'm wondering if journals are the best medium for me. I just don't have the access. It's hard enough to keep informed in the US, and I think that's still where the best information comes from, because there's just so much more of it there. It's hard work, but in the US there are other sources that never get in the mainstream press, but over here it's much more difficult. That's very frustrating, and sometimes it makes me wish I could go back so I could do more.

Here's another example. Maybe I've mentioned it before, but I ordered the Honegger book from here last Oct., and around May the bookstore sent me a note saying that after 12 reminders they had finally given up trying to order the book. Fortunately, I bought it in the States. That looks like damage control.

I wonder how worried Bush and Co. really are about Germany. Walters must be very busy, though I'm sure he has a lot of help. Maradona, the Argentine star, said Germany "bought" the world cup. I wouldn't be surprised. World champs and unification the same year — another one of those hard-to-swallow coincidences, like the stabbing of the only major politician (Lafontaine) to oppose unification (before the stabbing!), and the blowing up of the only major banker to promote debt reduction (Herrhausen).

I also keep wondering about Gorbachev. I can't help liking him, and suspecting that he is not only intelligent but honest. Can he really just be a puppet on a string like Bush? Maybe he has a deeper strategy. I know this may be wishful thinking, but maybe he thinks: Ok, capitalism has won this round (the last 45 years), so we'll just let it play itself out. That would be classical Marx anyway. The revolution won't come until the final stage, when the working class is so utterly destitute that revolution is inevitable. What the so-called communists have been trying to do, apparently, is speed up the process by force, which doesn't work. You end up with statism, totalitarianism, Stalinism. Marx took a much longer view, and maybe Gorbachev recognizes this. On second thought, I guess it doesn't make any difference; he's still rolling over and playing dead, whether he's dead or not, and we'll never know the difference. Maybe AIDS has more to do with this than we realize, too. I have a feeling it's very, very important. Suppose Gorbachev simply knows that the US is so far ahead in biological weaponry that there is no point in trying to catch up. Suppose the US told him, "Look, see AIDS? We did it, and we can do much more. And we will, if you don't play ball." What could he have done in the face of this?

But if that is true, he is a consummate actor. It's hard to look at him and think that his actions are motivated by such an absolute horror vision. I know that sounds naive, but I do place some trust in appearances, even on TV. Bush vs. Gorbachev, for example, there is something to be seen in their faces, their voices.

Take Segal, for example. He was here last month and gave a

talk, and I video-taped it. He writes extremely well — even I can judge that, as a non-native speaker — but to see him say the same thing on camera does give you more information, though it is hard to define, since it is more what we call an "impression." The media control and abuse this enormously, of course, by timing and selection, but if you just point the camera at somebody and let them talk long enough, you do learn something about the man (or woman) that you can't get from print. Segal gives the impression that he is telling the truth, or what he honestly thinks is the truth, that he is a man who should be taken seriously. (You gave me the same impression in your appearance in the Turner film, by the way.)

Back to Chomsky, I've written to him about the Segal thing (he didn't know about it) and sent him the materials, but he wouldn't commit himself. He said it "sent a chill up his spine," but I was a little disappointed that he couldn't seem to form a firmer opinion on the science of it than I can. Biology is not his field either, but he is much more of a (language) scientist than I am, and he believes in scientific truth. He has often said, for example, that linguistics should emulate the natural sciences in its methods and aims. I thought at MIT he would at least have access to colleagues whose opinions would be scientifically reliable. It might just be hard for him to admit that the natural sciences are as corrupt, just as subject to lies and manipulation, as everything else, especially now, when high tech knowledge is only available to a tiny group of specialists who are furthermore completely dependent on government and corporate funding. I wonder if he isn't tempted to retain this last strand of idealism, the idea of "pure science."

Segal says quite openly that nobody will agree with him, even debate with him, in public, because every one of them that is in a position to know anything is completely gagged by their dependence on the sources of their research funds. Chomsky is the last person in the world I would accuse of being naive, but I do wonder if he would still like to think that scientific truth is the one kind of truth that cannot be suppressed. I found this difficult to accept, too, but I'm getting used to it. I have not found a microbiologist yet, and I've tried a few, who is willing or able to discuss Segal's theory seriously, much less refute it in an even half-way convincing way. That is exactly what Segal says, the way they all react to him. The more I see of that, the more I am convinced that Segal is right. All somebody has to do is make the slightest, most unsubstantiated squeak about AIDS being around earlier than 1979, and it makes the headlines. Everybody believes that, no questions asked. My god! If Segal is right, of course they will arrange to "find" evidence of AIDS before 1979. It's like those phony pictures of Oswald holding up the supposed murder weapon and copies of the Socialist Worker, with a chin shadow showing noon and a body shadow showing late afternoon! Or JFK's brain disappearing! Whoops, whar is that damn thing...had it just a minute ago. It's just a circus. Maybe we should be laughing, but I can't. I've talked to some people who do seem to take it all very lightly, especially the assassinations, even the war. Oh yeah, of course, it's all corrupt, everything is manipulated. Terrible, ain't it. But you can see that it hasn't really gotten them, they don't really see it yet, or feel it. That's even more frustrating sometimes than the ones that refuse to see it. How can they know and pretend not to care, as if they were living in a different world? (Maybe they are.) AIDS does get to them, though. They do their best to brush that off too, but it's more difficult. What gets to them most I think is the black and white proof that the DOD asked for $5-10 million to create an AIDS-like virus on June 9, 1969. They don't know about it, if they haven't read Segal, and that alone scares them, as it should.

We're going to Ireland this week, west coast. Rent a car and do some biking. We like that. You talked about the transportation bind in your last letter. How true. The bicycle is the most civilized form of transportation. Maximum efficiency, minimum upkeep, ideal speed, no pollution. I really get a nice feeling on a bike, for a lot of reasons. Think what it would do to the HC if a sizable amount of people just decided to take their bikes instead of cars! That might be the most subversive thing we could do. How would they stop us? If the HC is beyond stopping by direct political confrontation, ecology might be the answer. That's the way the Greens started out, and I think they would have been more effective in the long run if they'd stuck with it, because ecology eventually confronts politics anyway, and it's harder to combat, to criminalize or demonize. What are you going to do to stop a mass movement of people who just want to ride bicycles, swim in rivers, breathe fresh air, not die of radiation poisoning, etc.? If the ecology issues are ridden hard, many of the political ones will follow automatically. You could base an entire political philosophy just on the bicycle, and it would have results. Every time you ride your bike, you take something away from Oil, Steel, Roads, Cars, the whole shebang. The problem is, such issues expand and get diffused to the point where they cannot penetrate and have any real effect. Bikes expands to the whole environment, and the environment expands to politics in general (that's what happened to the Greens). Result: poof! If you could get X number of people to do a simple thing like ride bikes Y percent more of the time than they do now, you could probably even calculate pretty precisely how things would change — for the better.

Hope you're feeling well.
Michael

1990.07.23 TO WEISBERG

July 23, 1990

Dear Mr. Weisberg,

Thank you very much for your very interesting letter. I hope you are recovering well from the operation.

I am very interested to know that you are convinced Ray didn't kill King. There's no question in my mind that Oswald and Sirhan (where is he now?) didn't kill anyone, either, but I have only read Melanson on King and that didn't seem conclusive.

I respect your opinion, though, and I know you have talked with Ray and investigated the case thoroughly. Especially since you seem to have a relatively conservative view of the other assassinations — I mean, a skeptical view of the literature — that makes what you say about Ray all the more convincing.

We can't all investigate everything. You make it very clear that private investigations of these covered-up crimes is a lifetime job and well-nigh impossible at that. Even reading the books is a major task. That means that at some point, we have to choose whom to believe, at least, whose opinion to accept as a working hypothesis.

People are not courts of law. I know I will never be able to prove anything about the assassinations, so I have to leave that to dedicated men like yourself, and thank God there are some. Nevertheless, I want to know the truth, I want to know what reality is, what kind of world I am living in. I cannot wait for a court of law or a Congressional committee to present the "truth" to me tied up with a blue ribbon. I have to take everything in that I can, which includes a lot more than what might be admissible as juridical evidence — fortunately — and form an opinion. I cannot NOT have an opinion. It's there, based on what I've read and seen and heard and thought and sensed. Of course, it can change, and I try to make sure it does change to correspond to new in- formation, which is sometimes hard, because we have a tendency to stay in the same ruts, for whatever reasons.

I'm saying all this because I think you have a different perspective. Your objective is proof, and as I say, thank God you're there. What I mean is, when I say I believe you, and I believe Ray didn't shoot King, partly because you say so, that is the truth, as far as I can figure it out.

If I waited for proof I'd never believe anything. This is not blind faith or anything like that. I'm extremely skeptical, as we'll all have to be after all the lies that the government and the media have served up to us.

I have no ax to grind. I just want to know the truth. So I do what I can. One result is, I write to Weisberg, a man I respect, he says he thinks Ray didn't kill King, and I believe him, because it also jives with what I've read and what I think about the other assassinations and the way the world is.

By the same token, you've put some doubt in my mind about the books you mention, but since some of that doesn't fit with what I've thought so far, it's a little different, so I'd like to ask you [to] say a bit more, if you would.

One book von didn't mention was Groden/Livingstone's *High Treason*. What do you think of that?

They first dismiss Lifton, then retract it saying it might have been that way, but that in any case it is certain that the body was altered and the autopsy photos and x-rays forged.

The details don't really matter all that much, e.g., whether the alteration was done at Walter Reed or Bethesda, or whether the ambulance came in the front or the back door and when.

Do you disagree with these conclusions?

I was surprised to see you refer to the Garrison book as "fiction." To me it seems the most plausible explanation of what happened and why. Prouty thinks the same thing, but goes even farther with the conspiracy thing. If you put Groden/Livingstone together with Garrison, it seems to me you've got as close to the truth as anyone is likely to get for the next 100 years, unless there's a revolution. That is because, if they are right, there is no way that the truth can be condoned, i.e., proved, without a revolution, because the accused party (the govt, CIA, FBI) is also the judge and prosecutor.

I would be very interested to know in detail what things you disagree with Garrison about, or Groden for that matter.

You say *Farewell America* is a fake by the SDECE. Why would they do that? Who is Lamarre? It is full of details about the assassination, including things like quotes of Secret Service agents right afterward. What is fabricated? That there were more than 3 shots, that the head shot came from the grassy knoll, that the Secret Service didn't react as fast as it should and could have, that they failed to check out the surrounding buildings? Who else was saying that in 1968? The next 20 years of research has borne it all out, hasn't it? Again, I would be very interested in a detailed critique.

Re the Bay of Pigs, Prouty is very explicit on this, and he was there. JFK agreed to the second air strike at noon on Sunday, the day before the landing, and Bundy canceled it the same night about 9 o'clock, according to Prouty, without JFK's permission, believe it or not. I haven't read *Operation Zapata* but he says it's all in there, and that is nothing else than Maxwell Taylor's personal report to the president.

Re Segal, cf. the House DOD Subcommittee Hearings on June 9, 1969. The DCD requested $5-10 million to develop an AIDS-like virus. That is incontrovertible fact. It doesn't mean they did it, but it does <u>prove</u> that they wanted to and that they thought it was feasible. Segal takes it from there, and is totally ignored by the press. This is a coverup at least as big as the assassinations. He could be proved wrong by scientific experiment.

I really do appreciate very much your writing to me, and I would be very pleased to hear more from you.

Do you know Peter Dale Scott? He has done the most regarding the connection between the assassinations and the war, I believe.

To my mind — again, I am just a guy trying to understand the world, not prove anything — JPK was killed, as Garrison says, primarily because he wanted to pull out of Vietnam. (That is fact, too, though suppressed and distorted if mentioned at all, in order to maintain the lie that LBJ merely continued JFK's escalation of the war, when in fact he reversed JFK's policy.)

I think MLK was killed because he had joined the anti-war camp and was a real threat, just like RFK. The govt was not ready to end the war in 1968, and not ready (still isn't) to make the kind of radical changes on social issues that MLK and RFK had the charisma to bring about. The mafia cannot have had anything to do with these things, except to the extent that they work for the govt, or <u>are</u> the govt.

As for the big question, who controls the govt, two things are certain: 1) it is not the people of the US, and 2) it is not the president or the Congress. Prouty calls it the High Cabal, others would say Big Business, or a Marxist would say capitalism. Whatever it is, it isn't working the way it should, and certainly not the way most people think it does.

Sincerely,
Michael Morrissey

1990.07.25 TO PROUTY

July 25, 1990

Dear Fletch,

I put my letter in the mail Monday afternoon and got yours, with the great news, on Tuesday morning! Now I'm up at 6 on Wednesday to get this off today because we're leaving tomorrow for Ireland for 3 weeks, so I won't be able to do justice to your letter but I want to answer it.

I'm extremely pleased that you want to go ahead with the oral history/memoirs/biography, so here's my enthusiastic confirmation! I am very serious about it and excited and honored to be able to have a part in it. The Time Line is fine; I'll keep an index and give you as much feedback and questions as I can.

Your reservations about writing better than you talk and not being able to revise are no problem. I would say forget it, that's the whole purpose of doing it orally. I'm not going to transcribe the tapes. Whatever I do with them will be a selection, paraphrase, or extrapolation from them as well as from your letters and, I hope, from conversations we might have in the future. It is raw material, and the whole point, I would think, is to get quantity more than quality in the sense of style and organization and all the things we have to worry about in writing. If I were the one behind the microphone, I can imagine that the real problem, if there is one, would be to get yourself to relax and really talk freely, just as if you were talking to a person in the room and nothing was being recorded.

As I mentioned in my letter, video adds a lot too, but that would be impractical (especially since US-German systems are different; I wouldn't be able to play the tapes). Audio, especially with cassettes, is a maximally efficient technology if you consider that we're trying to capture a personality (you) as well as a lot of information. Once we have that as a basis, getting something in writing of one kind or another is an entirely different affair.

So, yes indeed, sing a few, if you like, in fact, do whatever you like. Sometimes the most spontaneous ideas are the best, aren't they, and for this kind of thing, as far as I'm concerned at least, absolutely anything not only goes but would be very welcome. If your wife or son or daughters happen to be around, talk to them. Or anybody else. How about phone calls? You seem to have a lot, and if you could record those with decent quality, that would be fascinating, because it would have you interacting with other people. We don't have to ever publish any of that, and obviously we wouldn't without getting permissions if names are involved. I'd love to have heard your conversation with Stone, for example, though I know that was in person, simply because I'd like to know what interested him and what his reaction was to what you said. When I was there you got a call which I couldn't help overhearing, and in fact I meant to ask you about something: Did you say something about "4 men firing from a bridge" at JFK? I thought only the buildings behind and the grassy knoll were involved.

Maybe it will help you get started if I try to tell you what I am interested in. Not that you should try organizing anything, just to give you an idea of the kind of detail that one listener (me) is interested in. I would say there are three general areas, all of equal importance:

1) your personal experiences, including what you thought and

felt at the time as well as what you did or experienced

2) what happened, i.e., the historical facts that you can attest to through personal experience or documentation, especially things that differ or are omitted from other accounts

3) your interpretation of the facts, what you think has really been going on

I will be trying to accumulate as much detail in all three of these areas as I can and I will be trying to keep them separate in my mind. I think I've mentioned before that one thing I'm especially interested in is the development of your own thoughts and attitudes, which of course is a mixture of all three. I am interested in how, when, and why people change their minds about things, which is not an easy thing to describe. Don't we all have certain turning points in our lives which are immensely significant for us but trivial seen from the "outside"? In my case, for example, the night I watched the Turner film was one of these points, but it's very hard to describe, because the event itself — watching a TV film — is trivial, compared to its significance in relation to how I felt before and afterward about a lot of things. Since what we are talking about, ultimately, is mind control, or obliviousness, or propaganda, or whatever, it is important to see how people can and do change in spite of it. That is freedom, the ability to change.

As I get back to you, I may ask questions that seem provocative, but don't misunderstand that for antagonism. I will try to challenge you to make the best case possible for everything you say that differs from standard accounts, because that's the way it always is. If you say what everybody else says you don't have to substantiate anything, you just say it and people accept it. So you're probably going to get a lot of feedback asking for details, the more the better. Even if you describe a conversation, the more you can remember about exactly when it was, where, the weather, how people were dressed, what you had for breakfast, what you said/he/she said, what chair you sat in

— everything like that is important because it makes it all the more real and therefore credible. That's the big advantage of doing it this way. You can feel free to go on and on as long as you like, precisely because you're not worried about the verbatim result.

For example, if you'd like to start with memories of your childhood, parents, home, school, etc. that's fine. It doesn't have to relate directly to the "big stuff." What kind of kid was Prouty, what was he like as a young officer, etc. Of course it is useful to get other people's impressions, too, but your own recollections will in themselves build a kind of self-portrait that changes over time, at least that would be the goal.

I hope I'm not making it sound difficult — my intention is just the opposite. In sum, don't worry about speaking well, just talk. Here's another example which just pops into my mind. We've had an exchange about the Report from Iron Mountain, and you said you heard people at the time expressing similar sentiments. That is very important, but obviously you're not going to be able to document it, and you're talking about a novel. So everything depends on how much detail you can dig out of your memory about those conversations as they actually took place. Names, places, times, every detail would be relevant.

Re names, I realize that this can be problematic, but I will press you for them as well as for other detail (my job as gadfly!). If you don't want to identify somebody or something (secret document, event, etc.) specifically but want to talk about anyway, the best thing would be to say why you don't want to do so and use a fictitious name or as close a description as you can without giving away the identity.

Let me just run through your letter quickly.

Stone's *Born on the Fourth of July* is the best Vietnam film I've seen. I sent him, I think around the same time I first wrote to you, a copy of my review of the Turner film, and he did write back a short note, but just to say how busy he was, with no other comment.

Too bad Cavin didn't come through. It's discouraging, but don't give up. Maybe a foreign publisher would be easier. I wrote you about Black Rose, and you might also try Zed Books, 57 Caledonian Rd., London N1 9BU (US address 171 First Ave., Atlantic Highlands, NJ 07716). They did William Blum's *The CIA*, which by the way has a blurb from Oliver Stone — maybe he could help.

Oil must be the key to a lot. Farewell America has what seems like a good chapter on it, also in Hougan's Spooks, where he talks about the Achanarry Agreement back in the 20s up to the Onassis-Nixon feud (I'm sure Jackie didn't marry him just because he was rich). Both Onassis's children, son and daughter, seemed to have died mysteriously.

By the way, I wrote to Harold Weisberg recently to find out how to order his self-published books, and I took the opportunity to ask him about some of the literature. One of the few people he said anything good about was you, "as long as he sticks with what he was personally involved in, like the NSAMs." He dismisses Garrison and Marrs as "fiction," which surprised me. He said somebody named "Lamarre" and the French SDECE fabricated *Farewell America*. I wonder. Who else was saying there were more than three shots, placed two shooters the grassy knoll, mentioned the route change, and many other things, in 1968? If it was made up, I wish someone would say which part. He doesn't seem to think much of "conspiracy theorizing," as he calls it, but maybe he is at the other extreme — too cautious. If we wait for the truth to come out in a court of law or Congressional committee, we'll never get it, certainly not in our lifetimes.

He does say that he is convinced that Ray did not shoot King. That's worth a lot, because he did a lot of work on that, interviewed Ray, etc., and of the three (JFK, RFK, MLK) the "strongest" case is against Ray. So I'll just take Weisberg's word for that and make up my own mind on the other things.

I would like to get hold of some of that literature on Darwinism. Fuller talked about "reverse Darwinism" but I can't recall the argument. I wasn't convinced. Someone should do a book on all the books — the anti-Creationists/Darwinians, Segal, you — that can't get published. A great tribute to Free Speech.

I remember Fuller too talking about the Dhow, impressive example of no doubt myriad ways that so-called primitive cultures are far superior to ours. I wrote about bicycles in my letter the other day, and last night I saw a documentary about present-day Vietnam. Interesting that when you bomb a country back to the Stone Age, or at least to a pre-industrial age, the most evident vestige of post-industrial civilization that remains is the bicycle. You have people with almost nothing they don't make by hand, except for thousands of bicycles.

Our library doesn't have a copy of the Gravel *Pentagon Papers*, unfortunately, which makes steady reference impossible. Would it be possible to use the paperback NYT version (which is affordable), and fill in the gaps with references to Gravel which I could then try to zerox when I have the opportunity?

I still wonder what the "purpose" of Watergate was. It's hard to imagine that assassinations of presidents, wars, and now diseases can be contrived, i.e. planned by people as conspiracies, without believing that Watergate was planned, to accomplish exactly what it accomplished — get rid of Nixon. For the same reason, I connected the Bay of Pigs to Vietnam. How can we be sure there is not a connection?

Your point about ONI is well taken. Oswald would have been run by ONI too, right? And they go back to the first Mafia connections, with Lucky Luciano, as Alfred McCoy points out. By the way, you said you worked with McCoy. Where is he now? I've been trying to collect addresses. I wrote to Peter Scott c/o Dept. of English, U of CA Berkeley but haven't had a response.

Re Malthus, East India, Yale, P-2. If there's no lit on it, does anyone else share your theory, or does it originate with you?

The Lansdale photo in Garrison. That's big stuff, isn't it? That would make an Anderson column, surely, especially if you identified the other people who agree with you. Why can't you? I believe you, but a skeptic would ask you what it is about the back of the guy's head that makes you so sure. He is the "Focal Point" you allude to, isn't he?

What else has Honneger been writing on, and why do you think she has been set up? Do you have her address? The October Surprise story seems so hot that I cannot understand how they've managed to control it, or how the book got published in the first place. I guess I'm being naive again.

Voting is fine but who is to say that is not controlled too? When you had a lot of people counting votes by hand that was one thing, but the more mechanized and computerized it becomes, the more chances there are to control it. Just control the guys who write the programs. Frankly, I think the 1972 election was a fraud. I just can't believe Nixon got more votes than McGovern, much less a landslide.

Everything goes back to the coup in 63. Given that, plus coverup, everything is not only possible but likely. Election fraud? No problem. Evidence of AIDS before 1979? No problem. Program a crazy woman to stab a dangerous Social Democrat politician in the neck? No problem. Blow up a banker? No problem.

The gene pool business, Far East Clan, T.V. Soong sounds very close to the Yellow Peril. Since that's one of the many bug-a-boos which have been foisted on us, along with the Red Peril, Black Peril, Jewish Peril, and Catholic Peril, to create the mind control that we are trying to free ourselves from, it's hard to swallow. I will chew on that carefully. I still haven't read LaRouche in the original, but it's one thing to say the government and business and their institutions (CFR etc.) share the same values (protecting big business profits) and act within the parameters, and Chomsky would say this doesn't even have to be called a conspiracy (though I have a problem with that too, as I said). It's quite another to attribute these similar actions, conspiratorial or not, to a group that one identifies as "Jewish" or on racial grounds. That is more likely a reflection of sheer desperation, the basis of fascism, exactly what Chomsky says and also what Peter Drucker said. Whatever LaRouche says, when he starts talking about the Jews or whatever being behind it all, he loses all credibility. We know the profit motive explains a lot, and we know the government protects and supports that, and we even know that much of what the government does is conspiratorial. That's enough! Why do we need the High Cabal? Money and greed, capitalism, doesn't that explain it? It's hard enough to get the details on how Big Business, banks, law firms, etc. work together with the government, CIA, etc. in particular cases, but what evidence is there of an HC? If you postulate an HC with racial overtones, i.e. a Jewish Cabal or whatever, you've taken the leap into the irrational. We're trying to tell people, Look, what you believe about Free and Democratic America is not rational and doesn't square with the evidence. If we then propose something which is equally irrational and for which we can also produce no evidence, everything collapses. There is plenty of evidence that white Christian men have conspired against non-white non-Christian men, but what evidence is there going the other way?

This is a very important point, I think. It may be what happened to LaRouche. Maybe he had a reasonable analysis of what the world really works, up to the point where his feeling of helplessness and frustration caused him to cross that crucial line, to grab at a simple solution: just get rid of the Jews and everything will be fine. Chomsky's right, that is fascism. He is anti-Israel, but that's different. He has extremely well-reasoned and documented arguments for opposing Israeli as well as US foreign policy, the areas he has been most concerned about.

I wonder what Krulak would think of Saigon Solution. And, for that matter, Bundy, McNamara, De Silva, and the rest of them?

I read that article about putting military spies in business in the *Inter. Herald Tribune* (which takes stuff from the NYT and *Wash. Post*): author, George Lardner Jr.!

One assumes, reading the textbooks, that JFK ordered the Cabinet to Honolulu. The problem is to show why that could not have been the case.

I forced myself to finish *Foucault's Pendulum* but am none the wiser. A complete mystery, and there are so many real mysteries much closer to home that I can't get interested in concocted ones or innuendoes. It's not well written, in my opinion, so the only thing left is a hotch-potch of information, but I don't see the connection, and I don't like puzzles for their own sake. If Eco had something to say, he didn't say it, as far as I'm concerned. Creating more puzzles doesn't help. It's like all these books hinting at "dark implications" regarding the assassinations. Hell, somebody's got to say it, then at least we can talk about it. Garrison, you, Groden, Marrs, you've all said it. The problem is getting the word out and getting people to listen.

What I have...I have *The Secret Team* (thanks again), Saigon Solution, article about travel safety, Alumnus tribute to Barney Troy, copy of your letter to *Wash. Post* May 13, 1990, and your letters to me — that's it.

Got to finish. Again, I'm really happy about this. Let's do it. I'll try to be a good gadfly for you. I'll be looking forward to getting the first tapes.

I was just starting to print this when I checked the mail, which had the issue of *Lies of Our Times* with my article — enclosed.

Best,
Michael

1990.08.24 TO WEISBERG

Aug. 24, 1990

Dear Mr. Weisberg,

Thank you for your letter of July 30. I am sending you an international postal money order today for $12 for *Post Mortem*, which you should receive separately about the same time you receive this letter.

I've enclosed some pages from *JFK: The Mystery Unraveled*, Liberty Lobby, 1986, which consists of reprints from *The Spotlight*. The whole chapter is about you, and I would be very interested to know if it accurately reflects your views.

I believe *The Spotlight* and Liberty Lobby are LaRouche organizations. The only other things I know about LaRouche is what Dennis King says in *Lyndon LaRouche and the New American Racism*, which depicts him as a neo-Nazi, anti-Semitic kook. He is one who tried to pin AIDS on the KGB in 1986, shortly before Jakob Segal suggested the far more plausible theory that it originated at Ft. Detrick. But some people I respect have a more complicated opinion of him, that he has some good as well as kooky ideas. I believe Walter Marchetti is or has been associated with them, for example. Is there any good literature on this Bilderberger, CPC, Rockefeller etc. conspiracy stuff? The CIA is enough of a conspiracy for me, though who knows what forces control them. Not the President, certainly.

I also enclose an article I published in the last issue of *Lies of Our Times*, a new journal put out by Ellen Ray and Bill Schaap of *CovertActlon Information Bulletin* . What do you think of them?

As you can see, I have no inside information — the point is simply that we are so brainwashed that it is hard for anything even to occur to us that does not appear in the mainstream press. If you haven't been "radicalized" by JEK, RFK, MLK etc., you just never consider other possibilities.

Similarly now, with the Kuwait thing. I don't know what will happen, but two things have already happened: oil prices went up, and I don't think there will be any more talk of cuts in the Defense budget.

I don't believe you've mentioned Jim Marrs, *Crossfire*. Seems a good comprehensive summary to me — what do you think?

Have you read Barbara Honegger, *October Surprise*? Seems like it disappeared as soon as it appeared.

I don't understand your remarks about Groden/Livingstone. Their argument that the autopsy photos and X-rays were faked defeats the official story, but you seem to be asking, why would the govt do this? I don't get it. If you mean, why did they do such a bad job of faking everything, including (possibly) altering the body as Lifton contends, that is understandable enough. They wouldn't have had time. But in any case here you are talking about motives. What about the photographic analysis and the testimony of the Dallas doctors — do you feel that Groden presents any of this evidence inaccurately?

I hope you are recovering your health. I understand that it is difficult for you to write, and I appreciate it very much.

Sincerely,
Michael Morrissey

1990.09 Burying the Public Record

[This was written in September 1990, essentially a shorter version of what I had written a year earlier (1989.09). I hoped it might be more acceptable for publication if I focused more on the media (non-) reaction to the MacArthur testimony rather than the Segal theory. It was never published, except on my website.]

There is a brief but potentially explosive piece of testimony buried in the Congressional Record of 1969 that has never made the papers; it will not be hard to see why:

> Molecular biology is a field that is advancing very rapidly, and eminent biologists believe that within a period of 5 to 10 years it would be possible to produce a synthetic biological agent, an agent that does not naturally exist and for which no natural immunity could have been acquired...a new infective microorganism which could differ in certain important aspects from any known disease-causing organisms. Most important of these is that it might be refractory [resistant] to the immunological and therapeutic processes upon which we depend to maintain our relative freedom from infectious disease.
>
> A research program to explore the feasibility of this could be completed in approximately 5 years at a total cost of $10 million.

This was part of the testimony of Dr. D. M. MacArthur, then Deputy Director of Research and Technology for the Dept. of Defense, before the House Subcommittee on Appropriations on June 9, 1969. Let us be clear about what it means. It does NOT mean that the U.S. government created AIDS. It DOES mean that the U.S. government wanted, and considered it feasible, to create an AIDS-like virus as early as 1969.

It would hardly be surprising if the government wanted to keep this quiet, but what about the press? The significance of MacArthur's testimony has not been overlooked by everyone — only by the mass media. Robert Harris and Jeremy Paxman mention it in their 1982 book *A Higher Form of Killing: The Secret Story of Chemical & Biological Warfare* (NY: Hill & Wang); cf. also Robert Lederer, "The Origin and Spread of AIDS," in *CovertAction Information Bulletin* (Summer 1987). On Feb. 10, 1988, Jeremy Rifkin petitioned the Secretary of Defense (Carlucci) on behalf of the Foundation on Economic Trends, demanding information as to the further disposition of the 1969 MacArthur/DOD proposal. Needless to say, there was no substantive reply.

If this is the tip of the iceberg, Jakob Segal has outlined the rest, but we do not find his name in the NYT Index, nor his articles in the scientific journals, nor his books (very likely) in the library. He has been saying since 1986 that AIDS is an accidental product of U.S. biological warfare research (a.k.a. "defense research" — on which 90.6 million tax dollars were spent in fiscal 1985-86, for example). Segal is a biologist (professor emeritus at Humboldt University in East Berlin), but as far as the "scientific community" is concerned, he is a non-entity. This would not normally bar him from the popular press as well, but in this case, larger forces seem to be at work.

Why is Segal taboo? If he is right, the U.S. government is responsible for AIDS, which makes the answer obvious enough. If he is wrong, one would expect to hear more from the experts than dismissive snorts and echoes of arguments that have long been repudiated (such as the claims of African origin in green monkeys or "isolated villages"). There is no middle ground. If it cannot be shown that he is either right or wrong, i.e. if he may be right, or even partially right, the cat is out of the bag. As a matter of fact, the whole question of the origin of AIDS seems to have become taboo. The African monkey business has stuck in the public's mind, and it is convenient to leave it at that.

Consider the Peter Duesberg theory, by way of contrast. Duesberg suggested in 1987 that AIDS is not caused by a virus at all, a highly speculative, but convenient, thesis. If the virus (HIV-I) does not cause the disease, the question of the virus being a laboratory product is defused. Perhaps this explains why the Duesberg thesis was hotly debated in both the scientific and the popular press, while Segal has been completely ignored.

This is not the place to go into detail (see Jakob Segal, *AIDS: Die Spur fuehrt ins Pentagon*, Neuer Weg, 1990]). The arguments are technical, and the place for the debate is the technical journals. My point is that this debate has not taken place. Segal is not only ignored by the journals; he cannot find an English or American publisher for his book, and no one has been willing to debate with him publicly for three years.

If anyone should be interested in such a debate, it is Robert Gallo. Richard Crewdson's articles in the *Chicago Herald Tribune* last November have put Gallo's claim as the co-discoverer (with Luc Montagnier of the Pasteur Institute in Paris) of the AIDS virus in a very suspicious light, but Segal says Gallo actually made the damn thing (in 1978). (Why he would want to, or have to, "re-discover" in 1984 something he himself created in 1978 is not clear.) Gallo is generally credited with being the first to isolate a human retrovirus, HTLV-I, as early as 1978/79 (the publications appearing somewhat later), but Segal maintains that two of Gallo's publications indicate that he had already accomplished this in 1975. By early 1978, according to the Segal scenario, Gallo succeeded in splicing HTLV-I into Visna (a virus causing AIDS-like symptoms in sheep), thereby making the deadly sheep virus infectious to humans. This was HIV-I, the "synthetic biological agent," the "new infective microorganism," which the DOD had proposed developing in 1969.

Gallo, as head of the National Cancer Institute, also had authority over the Frederick Cancer Research Facilities, formerly (before 1975) the virus section of USAMARID, the Army biological warfare research center at Fort Detrick, Maryland, which would have given him access to the P-4 (top security) laboratory that went into operation at Fort Detrick in the fall of 1977. When the virus was ready in early 1978, Segal says, prisoners who had volunteered as guinea pigs in exchange for their freedom were injected with it and, when no symptoms of disease appeared after 6 months or so, released. Some of them entered the homosexual scene in New York, where the disease broke out in the spring of 1979. (An incubation period of one year, though short for AIDS, is conceivable if the infection was by injection of large doses of the virus.)

In short, according to Segal, the 1969 DOD project was carried out successfully, thanks to the genius of Robert Gallo, and AIDS is the result of a biological warfare experiment gone awry. These are horrendous accusations, but Segal says he is willing to go to court, anytime, anywhere, to prove them. Incredibly, there has not been a peep out of anyone.

The only newspaper with any readership at all that will print Segal is a (West) German Marxist weekly called *Rote Fahne*. This, needless to say, does not enhance his credibility for 99% of the population, but he has no choice. His latest article (8/25/90) challenges the findings of Corbitt et al. published earlier this year in *The Lancet*, a respected English medical journal. Corbitt et al. claim to show that a British sailor died indisputably of AIDS in 1959. Segal argues that this, like all of the other evidence adduced to prove the existence of AIDS before 1979, is inconclusive. Again, the argument is technical, so there is no point going into detail, but Segal's conclusion is that Corbitt et al. proved only that the sailor was infected with a retrovirus, not necessarily one that causes AIDS. (It is now known that many people, perhaps half the population, are carriers of non-pathogenic retroviruses which have nothing to do with AIDS.)

One must note that this is Segal responding to the "scientific community," but where is the response to Segal? One virologist I wrote to (who has been a consultant to the Frederick Cancer Research Facilities) deigned to say that "Visna plus HTLV-I in any arrangement does not make HIV-I, now or in 1978." This is less than enlightening if you have read Segal's painstaking description of gene-mapping and other procedures which, he says, prove the opposite. Segal says that any trained lab technician could make HIV-I in two weeks today, and that in 1978 it would have taken about 6 months. My correspondent's response to this was: "If Segal is so convinced, why doesn't he make the construct and see what kind of virus it makes." Fine. And who will provide him with the P-4 laboratory and component viruses to conduct the experiment? The question is more interesting turned around: Why doesn't somebody with access to the requisite facilities (e.g. the U.S. government) do the experiment and prove Segal wrong? Segal could be invited to participate and, if the experiment failed, forced to retract his monstrous allegations.

There will be no such experiment, of that we can be sure. Segal will be dead in a few years (he is 79), and it is unlikely that anyone equally competent will take up the cudgels, but his theory will smolder on, leaving all the seemingly answerable questions unanswered, year after year.

Wait a minute ... we've been here before. This is not the Wonderful World of Science — it's Dallas. We're caught between a "lone nut" (Segal is wrong) and a coverup of the usual mammoth proportions (Segal is right).

1990.09.15 TO PROUTY

Sept. 15, 1990

Dear Fletch,

The same time your letter came I got *Operation Zapata* and Vols. 1-4 of the *Pentagon Papers* through inter-library loan. I can only keep them 3 weeks, unfortunately, but I've made some notes on *Zapata* to coincide with yours.

Re ship names: We have to find out what Barbara Bush's middle name is. *Who's Who* only gives her maiden name (Pierce) as a "middle name," but she must have had a middle name before she got married (Jan. 6, 1945). Dulles says (p. 286) that the ships were meant to look Cuban, but "Houston" doesn't sound very Cuban.

Re Taylor's plan for Strategic Resources Group: Smith makes some ominous remarks (p. 277) about moving CIA's covert ops somewhere else. I wonder if that's what actually happened. Just as intelligence has always been a cover for covert action, maybe now the whole CIA is a cover for some other locus of the real action (e.g. Office of Naval Intelligence).

1c, 2d CIA did NOT support the Cuban Revolutionary Front in in internal resistance:

> Mr. Ray: We had a plan to take the Isle of Pines, but this was constantly postponed and we never got the supplies that we were supposed to. Later on we asked for

help in the Escambrays, for airdrops between September and February, and during all this period we never received any airdrops. Then in early April we presented a plan of sabotage in Cuba which we call Cuban Flames. We felt we could be very successful in this because we had made a very deep penetration in the labor movement; however, we never received the support we needed for this either (p. 339).

The Front did NOT want an invasion, they wanted a true counter-revolution:

Mr. Ray: We still believe that we can cause an uprising within Cuba amongst the Cuban people but we believe that the leaders must be developed within Cuba itself. We believe that the invasion concept was wrong (p. 339).

The CIA did not even allow the Front to participate in selecting the invasion force:

Mr. Ray: Another thing that was wrong with this operation was the fact that many of the elements in the invasion force represented the old [Batista] army. We felt it was wrong to give the impression that the old army was coming back and we protested (p. 339).

Even the leader of the Brigade was a Batista man:

Question: Did you approve of Pepe San Roman as the commander?

Mr. Ray: No. Everyone knew that he liked Batista. His brother had also fought against Castro in the Sierra Maestra (p. 340).

How could anyone have believed that an invasion by Batista people could be successful?

4 Interesting that Lansdale was involved in setting up Swan as well as training facilities (p. 194). Were you in Erskine's office

then too?

6 See Ray's comments above. If the airdrops weren't effective (Ray implies the effort was minimal or non-existent) then, how did they expect them to be effective in the Zapata swamp or in the Escambrays if the force went guerrilla?

8 Ranelagh (*The Agency*) mentions another marine colonel: Jack Hawkins. What was the role of Howard Hunt and David Phillips? Jim Marrs says "the former CIA station chief in Caracas" was Bissell's direct subordinate — who was that?

10 I don't get your point here. What's the punch line? There's no mention of total elimination — are you referring to a different paragraph?

16 Everybody agreed on the importance of "control of the air," including Bundy (p. 177). The crucial question is what precisely was necessary to achieve control.

16a and 18 Rusk (p. 221), Dulles (p. 222), and McNamara (p. 203) all say they underestimated the performance of Castro's planes, and Bundy mentions specifically the T-33s (p. 178). If Bundy is lying, he is covered by White and Lemnitzer. White didn't even know the T-33s were armed ((p. 259). Lemnitzer says he knew they were armed (p. 326), but did not think all of them had to be destroyed (p. 325):

> Question: What did you think would happen if you weren't 100 percent successful and didn't get a couple of T-33s?
>
> Gen. Lemnitzer: In war, you never expect 100 percent success. However, a couple of T-33s are not going to be decisive elements in an operation of this kind.

How do you explain this re 18?

19 Bundy clearly concurs (p. 177), and he could hardly have been lying since he knew JFK would see his letter. Rusk (p. 223) and McNamara (p. 203) also wanted maximum deniability.

There is no indication that AWD was pushing harder for deniability than State, Defense, or the White House.

The more important point in this seems to me the sentence beginning "In due course..." If pre-D-Day strikes were excluded, why were they included again later?

What "could not have been factual"?

22 If the goal was "to seize a beachhead contiguous to terrain suitable for guerrilla operations," the Zapata swamp should never have been considered.

30 What were the "political advantages"? The D-2 strikes were CIA's and Bundy's idea (p. 257). It doesn't make sense. First they are excluded (because not deniable — cf. 29 and 19), then included for "political advantages"...

33 If the D-Day strikes were crucial, why are they referred to here as "limited"?

35 The whole idea of this D-2 landing seems screwball. Were those 160 men supposed to commit suicide? No wonder they didn't do it. Nobody seems to have asked what these men were supposed to do after landing, which is very odd.

43-44 Taylor neglects to mention that Rusk didn't even know about the D-2 strikes and I think misrepresents what Rusk actually said (p. 221-222):

> Question: Was it understood that control of the air was considered essential to the success of the landing?
>
> Sec. Rusk: Yes, it was understood that it was essential to the success of the landing, but there was an inadequate appreciation of the enemy's capability in the air. Furthermore, neither the President nor I was clear that there was a D-2 air strike. We did have it in our minds that there would be a D-Day air strike. Following the D-2 air strike there was considerable confusion. It wasn't realized that there was to be more than one air

strike in the Havana area. The President was called on this matter and he didn't think there should be second strikes in the area unless there were overriding considerations. We talked about the relative importance of the air strikes with Mr. Bissell and General Cabell at the time. However, they indicated that the air strikes would be important, not critical. I offered to let them call the President, but they indicated they didn't think the matter was that important. They said that they preferred not to call the President.

Question: Did you attempt to advise the President as to the importance of the air strikes?

Sec. Rusk: I had talked to him and he had stated that if there weren't overriding considerations the second strikes shouldn't be made. Since Mr. Bissell and General Cabell didn't want to talk to the President on the matter, I felt there were no overriding considerations to advise him of. I didn't think they believed the dawn air strikes were too important. I believe that Castro turned out to have more operational air strength than we figured.

Question: Do you recall why the question of air strikes was withheld until Sunday evening?

Sec. Rusk: As far as I was concerned, I was caught by surprise with the first air strikes. I was trying to advise Adlai Stevenson at the UN on what was happening and suddenly found out there were additional air strikes coming up. We didn't want him to have to lie to the UN.

There is another rendition of what happened in Rusk's office, anonymous but I suspect it was Tracy Barnes — who was at the meeting that day (p. 130):

Question: What led to the cancellation of the air strikes?

Answer: At 1300 Sunday it was understood that the plan, including the air strikes for dawn of D-Day, had been approved. At about 7:00 p.m. CIA representatives were called to Mr. Rusk's office. He was concerned over the apparent defection of two rather than one B-26 and an additional cargo plane because he felt these additional defections had caused him to mislead Mr. Stevenson. At 10:30 p.m. the CIA tactical commander was advised that the air strikes had been called off. He most strongly urged that this decision be reconsidered and reversed. In debating the air strikes question and in discussing the action to be taken to strengthen Mr. Stevenson's position, the President was contacted. In discussing the air strike question the President said he wasn't aware that there were going to be any air strikes on the morning of D-Day. At 2315 Mr. Rusk announced that there would be no dawn air strikes. At this time the invasion ships were within 5,000 yards of their landing beaches and it was physically impossible to call off the strikes [sic — should this be "landing"?].

I think it was Barnes because of his widely quoted "verbatim" rendition of the scene (originally in Wyden's *Bay of Pigs*), e.g. Ranelagh (p. 374).

If you compare carefully what Rusk says to the other two versions, it is not clear how many calls to JFK were made, when, or what was discussed. E.g., Rusk talks about second strikes "in the Havana area"; this doesn't sound like the D-Day strikes to protect the landing. Where exactly were those T-33s — in the "Havana area"?

Note the timing in the version on p. 130, which implies that Cabell and Bissel were summoned by (not looking for) Rusk at 7: OO p.m. (44 says 10:15) and the strikes were definitely cancelled by 2315.

The most damning thing is that Rusk says Cabell and Bissell

told him the dawn strikes were not crucial! In such a crisis situation, this could not have been a misunderstanding. Either Rusk or Cabell and Bissell are lying. Bissell, quoted in Ranelagh, p. 374, says: "The Taylor Committee report was probably correct in concluding that Cabell and Bissell were negligent in failing to make a last attempt to persuade the president by telephone to reverse his decision." This doesn't wash. Whatever Bundy's motives were, Cabell and Bissell had the final opportunity — and obligation — to make the situation clear. If they told Rusk at that point that the strikes were not crucial, as Rusk says, they were not telling the truth. Whether that is "lying" or cowardice or whatever depends on what their motives were.

Cowardice or reticence etc. are unlikely explanations, as their subsequent actions show.

45 Cabell is bold enough to call both Rusk and the President at home at 0430 for air cover (presumably US Navy here) and destroyers. Why would he have been less bold earlier in the evening?

This B-26 coverage — I don't get it. Why didn't they need permission for that? The dawn strikes were supposed to be B-26s too, weren't they? If they could call them out then, why not a few hours earlier? And where did they come from? I thought they would have had to take off by 0130 to make it from Nicaragua by dawn.

48 I thought it was three T-33s that did all the damage.

56 Here again, two Sea Furies and two B-26s — where did they come from?

And again, if Brigade B-26s could "rotate over the beachhead through D-Day," why the hell couldn't they have done so at dawn, and where did they come from, if they never got permission to take off?

57 CIA decides to bomb Castro's aircraft D-Day night! Here there is no question of seeking permission, so why all the

folderol the night before? This cannot be a question of deniability. The planes had to come from somewhere, and if the cover story was supposed to be that they originated from the Blue Beach airfield, it wouldn't have made a whit of difference whether they appeared before or after the first troops set foot on shore.

68-70 These are very revealing, I think, if compared to Memo 2, 6-7 (p. 36). In the latter, Taylor seems to be covering for CIA. 7 implies that CIA called off the resupply convoy because a daylight unloading would be futile, and therefore didn't request the jet and destroyer support. That isn't what 69 in Memo 1 says. That says they thought it was futile to request the support, and therefore the mission would also be futile. That's a very big difference. Why did Taylor turn it around in Memo 2?

Furthermore, Bissell's actions here are again contradictory. If he ("CIA leaders") thought it was futile to ask for air support for the ammunition convoy, why did he not think it was futile to ask for it for the air resupply?

Also, the textbooks have it that JFK reluctantly allowed this one hour of US jet coverage, but 70 reads quite clearly that Bissell asked for one hour, with no indication that he asked for more or had trouble getting it.

I would like very much to have your detailed feedback on all this, but I'm also wondering where it leads us.

To me, it leads back to the same question everything leads back to. Incredible stupidity, bungling, and competence — or a giant plot. If we did not know, because of all the independent research that has been done, that the JFK assassination was a giant plot, it might still be possible to accept the first alternative — that is why the assassination is still so important. Also, your *Secret Team* makes it very hard to accept the first alternative. If the Powers U-2 shootdown was a plot, the assassinations were plots, Vietnam was a plot, surely the Bay of Pigs must have been a plot.

Incidentally, it is interesting that Dulles refers to the D-2 strikes as a "plot" (p. 249), and admits the idea came from CIA and Bundy (p. 257).

It is also interesting to see Vietnam come up several times in the testimony. Vietnam was, after all, a guerrilla war. Here we have Lemnitzer arguing that guerrillas in Zapata could survive just like the VC (p. 319). Burke points out that they couldn't survive without indigenous support, a problem which they agree could be solved in Zapata with airdrops and in Vietnam by fencing in the food (the strategic hamlets idea). How incredibly naive, in both cases! The real question, not one of how to get food, but do the people support them, is not even asked.

I know you think well of Lemnitzer, but the only person in the Zapata report other than the Front leaders Varona and Ray who seem to have even thought seriously about this, the most fundamental question of all, is Lansdale:

> In developing a military capability in the various nations of the world, I believe you have to start on a political base. The people in the country concerned must feel that they have something worth fighting for and we must use the local people (p. 196).

This is wrong, of course, but at least he is thinking a little bit! Everyone else, military and administration, seem to have just accepted CIA's incredibly and crucially wrong estimate concerning popular support.

The final irony, if you are right, is that this man helped to engineer the murder of the one president who would have agreed with him. Whether MONGOOSE was behind the JFK assassination or not, I don't understand how Lansdale got involved. He was an ad man, a leaflet writer. Did he ever see combat? Conein seems more the assassin type. I realize that neither would have had to pull the trigger himself, but frankly my impression of Lansdale, from what I've read, is that he was rather a nonviolent type. You knew him, how do you see it? Incidentally, would you be willing to go public with your views on Lansdale's role in the assassination? Who else agrees with you and who or what could back up your assertions? I've never asked you why you think it was MONGOOSE.

My own tentative conclusion re the Bay of Pigs is that it was a calculated failure, just as Vietnam was a calculated failure. Vietnam was for the money, and the Bay of Pigs was intended either as a smaller scale Vietnam, or as an excuse for Vietnam (and whatever other anti-communist wars to come). Reasons:

1. CIA lied or was incredibly stupid about the possibility of an uprising.

2. CIA lied or was incredibly stupid about the possibility of going guerrilla.

3. CIA lied or was incredibly stupid about not going ahead with the D-Day air strikes.

I think the D-Day strikes cancellation was a story manufactured as an excuse for the failure of the invasion. 1 (and 2) are the real reasons why it could never have worked in the first place. This is what we are not supposed to think about, because it is obvious when we do think about it. Land a hopelessly outnumbered force of Batista supporters and topple a popular (though communist) folk hero?

As Kennedy later said, how could he have been stupid enough to let them go ahead with it? How could the JCS and everybody except apparently Fulbright and Rusk and a couple of others have been so stupid? I guess the answer is just that CIA jived and lied its way through, and once the President was convinced, EVERYBODY just stopped thinking.

Since I cannot, in hindsight, accept the "incredibly stupid" explanation as far as the CIA is concerned, I speculate that they figured, from the beginning, on 2 possible outcomes:

1) the landing would fail, and JFK would be drawn into a total

commitment of US forces, and Batista or someone like him would be back in power;

2) the entire mission would fail (which is what happened), and Cuba would serve as an everlasting example of the necessity to combat communism (as in Vietnam). Either outcome would have suited CIA's one real purpose, which is to serve Big Business (including the defense industry and the Mafia).

A further consideration was that if 2) occurred and JFK proved difficult to manipulate about Vietnam (which is what happened), there would be a permanent cadre of intense CIA loyalists and anti-Castro (pro-Batista) fascists who would 1) be willing to help assassinate him, and 2) provide a scapegoat to blame for the assassinate whenever, if ever, one was needed. (So far, Oswald has been enough. The stupidity of the American people was underestimated.)

What do you think?

I'm afraid I'm not going to be able to follow you so closely on the Pentagon Papers (this has already taken me a week!), because I've only got the books for a few weeks. Maybe I should consider buying a set. It doesn't matter. If it's on tape, it will be there for posterity. But frankly, now that I've gone through *Zapata*, I wonder if this close reading is really worth it. What is the point, unless something can be proved? Peter Scott's paper in Vol. 5 seems as close as one can get to proving the thesis that LBJ reversed JFK's withdrawal decision, and that is the main point. The more general point about the evils of secret government is made clearly enough in Gravel's introduction. Your point is that they are a scam, a purposeful exoneration of the CIA. How could you substantiate that? It is widely recognized that the PP show that the CIA questioned the winnability of the war since at least 1965. If they pursued it anyway, that is easy to explain: it was their duty, even though it was against their better judgement. You want to say that was a lie, that Dr. Jekyll was just a cover (as usual) for Mr. Hyde, that the PP themselves are nothing but Dr. Jekyll covering for Mr. Hyde. But how will a detailed analysis of the documents support these claims? This is a question of motives.

I'm not trying to discourage you, but I think your personal story — what you thought at various times and how and why your thinking changed — is potentially more valuable than trying to make a historical case, though obviously both are intertwined, since your thinking concerns the historical events. What I mean is, if a biographical approach, supported (or illustrated) with a reexamination of the historical events, can establish your credibility (in the largest sense), that would be enough. A lot, if not most, of what you (and I) think will remain speculation forever (as long as the current power structure remains in place), so our job must be to cause people to take that speculation seriously. The way to "prove" what happened the night of April 17, 1961 is to put the surviving actors — Rusk, Bundy, McNamara, (Bissell? Barnes?) — on the witness stand and grill them. But who is going to do that?

Next topic — but I'm going to quit soon — oil. I agree with you, what a scam. We never learn. I hope the Great American Populace will begin to come to its senses again. But after all, it took 4 years of war (1964-68) for them to start thinking about Vietnam. Obviously, we haven't learned anything.

Why do we have armed forces? To protect our national interests. What is (should be) our primary national interest? Our citizens. So why is Bush letting them (the hostages) rot. If he wanted to use force, he would have used it to get them out. That I could have supported, though it wouldn't have been necessary. They were taken hostage after Bush called out the cannons, so Bush is the one to blame for their being taken hostage.

As for oil, who cares. We should cut down anyway. Furthermore, we have the reserves, and it's ridiculous to be afraid of Hussein jacking the price up. It went up anyway!

As for the Kuwaiti (and Saudi) governments, who cares. I don't.

I believe in democracy, not dictatorship.

As for the US concern for international law and the UN, and as for the entire world "free press" for not pointing out the hypocrisy of this "moral" stance against Iraq, I can only laugh (actually, I can't).

The two obvious results of this "crisis" are: 1) oil prices went up, and 2) there will be no more talk of reducing the defense budget. Cui bono?

Thanks for your fascinating articles on the oil history and the air crashes. I'll have to get back to these later. You're right, oil is at the heart of things. Hepburn's chapter on that in *Farewell America* is good, going back to the Achnacarry Agreement. There are so many things that tie in, the Iraq situation just being the latest: Onassis-Nixon-Jackie, Howard Hughes in Nicaragua; John McCone-Standard of CA-Vietnam, Kissinger-Rockefeller-Standard of NJ, etc. Your point about the pipelines reminds me of Fuller's idea of a world-wide electricity net connected with solar sources. World-wide pipelines, at least in Europe and Asia, seems equally feasible. As long as they can make us believe we need oil, and need ships to transport the oil, they've got us.

I am quite sure we don't need oil at all, at least only a tiny fraction of what we now use. But that is not the point. Of course we need oil, just like we need poison gas (Hussein got his from German companies) and everything they are killing us with.

Great that your ST is being reprinted. Maybe they would do your SS too. I would like to go to that convention. Just how close are they to LaRouche? Did I tell you I got *JFK: The Mystery Unraveled*? Marchetti says in there that "renegade" elements in the CIA did JFK in. I don't buy that. If "renegades" do something like that, and the organization covers up for them, who are the "renegades"? Just because he, Marchetti, didn't know about it doesn't mean Helms and Bissell and Cabell and Dulles and Hoover and Johnson and Bundy and a lot of other people weren't involved. I think it is fair, logical, and healthy to say the CIA did it, that they in fact did (and do) everything, just as Toynbee said. They are exactly what the world has long thought they were: evil incarnate. There may well be a High Cabal behind them, but as long as they exist, we will never know who the HC is or how they work. The CIA must be considered the first and foremost enemy, and by CIA I mean the ST, the intelligence community and its allies. In fact, forget the allies. It is the legitimate secret institutions of the US government, paid for with US tax dollars, that are the real enemy. Whether they actually do things or just cover for others who do things doesn't matter. It is because they exist that the others, whoever they are, exist.

Maybe this is naive of me, searching for a concrete enemy, but I feel at least on solid ground. They take our money and don't tell us what they do with it — that's where we should start. And if we pull that string hard enough I think the whole spider's web would come along. And you have to start somewhere.

Your point about the Naval War College is very important, I think. There must have been all sorts of signs that Hussein was going to move.

Newsweek's report that Bush gave CIA the go-ahead to assassinate Hussein must mean, if anything, that they don't want him assassinated — yet. He must be working for them, just like Noriega was. He has what he wants and Bush has what his handlers want — more expensive oil and a permanent military presence (and maybe a war) in the Middle East.

I wonder what Stone is up too. Born on the 4th of July is the true story of Ron Kovic, who joined the Marines with his mother's and (less so) his father's blessing, got shot (and shot one of his own men by mistake), was paralyzed from the chest down, and became anti-war. It's the best Vietnam film, simply because it shows that — his suffering and tragedy, and the stupidity of his parents (especially mamma) — better than all the blood and guts. When I see these nitwit "representative" editors on McNeil-Lehrer, some of them women, saying "Yes, our mission in the Middle East does justify the sacrifice of American (or any) lives," I tell you, THAT makes me feel violent. I would like to push their faces in the bedpans of the vets who are still suffering from Vietnam and will suffer from what we're doing now, and let them argue their cause from there. I guess some of them still would.

I'm going to stop here. I'm exhausted myself on the Zapata thing.

You mentioned the idea of an archives — good idea. The ideal accompaniment to the tapes. I'd be glad to be the "curator," if you like, until we (hopefully) can find an institutional one.

Best regards,
Michael

1990.10.29 TO WEISBERG

29 Oct. 1990

Dear Mr. Weisberg,

I've been waiting to answer your letter of Aug. 30 until your book arrives, but it still hasn't. If you did not receive the postal money order (should have come with the mailman), please let me know.

Since Herrhausen we have had the stabbing of Oscar Lafontaine and just recently the shooting of Stäuble, both by lone nuts. This is presumed to explain everything — even better than the terrorist explanation. People have forgotten — more likely, they never knew — about Sirhan Sirhan, who can't remember anything about that night after the moment he met the woman in the polka dot dress at the coffee machine. This triggered his program which had been installed by CIA hypnotists, but they had Cesar do the job from behind anyway. Here they had not just one but three magic bullets, which hit RFK from behind at point blank range from a gun supposedly fired several meters in front of him, a gun which could also fire more bullets than it could hold.

Honneger's *October Surprise*, about the deal that Casey and Bush made with Khomeini not to release the embassy hostages until after the 1980 election, was "available" in the US last February when I was there, but I had not been able to order it from Europe. This subject of the suppression of books is one that needs exposure. I suspect that you are well aware of the problem, since you have had to publish yourself. Even the books that get published don't necessarily get advertised, reviewed, presented on TV talk shows, or in the bookstores. How are you supposed to even know about them? (We are not, of course.)

I'm afraid I still do not understand your point about the JFK autopsy photos and x-rays. Take the drawing/photo of the back of JFK's head, showing only a small entrance wound — that <u>does</u> support the mythology, but it does not show the wound described by the Dallas doctors or the one visible in Zapruder Frame 335. If that autopsy drawing/photo (cf. Groden, after p. 23 and 389) is not a fake, it must be of someone else.

As for the Dallas doctors, I believe what I saw and heard two of them say in the Turner (ITV) film (McClelland and Perry, I think). I didn't see the Nova show, and I don't know what the doctors saw at the Archives, or which doctors you mean, but if any of them were tricked or intimidated into changing their stories I wouldn't be surprised. Enough credible eyewitnesses have described the huge exit wound in the back of JFK's head to make that official autopsy photo impossible.

If there are things in the photos and x-rays that do not support the govt's theory consistently, I don't find that surprising either. They didn't have much time and had to improvise as events developed and facts leaked out. Obviously, the coverup was far from perfect, but why is this surprising?

In fact, in retrospect, the entire assassination and coverup seem so crudely done that I wonder if the crudeness wasn't intentional. What better way to let us know, without admitting it outright, that they had (and have) us by the balls? Maybe they were saying: "Look what we can do. We blew his brains out in broad daylight, created a fairy tale, and got away with it. You can be as suspicious as you like, but we're in total control, and there's nothing you can do about it."

After all, they could have just dropped a pill in his coffee. CIA and their friends certainly had the techniques for causing "natural" deaths in 1963 just as they do now. Why go to the trouble of a public ambush and massive coverup when it could have been done without anyone even suspecting foul play?

The Lifton book is weak because he doesn't go beyond the usual innuendoes about "dark forces." But if he is wrong about the body being altered, why did it arrive at Bethesda in a different casket and in different wrappings from what it left Parkland in?

I know it's asking a lot, and maybe when I get your book that will take care of it, but I wish you would explain why you find Garrison, Groden/Livingstone, and Marrs "fictional." Their conclusion is the same — that it was a coup d'état. Do you disagree with that?

I think Garrison rightly puts the finger on the CIA (Groden points more at Nixon, Marrs more at Johnson). Fletcher Prouty wrote a series of articles which he has been trying (unsuccessfully so far) to get published in book form, in which he carries further his notion of the "Secret Team: The CIA and Its Allies in Control of the USA and the World" (his 1972 book). That about says it all. The CIA. (and allies) control the Presidency — this was Allen Dulles and Co.'s objective from the beginning. Now we have an ex-DCI (do they ever retire?) in the White House, and nobody bats an eye. After all that has been revealed about the CIA, it is riding higher than ever. Presidents come and go, but the secret police remain, responsible to no one — certainly not to the President (regardless of what the law says).

What do you think of Prouty's essay in the Groden book, by the way?

Prouty calls the people behind the CIA, i.e. behind everything, the High Cabal, using Churchill's term. He thinks they all take Orders — Bush, Gorbachev, everybody. He reiterates that they need not all be Americans. I don't think he has names, but he did mention that T.V. Soong may have been one of them.

Prouty has told me and others privately that MONGOOSE was the operation, or the cover for the operation, that assassinated JFK. He is sure that the man walking away from the camera in the picture of the "tramps" in Garrison's book is Lansdale (whom he knew). I don't know how many other people share this view.

You mention some "internal CIA papers" re. Kimble. I don't know about the Kimble thing, but in general, how much trust can you put in anything that CIA puts out?

If the government, or any part of it, had anything to do with the assassination or the coverup — and we know they did — there are only three people in the world who had then and have now the legal right to be on the other side of the "national security" wall: the President, the Nat. Sec. Advisor, and the DCI. Of these, the DCI is the most powerful, because he sets the information first and can therefore control it. Add this to unlimited funds, zero accountability, and total secrecy, all of which the CIA has, and you have total power.

The people who scoff at "conspiracists," as if they were overly imaginative fanatics, make me laugh. Poindexter was convicted of conspiracy. Furthermore, the CIA is itself a conspiracy, by definition ("two or more people who plan something immoral or illegal"). It is an institutionalized, legal conspiracy existing with the support of our tax dollars within our own government.

That makes the government itself a conspiracy, or an important part of it (the most important part being secret). I don't think this is just playing with words.

Vietnam was probably the immediate reason for JFK's execution, but his threat to break the CIA into "a thousand pieces" was the real danger. Without the protection of CIA, the corporate oligarchy and organized crime could not function as they do. I see this as exactly analogous to a corrupt police force. Instead of protecting us, they protect the criminals — the people who exploit us and do not care for our welfare at all except as it furthers that purpose.

It is almost impossible for us Americans to believe that our govt is the Enemy. That's media control and "education." It is very effective.

I don't think it matters if we say the Enemy is "the govt," "elements of the govt," "the CIA," "the intelligence community," or some combination of these. The depth of corruption and control is obviously so great that it cannot be a matter of "renegade" elements, loose wires, etc. As long as the "renegade elements" remain secret, the top of the govt must be protecting them, and that means working with them.

I keep trying to see a light at the end of this tunnel, but if my worst suspicions are correct, no change is likely unless a war or major catastrophe starts burning directly under our asses again. That might happen in the Gulf.

I'll look forward to receiving *Post Mortem* and any comments you might have on what I've said here.

Sincerely ,
Michael Morrissey

1990.11.24 TO THE HESSISCHE ALLGEMEINE

[My translation. I sent a copy of this to Chomsky.]

As an American, I strongly condemn the fact that Bush is now violating our Constitution and the War Powers Act of 1973 for the second time (after Panama), securing billions in profits for the defense and oil industries (where he comes from). In whose pockets else does the $45 million a day ($1 billion if war breaks out) that the deployment "costs" end up? In July, there was much talk of drastic reductions in the Pentagon budget, but not since August 2: Goodbye Communism, Hello Hussein.

This is not about cheap but expensive oil. With the price increase, Hussein has achieved his goal and the oil industry in all countries has doubled the value of its reserves. Now oil can be extracted from the previously unprofitable oil fields in Louisiana and Russia.

It's not about the hostages, either. Bush knew as early as July that Hussein was planning to invade Kuwait. Why didn't he try to evacuate our citizens beforehand, or at least before he sent the troops there?

Bush knows there has to be war. As he spent Thanksgiving with the troops in the desert on 11/22, the former intelligence chief must have been thinking about that day in Dallas 27 years ago when Kennedy's (still covered-up) decision to pull all troops out of Vietnam by 1965 exploded along with his skull.

1990.11.30 TO CHOMSKY

[I had not written to Chomsky since the previous November. In the meantime the first Gulf War (2 August 1990 – 28 February 1991) had started.]

30 Nov. 1990

Dear Noam,

Enclosed is a letter that appeared in the local paper[9] which I thought you might like to see, since we both believe that every little bit helps. I'll bet the *New York Times* wouldn't have printed it.

I got a couple of calls from people who agree with me and are glad to know that not all Americans think like George Bush. I sent a longer version to all the TV talk shows, so if I get lucky I can spread that message further.

Congress doesn't need a new resolution. They can just take the Gulf of Tonkin text and make the appropriate substitutions. I did that in class the other day, with me playing President and the class Congress. I did my best, but nobody voted for it. Afterward, after about 6 tries, somebody guessed the original was about Vietnam. They were amazed when I told them it passed Congress 533 to 2. But, after all, they are only first semester students. By the time they finish here they will have learned the "On the one hand, on the other, therefore Dr. Kissinger must be right" formula for academic success.

It's incredible. There he is, saying exactly the same things he said 20-odd years ago about "losing the facedown" and the inevitable holocaust to follow.

On the second front, AIDS is getting bigger and bigger and quieter and quieter. I was glad LOOT published my thing on Herrhausen,[10] but I sent them another one on AIDS/Segal in Sept. which there's been no response to despite my queries, which puzzles me.[11] It may be too hot even for them. (Enclosed, in case you're interested.)

Segal is the Jim Garrison of AIDS. Fletcher Prouty has told a lot of people (including me) that MONGOOSE had the JFK contract and that Lansdale is the guy walking away in the "tramps" photo in Garrison's book (*On the Trail of the Assassins*). Segal, Garrison, Prouty — they're all crazy, of course. Me too.

Sincerely,
Michael

1990.12.13 TO WEISBERG

13 Dec. 1990

Dear Mr. Weisberg,

I still haven't received your book, and there is no way to check on it. Surprising, since I order a lot of books from the States and this will be the first time one has gotten lost in the 13 years I've lived here. Would it be asking too much to ask you to send another copy?

I agree that cui bono doesn't provide any magic solutions, but it is still the first and best question to ask in any investigation of possible wrongdoing. It is never pursued adequately when the State is the accused. Most people don't even stop to consider the obvious fact that the "cost" of anything is somebody's gain. Vietnam "cost" $220 billion. The Gulf is "costing" $4-5 million per day. We know where the money comes from, so we talk about it only in terms of "cost." Where does it end up? We sometimes talk vaguely about the "defense industry," but so much of this is secret anyway (have you read Tim Weiner, *Blank Check*?) that a detailed accounting is impossible. If we could study the balance sheets of all the corporations that end up pocketing our tax money, the question cui bono would be a lot more meaningful. This is precisely what the Constitution mandates, but who cares about that?

If we do not understand how our "democratic" America can have a secret police, secret armies, and a secret government, or how a president can flout the law of the land (Constitution, War Powers Act), why we fought in Vietnam (etc.), or why we are now in the Gulf, cui bono goes a long way toward clarifying matters — if we are willing to accept the unpleasant truth. The primary beneficiaries of the Gulf crisis are 1) the oil industry and everything dependent on it, all over the world.(The hitherto unprofitable oil fields in Siberia as well as Texas can now begin to be pumped, fuel prices are driving the airways into the hands of a handful of the biggest airlines, etc.); 2) the Pentagon and the defense industry, for whom Hussein is a godsend, a replacement for the Red Peril Just when people were starting to talk seriously about drastic defense budget reductions.

Back to JFK. I want to respond to your letter in detail because, frankly, I find it very confusing and I cannot believe that it is a true reflection of your thinking. I wish I had *Post Mortem* and your other books so I would have more indication of what you do think, as opposed to what you think is crap.

I did not see the Nova show (do you know where I could get a copy of it or any of the other assassination documentaries shown in the US?), so I don't know which Dallas doctors you are referring to, what they said, or what they saw at the Archives. You say the doctors said on camera that what they saw at the Archives is what they saw in Dallas, i.e. supporting the official version. In the next sentence you say two of them (which ones?) dispute the official version. Are you saying that because there is contradictory testimony, we cannot know which is true? If that were the case, we would never know anything. The adversarial system begins with contradictory evidence; it doesn't end there.

For my part, I really don't think it is a matter of "what I want to believe." Much more to the point is what most Americans do NOT want to believe, and therefore cannot believe. I saw and heard Dr. McClelland and Dr. Peters of Parkland Hospital describe and draw a picture of the head wound (in the British ITV film *The Men Who Killed Kennedy*, in which you also appear — I presume you've seen it) which corresponds exactly to the lower drawings in Groden, p. 23 f.

You say that for the film to have been faked, the CIA would have to have known where the autopsy would be performed and be able to control everyone involved. What makes you think they did not know? Do you think they would tell us that they knew? The question of control is crucial. First of all, it eliminates every suspect in the conspiracy below the highest levels of the US government: the Mafia, anti- (or pro-) Castro Cubans, Russians, "renegade" elements of the CIA, Big Oil, Minutemen, etc. None of these groups would have been able to participate at all in the conspiracy, much less carry it off alone, without the full power of the government behind them. The second question is, could even the full power of the government carry it off? The answer stares us in the face. The mission has been accomplished, to date. Of course people can be controlled. The FBI and CIA have plenty of practice at this. True, many people were involved, but not that many would have been in a position to put two and two together or, more importantly, had any concrete evidence and the courage to make it known. And how does any one brave individual make something known, even if he dares to, and resists threats, bribery, flattery, and appeals to patriotism? (Can you imagine being prevailed upon by the highest officials in government not to endanger the "national security" of your country?) Would the big newspapers and TV networks publish your information? Even if it were published, what then?

You seem to forget that not everyone was controlled. A lot of people have been killed and a lot more have simply been ignored. If they have not been completely ignored, it has been due solely to the efforts of private researchers like you. Absolute, 100% control is not necessary: the best way to keep the lid from blowing off is to let out a little steam. But the end effect, again, stares us in the face. Quite a few people have spoken "out of control." What happens? A book or two may be published and even sell (though the most dangerous ones, like Garrison and Groden/Livingstone and Marrs — and yours?) are not reviewed or advertised. We continue to have a mass of "contradictory evidence" and unanswered questions, with the end result — and that is what counts — that the mystery continues. That is control.

Re the body bag and casket. Why do you give the FBI more credence than Paul O'Connor? Do you believe the FBI agents who reported that there had been surgery to the top of the head and that the back wound wasn't longer than a finger (I don't have the precise reference)? Do you believe what William Webster et al . say about the CIA or what Victor Marchetti, Philip Agee, and other apostates say? Who has more reason to lie? Who has a proven record of deceit, conspiracy, violence, and collaboration with organized crime? You say yourself the CIA is the enemy of the people. Surely you don't think the FBI is any better. You say, "The FBI agents, unless you make them part of the conspiracy, also disprove that [the casket was changed]." That is the whole point. That is what Garrison, Groden/Livingstone, Marrs, etc. are saying. Of course they are part of it — not every agent, but the ones that count. We already know how they work, from the top down, but with plausible deniability, compartmentalization, self-defined accountability ("national security") and all the rest.

My question to you is: How can you believe that anything the FBI or CIA says has any credibility at all, especially when it supports the government's case? It is more logical to seek credibility in the few things they have produced which are self-contradictory.

It seems very strange to me that you call Prouty "a first-rate and courageous person" and at the same time imply that he is a nut, if that is your implication re. his Pentagon Papers theory. Prouty, as I mentioned in my last letter, has the most comprehensive "nut" theory of all: the CIA and its allies in control of the US and the world (the subtitle of his book). Behind them are what he calls the High Cabal (Big Bucks). What he says about the PP makes good sense. Cui bono? The CIA advised "against the war" since about 1965, hence they are wise and should be listened to and have even more power in the future. At the same time, they continued fighting the war, which they began, as hard as they could (their "duty," they would say). The PP made scapegoats of Johnson and Nixon and the Pentagon, two of whom have conveniently disappeared from the scene (leaving lots of questions about the real motives behind Watergate), and one of whom (the Pentagon) is invincible. No matter how stupid they are, we still need the armed forces. It is much more difficult to make this last argument about the CIA, but thanks to the PP, it is not necessary. They come out shining like choir boys. Whether Ellsberg did this knowingly or not is not clear, but it is clear that the PP exonerated the CIA with regard to Vietnam. And where are they now — in the White House.

Your next paragraph is very confusing, because you say that the FBI field agents automatically responded to Hoover's vision that Oswald was guilty because they knew "what was and was not expected of them." But then you say: "Do you want to include the entire FBI in the conspiracy...?" You answer the question yourself: if Hoover was in on it, the whole FBI would have been in on it. Hoover may have detested the CIA, a rival (and much more powerful, since the CIA Director is also DCI) secret force, but of course he would have cooperated with them. He hated Kennedy too. Hepburn says in *Farewell America* that Hoover knew all about it and cooperated by simply doing nothing. That seems likely. At least, the core of the conspiracy would have to have been in the more powerful (CIA) rather than less powerful organization .

I do not agree that an autopsy would have discovered a poison or other simpler cause of death. First, the CIA has long had toxic agents that can simulate natural deaths and are totally undetectable. Secondly, you again seem to be skirting the implications of the thesis that the government itself was the perpetrator (that it was a coup d'état). With this thesis, there need not even have been an autopsy, much less an honest one.

As for the tramps, or winos — what difference does that make? Winos don't have trimmed- haircuts either. Why do you avoid the most important question, which is why they were released without any record of their testimony or identities? As for Lansdale, no one has claimed he was "the shooter." If Prouty is right, he would have been the one, or one of the ones, in charge. "What in the world would have kept him from fleeing?" you ask. Obviously, nothing did! Let me ask you: Would you have believed, in a penny dreadful, that three tramps/winos could be "arrested" under such circumstances and released without a trace, and that whoever the other people were in the photographs have never been officially identified?

I appreciate very much the time you have taken to answer my letters, and I hope you will answer this one too. I hope too that I will be able to read your books, at least *Post Mortem*, before long, because what you have said so far has told me more about what you do not think than what you do think. Let me ask you straight out: What is your best guess as to who did it, and more importantly, who has been managing the coverup?

Sincerely,
Michael Morrissey

1991.01.03 TO CHOMSKY

3 Jan. 1991

Dear Noam,

Thanks very much for your letter and the articles. Good length to photocopy for class, and I will do so. (Page 4 is missing from "The Third World in the 'New World Order,'" though.)

I'll send another copy of my AIDS article to Edward Herman c/o LOOT.

I fully agree that the Cold War is not over; only the terms of the propaganda have changed. The real war has always been between the Haves and Have Nots and will not change soon.

The current pas de deux between Hussein and Bush, threatening to crush thousands beneath their stinking feet, has already achieved the major aims of both: pan-Arab leadership (of the people if not of the governments) for Hussein, a new credible threat for the US military, and higher oil prices for all.

I read Michael Klare's June 18 article "The U.S. Military Faces South" in *The Nation* after returning from vacation in late August. At first I thought it was an <u>analysis</u> of the invasion, rather than what amounts to a prediction!

The ideological fanaticism you speak of, quite evident among the government's media mouthpieces (less so, hopefully, in the general population), is as impressive as the passion of a used car salesman. This spectacle of King George the Wimp flouting the law of the land, not to mention common sense, while Congress and the press sit by and (mostly) applaud looks like a rerun of Chaplin's *The Great Dictator*. Fascism on low burn? Surely Hitler had no more "charisma" than Bush (or Reagan), and maybe that is the key: the Führer must be an empty shell in order to absorb all the contradictions, ignorance, and frustrations which have been engendered in the people, building up to the explosion.

The list of friends-turned-foes is complemented by the list of foes-turned-friends: Klaus Barbie, Reinhard Gehlen, etc.

The level of cynicism and hypocrisy and just plain lies is truly staggering. It does my heart good to see you lay into people like Moynihan — as convincing a moral giant as any other barfly.

I saw James Schlesinger giving a similar performance on TV the other day, lamenting the US "failure to respond" to the Indonesian slaughter in East Timor! I think he was Sec. of Defense at the time, fresh from CIA.

"The truth shall make you free," as written in the lobby at Langley. St. John claimed by the CIA (murderers of presidents et al.), Jesus Christ claimed by the Vatican (murderers of popes et al.), Moses claimed (I suppose) by Mossad, Mohammed claimed by Hussein, etc.

The friends-turned-foe list has to include Castro and Ho Chi Minh. Fidel can hardly be considered a real foe, since he has served an invaluable propaganda function, and I am not convinced that the Bay of Pigs was truly the "fiasco" it has been pictured as.

As for Ho, didn't we arm and encourage him in 1945, with half the equipment originally intended for the invasion of Japan? (A little-known fact, it appears.) The other half went to Syngman Rhee. A few years later there were wars in both countries. Then we armed the French, thereby re-arming Ho after the capture of Dien Bien Phu, and continued the war.

All of this makes no sense from the point of view of the victims (99.99% of the population).

Hussein is a threat to US hegemony, as you say, but at the same time an opportunity — for the same war economy and profiteers that created the "threat" of North Vietnam and North Korea.

If we confine morality to the propaganda department on both sides, it is clear that Hussein and Bush are both getting what they want, whether there is a war or not. Hussein clearly was encouraged to invade, and the excuse that this was April Glaspie's diplomatic mistake or that Hussein took more than was expected is simply ludicrous. Just as ludicrous as the idea propagated by the *Pentagon Papers* that US strategy in Vietnam (since 1965) was driven by a stupid Pentagon and stupid presidents, in defiance of the wise voice in the wilderness: CIA.

Where does the money go ($220 billion for Vietnam, $45 million per day for the Gulf, etc.)? The closer we get to pinning that down (with names and figures), the closer we will be to knowing the real reasons behind "foreign policy."

A caller on C-Span the other day dared to say the obvious — that the main beneficiaries of the Gulf crisis are the oil companies (and dependent industries). David Ignatius (*Wash. Post*) dismissed this straightforward observation as "conspiracy theorizing," which reminded me of Nicholas Lemann's crazy reaction to *Manufacturing Consent.*

Some (fortunately, a small minority) of the reactions to my letter to the local paper have forced me to see a further danger with espousing (or hinting at) conspiracy. Some of the people who agree with me, and not necessarily the least intelligent or least well-informed ones, turn out to be neo- or unreconstructed Nazis! This is very depressing, but I am trying to understand it.

I think it is difficult for such people, perhaps for most people, to conceive of a conspiracy of the king, or of those in the shadow of the king, against his subjects. If the government is bad, it cannot be the government itself which is to blame, but something else which controls the government. A scapegoat is needed; hence the fascist leap — typically, of course, fastening on "the Jews," equated with Zionism.

The basic problem seems to be a deep psychological barrier to accepting the idea that the government itself is the enemy — whether "conspiratorial" or not. (If "they" — the government consisting of more than one person — are the enemy, they are by definition conspiratorial.) I suppose this should not be surprising, given the propaganda machine. On the other hand, at some level, the inherent evil of government is common knowledge, reflected in truisms like "All politicians are crooks," "Money rules the world," etc.

I am interested in this as a psychological problem because it seems essential. No matter how many facts are brought to bear, there seems to be an attitudinal or emotional bedrock that remains unmoved by rational arguments. Perhaps it is just the fear of radicalization, of marginalization, of no longer being or feeling part of the larger community.

What David Yallop says in *In God's Name* about the relation-ship between the Vatican and P2 strikes me as an excellent analogy for the relationship between the US government and the CIA (i.e. the "intelligence community"), and also for the re-lationship of individuals to the institutions they "believe in," whether it is the Catholic Church or the USA. Not everybody in the Vatican is a crook, but the degree of corruption (and conspiracy) is such that, rationally, one would think that even a devout Catholic would feel compelled to reject the institution. Yet, for the most part, they don't. Somehow, they accommodate the contradiction between doubt and belief, be-tween reason and propaganda ("faith"), because they see no alternative. If Yallop is right, how can they continue being "good Catholics"?

The same is probably true of Americans' reaction to radical dissent, assassination theories, etc., all of which threaten to topple their fundamental belief in the goodness of their country, which they (wrongly) identify with the goodness of themselves, I suppose.

I have gotten an interesting reaction from some students in talking about the Segal thesis. I watch them trying to deal with it and try to get them to express what it is about it that troubles them (if it does at all — some are forever oblivious). A couple have said, "If this is true, I think I would commit suicide." This is a startling reaction, but an honest one, and I think (hope!) what they really mean is that they simply cannot conceive of a world where this is true, or where they believe it to be true, or even where they believe it <u>may</u> be true. Perhaps they would kill themselves only metaphorically, with a new self replacing the old — which doesn't sound so bad. Better than handing things over to the cockroaches, in any case, as you put it.

Sincerely,
Michael

1991.01.04 TO PROUTY

Jan. 4, 1991

Dear Fletch,

Just want to check in. I hope you're recovering well.

It's hard to believe they're doing it to us again. The Cold War is far from over; only the terms of the propaganda have changed. The real war has always been between the Haves and Have Nots and will not change soon.

The current pas de deux between Hussein and Bush, threatening to crush thousands beneath their stinking feet, has already achieved the major aims of both: pan-Arab leadership (of the people if not of the governments) for Hussein, a new credible threat for the US military, and higher oil prices for all.

I read Michael Klare's June 18 article "The U.S. Military Faces South" in *The Nation* after returning from vacation in late August. At first I thought it was an analysis of the invasion, rather than what amounts to a prediction!

This spectacle of King George the Wimp flouting the law of the land, not to mention common sense, while Congress and the press sit by and (mostly) applaud looks like a rerun of Chaplin's The Great Dictator. Fascism on low burn? Surely Hitler had no more "charisma" than Bush (or Reagan), and maybe that is the key: the Führer must be an empty shell in order to absorb all the contradictions, ignorance, and frustrations which have been engendered in the people, building up to the explosion.

If we confine morality to the propaganda department on both sides, it is clear that Hussein and Bush are both getting what they want, whether there is a war or not. Hussein clearly was encouraged to invade, and the excuse that this was April Glaspie's diplomatic mistake or that Hussein took more than was expected is simply ludicrous. Just as ludicrous as the idea that US Vietnam strategy was driven by a stupid Pentagon and stupid presidents, in defiance of the wise voice in the wilderness (CIA).

Where does the money go ($45 million per day for the Gulf)? The closer we get to pinning that down (with names and figures), the closer we will be to understanding "foreign policy."

I guess I've told you that I get snippets of C-Span here via USIA's WorldNet satellite. Once in a while something slips through — usually from a caller. A caller the other day dared to say the obvious — that the main beneficiaries of the Gulf crisis are the oil companies (and dependent industries), a straightforward observation which David Ignatius (Wash. Post) dismissed as "conspiracy theorizing."

Better to take the bull by the horns, as you do. Still, there are dangers. I wrote a letter to the local paper saying, in effect, that war is inevitable because Bush knows what happened to JFK when he tried to avoid Vietnam. Most of the reactions were positive and reasonable, but I am sorry to say that some of the people who agreed with me, and not necessarily the least intelligent or least well-informed ones, turned out to be neo- or unreconstructed Nazis! This is depressing, but I am trying to understand it.

I think you hit it right on the nose when you said that it is difficult to conceive of a conspiracy of the king (or in the shadow of the king) against his subjects. If the government is bad, it cannot be the government itself which is to blame, but something else which controls the government. A scapegoat is needed;

hence the fascist leap — typically, of course, fastening on "the Jews," equated with Zionism.

The basic problem seems to be a deep psychological barrier to accepting the idea that the government itself is the enemy — whether "conspiratorial" or not. (If "they" — the government consisting of more than one person — are the enemy, they are by definition conspiratorial.) I suppose this should not be surprising, given the propaganda machine. On the other hand, at some level, the inherent evil of government is common knowledge, reflected in truisms like "All politicians are crooks," "Money rules the world," etc.

I am interested in this as a psychological problem because it seems essential. No matter how many facts are brought to bear, there seems to be an attitudinal or emotional bedrock that remains unmoved by rational arguments. Perhaps it is just the fear of radicalization, of marginalization, of no longer being or feeling part of the larger community.

I've just finished David Yallop's *In God's Name*. I am convinced, and it seems to me that the Vatican's relation to P2 is an excellent analogue to the US government's relation to the CIA. It's also an excellent analogy for understanding how people relate to the institutions they "believe in," whether it is the Catholic Church or the USA. Not everybody in the Vatican is a crook, but the degree of corruption (and conspiracy) is such that, rationally, one would think that even a devout Catholic would feel compelled to reject the institution. Yet, for the most part, they don't. Somehow, they accommodate the contradiction between doubt and belief, between reason and propaganda ("faith"), because they see no alternative. If Yallop is right, how can they continue being "good Catholics"?

The same goes for Americans' reaction to radical dissent, assassination theories, etc., all of which threaten to topple their fundamental belief in the goodness of their country, which they (wrongly) identify with the goodness of themselves.

I have gotten an interesting reaction from some students in talking about the Segal thesis. I watch them trying to deal with it and try to get them to express what it is about it that troubles them (if it does at all — some are forever oblivious). A couple have said, "If this is true, I think I would commit suicide." This is a startling reaction, but an honest one, and I think what they really mean is that they simply cannot conceive of a world where this is true, or where they believe it to be true, or even where they believe it may be true. Perhaps they would kill themselves only metaphorically, with a new self replacing the old — which doesn't sound so bad.

I've also just finished John Ehrlichman's novel *The Company*. Interesting, in view of our own discussion, that he suggests (substituting real names for the fictional ones) that the CIA purposely sabotaged the Bay of Pigs ("Rio de Muerte") on the president's orders.

I recently got hold of the Nova film on the assassination, the one narrated by Walter Cronkite. A wonderful job of obfuscation. For every fact, a counterfact. Result: nobody knows, and therefore the "single bullet theory, despite the doubts, remains intact." Compared to this, the Turner film is dynamite, which of course is why it was kept off the air in the US.

The only disturbing thing to me in the Nova film was the testimony of Dr. McClelland and Dr. Peters of Parkland Hospital, who were shown going into the Archives, where they supposedly examined the autopsy photos, then came out and said they did correspond to the wounds they saw in Dallas after all, even explicitly saying they had been wrong. It's hard to evaluate this without knowing what pictures they actually saw in the Archives, but it is confusing — like everything else in the film. Groden/Livingstone say (p. 394 ff.) McClelland later denounced the Cronkite film, but it's hard to see how Cronkite et al. could have tricked these doctors into saying what they did. In any case, the result is not only contradictory testimony, but self-contradictory testimony. What more could a coverup artist ask for?

Enough for now.

All the best,
Michael

1991.01.04 TO WEISBERG

4 Jan. 1991

Dear Mr. Weisberg,

I guess I owe you an apology, so here it is. I really am sorry. I didn't mean to anger you, though I see now that it was stupid and presumptuous of me in the extreme to appear to challenge you without having read your work.

I hope to remedy that failing as soon as possible.

Thank you very much for sending another copy of *Post Mortem* I will let you know when I receive it. I'll order the other books, too, if I can't get them by interlibrary loan.

I realize that your health is not good and that you are still recovering from heart surgery and have no time to waste answering questions that you've already written about.

Please forgive me. I'll keep my mouth shut until I've read your books, then I'll re-read your generous letters and perhaps write again then if I have questions. In the meantime, thank you very much for taking the time and effort that you have .

Sincerely,
Michael Morrissey

1991.02.17 TO PROUTY

Feb. 17, 1991

Dear Fletch,

Sorry I'm so late in answering. The end of semester (Friday) was particularly hectic, not so much with exams but the students have kept me busy giving talks against the war. Last Monday I gave the same speech three times — at two local high schools and at the university. I am only too happy to oblige, but it takes a lot of time to write it all up in German. We had a strike/teach-in week — just like the old days! — right after the war broke out, which then continued parallel to business as usual, for those that wanted it.

I have to admit, I'm tired already, and remembering that Vietnam lasted 9 years...

Let me at least try to talk about something else. I'm glad you're feeling better. Your work with Stone may be a ray of hope, and I will be interested to see the final product, knowing that you were so involved. To be honest, though, I cannot imagine that much of the truth will actually come out on the screen, however well-intentioned Stone may be, and I hope you are preparing yourself for that. It would be interesting to keep an underground record of how the film develops, just to illustrate how the pressures work.

As we both keep pointing out — I guess because it just continues to amaze us — the powers of self-deception seem end-less. The clearest demonstration of this is the spontaneous reaction I have gotten from several students when I told them about the Segal theory. They say, "If this were true, I think I would kill myself." The truth is simply too much for 99.99% of the population. Look at the neo-Nazis. They get a glimpse of the horrible truth and blame it on the first scapegoat that comes to mind: "the Jews." The fascists are infiltrating the anti-war movement too, according to *Newsweek*, and it's a good bet they are tools, willy nilly, of P1.

By P1 I mean the Secret Team, the big brother of P2. I can't find the clipping now, but recently I read about a group of Gladio, the NATO secret army, which was referred to as P26, without explanation. The analogy of Vatican/P2 : USA/CIA is so telling that I would add World/P1, where the High Cabal would be the board of governors of P1.

Your remarks about religion, especially Catholicism, make even more sense to me having read Yallop's *In God's Name*. How the hell did he ever get that published? Also, the most pro-war group of students I have run into were at a Catholic high school. The Chairman of the German Bishops Conference (Leh-mann) is also pro-war. This is a far cry from Latin American or even American Catholicism, I suppose because they are far-ther away from the Pope. I agree with you. Religion, at its best, is poetry — and I mean that in the most positive sense. At its worst, it is a particularly virulent form of propaganda, not only the opium of the masses but, when necessary, speed, LSD, etc.

The racial thing is interesting, like the origin of oil and nega-tive evolution. What you say is of course taboo, within the edu-cational (read "propaganda") system. To interpret the domin-ance of particular gene, like skin color, as superiority would be dismissed as racist nonsense by the scientific establishment, but a Harvard professor can speculate about an infinitely more complex "trait," namely intelligence, and get away with it, since in this case he is asserting the superiority of whites. The cases of genetic dominance that all can see are treated as unimportant because, as you say, they could be used to assert the superiority of non-whites. Unless we are devolving instead of evolving. These are fascinating subjects.

Lies of Our Times, run by the CAIB people, rejected my article on Segal and the possible "AIDS contract," and Bill Schaap wrote me a two-page letter explaining why, but frankly I'm not convinced. I countered, and I hope he writes back, but I doubt that he will. I have great respect for them, but I think this is too hot even for them. Maybe it's just as well — for my own good.

The other day on World Net (USIA) there was a guy on that looked like a llama and was the USIA "specialist for countering disinformation." To explain what disinformation is, he described (very superficially, of course), the Segal theory, which he said began in 1983 in an Indian newspaper called "The Patriot," funded by the KGB. Segal's "pseudo-scientific" theory expanded on that (he also being a paid KGB agent) until even the Soviets decided it was too outlandish to continue. He didn't mention that Segal continues to run a rather successful one-man campaign here in Germany. The llama's only excursion into the "science" of the matter was to say that the AIDS virus is "far too complex to have been invented by a scientist." This is exactly what my boyhood friend Antonio DiAngelo,[12] now a viral surgeon, told me at first, but he never reacted to my counter that nobody says it was invented, but spliced from existing organisms, just as you don't have to invent a horse or a donkey to "make" a mule. Seems they have been schooled to react in stages, using the most stupid arguments first (since they don't have many). When you counter, they just ignore you and go on to the next stupid argument. When they run out of stupid arguments, they simply express amazement that you continue to be obsessed with such obvious nonsense that makes no scientific sense, which brings you back to the beginning. At that point the dialogue ends. That is exactly what happened in my correspondence with Tony, and Segal cannot get anyone to debate with him either.

Re Weisberg, thanks for putting that in perspective. I won't write to him again. His last letter was two single-spaced pages of the most personally insulting and irrational garbage I have ever heard. It depressed me terribly, not just because he attacked me, but I feel sorry for him, and I wonder if what has happened to him is partly a consequence of a lifetime spent bucking the system (to put it mildly). He was furious that I had mentioned what he had said to me in my letter to Livingstone, who sent him the page. Maybe I shouldn't have done that, but I was assuming that he (Weisberg) had reasons for what he said that I was not proving able to squeeze out of him. Livingstone, for his part, knew of Weisberg's condition and should not have passed on my letter, but he was understandably pissed off that Weisberg was telling people that his book (and others — Garrison, Marrs, Hepburn, Lifton) was a load of crap. Anyway, I feel very bad for having hurt Weisburg without meaning to, not realizing his state of mind, but I cannot write to him again since that would no doubt make it worse.

Another illusion shattered. I had thought the assassination buffs would be a close-nit community, but that was obviously naive. I have also written to Peter Scott (twice) and Jim Marrs, but no response. Livingstone suggested I subscribe to *The Third Decade* (State University of New York, Fredonia, NY 14063). Do you know it?

I have gotten a couple of things from Liberty Lobby which look very good, despite their neo-fascist reputation. One is the documentation on the Bilderbergers (McGeorge Bundy et al.!) and Gen. Smedley Butler's wonderful essay on *War Is a Racket*. I had asked them too for a sample issue of *Spotlight*, but they didn't send it, though they included *Kiss the Boys Goodbye*, by Monika Jensen-Stevenson and William Stevenson (Dutton, 1990), which looks good. They also distribute Garrison's *On the Trail* and a video called "The Plot to Kill JFK: Rush to Judgment" (know it?). I am curious about them — which is why I want to see the newspaper (100,000 subscribers, apparently). The "patriotism" theme turns me off, as would anything that smells anti-black or anti-Semitic, but what the hell. They're obviously putting out good stuff too — including your book. I've had a taste of "fellow conspiracists" who are in fact old and neo-Nazis, which is very depressing.

I guess I am trying to do the impossible — get a handle from here on the fabric of dissent in the US. A broad spectrum, of course, but it narrows considerably if you limit it to those who have concluded, with us, that the JFK murder was a putsch. Call it that or a conspiracy or whatever, the point is that if you believe "our side" did it you have crossed a crucial boundary. Weisburg is a case in point. I finally received his book *Post Mortem*, which looks good, but his crazy letters sound quite different. That's why I'm curious about people like Livingstone, Scott, etc. and also people like Oliver Stone.

It's much the same here, though at one remove. The German gut is not so much affected by JFK, Vietnam, etc., but the reactions are much the same. If anything, they are more ready to accept radical ideas, but that is partly because their guts are not involved — yet.

The longer I stay in this brave new world — I like to compare it to a fly waking up in a spider's net — the more I admire you. (Sounds like flattery, but so what.) You've been in it for a damn long time, and you haven't copped out or sold out (to yourself or to others) or ended up like Weisberg (I don't mean that disrespectfully to him; he strikes me as another victim). It's one thing to recognize injustice in the world, but to recognize that it is a plot, or even that it may be a plot, and such a gigantic one at that, takes guts. You're a damn fine soldier — if you don't mind the irony of that coming from me.

Which brings us back to the news of the day, and I'd better stop if I want to finish this today. I can give as many speeches as I want here, but it's not the same. Maybe it will do more good, but just for my own sentimental reasons I wish I was there, walking behind the antiwar Vietnam vets. One of them spoke in Bonn on Jan. 26, a member of a black rap group. 250,000 people in what *Newsweek* called an "anti-American demonstration" — what an outrageous lie.

I guess they'll launch the ground war by the time you get this. Hitler must be stopped, before he exterminates us all! I agree. Bomb the White House. (And 55% of the Capitol building.) What a patriotic and thoroughly American idea — but I guess I wouldn't do it, any more than I would have gone to Vietnam or the Gulf. What will change things is when the gals start coming back in bags. The "issues," which are all lies, will disappear in direct proportion to the number of returning corpses. Everybody knows that too, but it doesn't matter. Everything is on automatic.

One thing that struck me, and I've mentioned it in a couple of my talks, though I may be wrong about it, is the way the media treated the "tortured prisoners" episode. Obviously they were tortured, but my question is, why weren't those pictures censored? I assume that the US govt could have prevailed upon CNN et al. not to show them if they had wanted to. So, why did they not only allow them to be shown but make such an issue out of it? Imagine being taken prisoner, tortured, and forced to make such statements, and then have the video played and replayed and discussed for hours by 240 million of your fellow citizens, family and friends. Generals and admirals sitting around on the McNeill-Lehrer show discussing the morality of your actions, etc. Why, if it could have been prevented, which I think it could have, easily.

Answer: Propaganda. Our first reaction is to hate Saddam for it. We are not supposed to ask the question I have asked: Why did OUR govt choose not to suppress the pictures? Because that question reveals how little OUR govt cares about its own soldiers. How dare they parade them before the public in such a state of humiliation and compromise, after they have done everything that was asked of them, and will probably pay the highest price? Anyone who realizes how callous and disloyal this was of our own govt has to end up madder at Bush than Saddam.

I think CNN is CIA, just like Radio Liberty and Radio Free Europe were. How did they manage such super success without inside help and funding? Somebody from Nat. Public Radio made the interesting comment that "CNN seems to get the news 10 minutes before the National Security Council does." We know where the NSC gets their news. In fact, I think it's fine to have a govt news station, as long as they admit it, since that would stimulate competition, even if the competition had to go underground, as in an overtly totalitarian state, where at least the people know what they are dealing with.

I've decided to give a whole course on the JFK assassination next semester. It still seems like the key, at least the best one to try to turn, since there has been so much independent research.

All the best,
Michael

1991.03.26 TO PROUTY

March 26, 1991

Dear Fletch,

It's great to hear from you again and that you are apparently back in stride again. By-passes are so common now that I think we tend to underestimate how traumatic they are, so I wouldn't be too surprised that it takes a good while to recover. My father-in-law has had several (and several heart attacks). His mistake was not to lose weight drastically after the first one and keep it down. Now he has, but if he didn't have the constitution of an ox he'd have been long gone. I shouldn't talk, I should lose about 20 lbs. myself.

I am really grateful for my correspondence with you. I haven't found anyone that I feel has the grasp of things the way you do, and since I agree with you it makes for a club with a pretty small membership. Livingstone does. Weisberg was a real shock, though as I mentioned to you, you are virtually the only person he had anything good to say about. Jerry Rose of SUNY (Fredonia, NY 14063) puts out what is apparently the only on-going JFK assassination research journal, *The Third Decade*. Seems ok, but I will keep in mind what you say about being skeptical. He is loosely associated with the Assassinations Archives, whom I have written to about video materials.

I have the Turner/De Antonio film *The Plot to Kill JFK* from Liberty Lobby, which is interesting because the interviews were done 1964-66.

Did you see *Executive Action*? I think Turner worked on that too, though I believe it was fiction. I have seen a similar one, a French production starring Yves Montand, and one called *The Trial of Lee Harvey Oswald* starring Ben Gazzarra (what the trial might have been like had it occurred). I am collecting these for my own interest and for my assassination course, which I hope to make a regular thing.

I will certainly use both *Secret Team* and Saigon Solution in my course. By the way, ST is probably not on the LL book list because the list is old — but it was advertised big in one of the sample issues of *The Spotlight* they sent me. I have decided to subscribe. I don't think much of their apparent enthusiasm for David Duke or Pat Buchanan, but your comments are exactly right. Playing them against each other, that's the only way to do it.

I also subscribe to a thing called *Rote Fahne* (Red Flag), which is the official organ of the German Marxist-Leninist Party. It has its foibles too, but as with *The Spotlight*, you can read things there that just don't appear elsewhere. They are as critical of what they call revisionist or capitalist (since 1956) Communism as they are of western capitalism, by the way.

I agree with you. There is no need whatever to choose any party line. I'll take whatever sounds like the truth wherever I find it, and to hell with the rest. The Gulf War was a very interesting case. The far left and far right were both against it and had almost identical analyses, both opposed the whole of mainstream (left-right) thought. The left has a "structural" analysis of what is wrong with the world, whereas the right tends more to conspiracy theories. I tend to agree with both of them. It's unfortunate that the conspiracists tend to discredit themselves by what I call the "fascist leap" — trying desperately to find a scapegoat, for which role of course the Jews offer a historical precedent. There is a group of these people here who are nothing more than unreconstructed Nazis. I believe some of them may be financed by the CIA and friends, for obvious reasons. What better way to discredit all talk of conspiracy, and in particular of war as conspiracy, than to associate it with raving anti-Semites and racists?

I am looking forward to the Stone film. Somehow, they will have to underplay it. If it propagates the Garrison thesis, how can it come out without being muffled, just as his book (and yours and others) was? Of course, disguised as fiction, it might get through. Weisberg said *Farewell America* was fiction, but in this situation fiction may be truer than "fact." There will be no official truth about any of the assassinations or Vietnam or AIDS or any other the rest of it unless there is a revolution, and that doesn't seem very likely. I think you mentioned once that Marx underestimated the rise of the middle class (or was it Drucker?). The appeal of Marxism is that it offers the hope of inevitable revolution, when capitalism plays itself out, but that may not be the case at all. After all, the pyramid is a stable structure. Why should the underclass necessarily ever get out from under?

I have started (actually, I've started a number of times) a semi-autobiographical novel, which may be the best way to say things that just can't be said as "fact." If you have had such difficulty telling it like it is, and you are a first-hand witness, what chance would I have? You will be one of the main characters, of course. This may be a better way to get it out than the straightforward biography we talked about, which would be difficult without face-to-face interviews anyway. Still, I can use all the material you would like to send me — tapes, files, etc. — in one way or another. If I bomb as a novelist at least your stuff will be archived and could come out in other forms.

I can imagine the Stone film coming out this way — quietly but at least there for those who know or want to know, like so much else. Part of the Underground Library.

By the way, I remember wondering, when I first read ST, why you didn't go into the JFK assassination then. Something must have induced you to change your mind and talk about it openly after that.

Re P-2 et al., there was a note in the paper the other day about one of the Italian ministers defending them as patriots, in the context of an investigation of the recently discovered secret NATO army Gladio, which I have also seen referred to as "P-26." Can that be coincidence?

While the war was still going on I watched several economists on the McNeill-Lehrer show discuss the question of costs, and to my amazement several of them said that the costs were not nearly as high as people were estimating. Just stocks being used up, much of which would not be replaced. They really take us for fools. Now they are busily rehabilitating Saddam Hussein and the Shiites. I was proud of the German peace movement (biggest demonstrations anywhere), but now they've faded, just when the government is about to pay the biggest tribute to Bush's war policy that it possibly could — by changing the German Constitution so that Germans will be able to fight, too, the next time. I've written an article about this saying they will be throwing away the greatest contribution to reason and civilization Germany has made since WW2 (refusal to fight except in case of national defense), but I'm afraid it's going to happen. They want to be just like everybody else, which is too damn bad.

I had never heard that story about Carter's CIA remarks being cut off. Amazing.

I wonder how your views on religion would sit with the Liberty Lobby people. I wouldn't be surprised if a good number of them weren't Creationists (hence the anti-Darwinism), which strikes me as sillier than the idea of the Eucharist. The primary target within the pool of heretics, of course, is traditionally the

"Christ-killers," the Jews. You are absolutely right that all religions are barbaric, at least as they are used for political ends, which they are (Middle East, Ulster).

As for the 6 million holocaust victims, I see no reason to doubt it. Most of them came from Eastern Europe, didn't they? This is a very touchy subject, because the full-fledged neo-Nazis in this country (and probably everywhere) also talk about the "Auschwitz lie." I have heard from several of these people, who have responded to a couple of letters to the editor I've gotten into the local paper, and it is very depressing. They will talk and write quite rationally about the Gulf War and in the next breath defend Hitler. Sure Big Money is behind everything. And who is Big Money? The Jews. Israel controls US foreign policy.

Why do they need that? Isn't it bad enough that the US controls US foreign policy? In the end it seems to be a kind of perverted nationalism. They can't really face the idea that their own government is the enemy, so they have to invent a scapegoat. Our guys are bad, but they are bad because the really bad guys (who are Others) are controlling them. This converts easily to fascism: re-take control of the government and keep the evil conspirators out, namely Jews, Freemasons (another favorite scapegoat of one group here), whatever. Why doesn't it occur to them that the CIA is the most powerful institutionalized governmental conspiracy in the history of mankind? Why make a game of finding "Jewish" names on the Federal Reserve Board? How many "Jewish" names are there in the CIA? The Vatican/P2 conspiracy is certainly not Jewish either. How absurd to imagine that Israel controls US policy, rather than the other way around.

Your point about the Israelis blocking the Arab pipelines is well taken, and proves that the US controls them rather than vice versa. Israel would be better off as the keeper of the pipelines. The tanker monopoly is US, isn't it?

I am keeping an open mind about Liberty Lobby, though. They put out good stuff and deal with good people, and if there are a few kooks among them, so what?

Stern magazine had an interview with CNN's Peter Arnett recently, who said CNN had an exclusive deal with the US military to broadcast from Baghdad. Since when does the US govt grant exclusive coverage to individual networks? I didn't know that Casey was a broadcasting mogul, but it fits. As far as TV goes (and it goes a long way), they've really got us by the balls. The "epitome of propaganda" is right.

But that brings us back to the Stone movie. How else can you reach a befuddled public with, as you say, a "studio mentality," except through the same medium that befuddles them? Somehow that overarching priority that TV has in people's minds has to be broken, and the best way to do that is through TV itself. I say TV deliberately, because cinema is different. You don't hear the news every night in the movie theater. That's why the real impact of Stone's film, if it gets out at all, may eventually be as a video, where it can hit people where they live. I cannot forget what the Turner film did to me. That is the power of TV. ABC weapons only affect our bodies, but TV is directly wired to the brain. The German documentary about Segal is powerful stuff, too, and I understand it has been translated and is circulating in Sweden, but I doubt if it will get into the US. He can't even get his book out in English. I would send you a copy of the film, but it is in German and German norm, so you couldn't play it.

Have to leave it here and start packing for Sardinia. We've rented an apartment from a friend to escape the gray German drizzle for a couple of weeks.

Best,
Michael

1991.05.13 TO PROUTY

13 May 1991

Dear Fletch,

I'm way overdue on this. I hope in the meantime your work on the Stone film has been progressing. I've seen short articles on it in *Newsweek* and the *International Herald Tribune*, so the news is out to some extent. I'm really looking forward to it and I hope, as you do, that it fulfills its promise.

Enclosed is a review of *Crossfire* that the publisher sent me and which I found quite interesting. You may have seen it in the *New Federalist*, since you say you get that. I didn't know it was a LaRouche organ. It is published here by the Schiller Institute as *Neue Solidarität*. Pretty good for a guy behind bars.

I didn't realize the significance of JFK's attempt to combat the Fed that Marrs mentions and Salisbury picks up on. I wish I understood more about how banking works. My theory is that we are not supposed to understand it, or anything about economics for that matter. A good example of that was a discussion I heard on McNeill-Lehrer during the gulf war, where one economist said the war is costing us our shirts, and the other one said it's costing virtually nothing (just using up stock). There's a lie for every truth, I guess.

I also read an excellent exposé of the Gulf war lies published by this Schiller Institute, which is probably a translation from English. I have [read] nothing but terrible things about LaRouche, but I found nothing anti-Semitic in this work and a number of important things I haven't seen elsewhere.

Also enclosed is the article on Segal I recently rewrote and sent off to several "radical left" magazines, which probably won't take it — in which case I guess I should consider sending it to the "radical right" ones![13]

I don't know much about LaRouche, except for the terrible things I read about him in Dennis King's book *Lyndon LaRouche and the New American Fascism*, but I have learned, as you have, to take what looks like the truth from wherever I can get it.

What's happening now with the Kurds reminds me of your description of the situation in Vietnam from 1954 to 1960. First the contrived flood of refugees, then the protective camps (strategic hamlets), then the commitment to defend them. This may be the beginning of another long haul.

It's pretty clear that big winds were blowing after the end of the victory. Bush was riding high and no doubt enjoying it. Then came the Kurds, then Gary Sick's rekindling of the October Surprise story, then (the very next day) Bush changes his mind and sends in the troops, starts having health problems, and Webster retires from the CIA. I don't know how Webster fits in, but it looks like Bush was getting a bit of the treatment. There's a Watergate/Iran-contra waiting for him too if he doesn't behave.

We had a professor couple (English lit) from California over the other night, and I guess I harangued them a bit. They said the same thing I said for about 25 years — the govt is so incredibly stupid, etc. They could not buy into the conspiracy idea, but I could see that it troubled them, and that they were totally unaccustomed to hearing about it. I guess I depressed them, and in fact I depressed myself. Two presumably sensitive, intelligent people, and yet so far away! It's hard to remember that just short while ago I was in the same place.

I'll stop here and send this off. More anon.

Best,
Michael

1991.10.01 TO PROUTY

1 Oct. 1991

Dear Fletch,

I guess you've been pretty busy lately with the film, and I keep seeing your name in *The Spotlight*. I tried to get the radio program on short wave but I guess the signal doesn't reach over here. Too bad.

The Sept. issue of *Lies of Our Times* has several articles on the unprecedented beating the Stone film is getting even before release. A good sign, I'm sure. You've got their hackles up. It's supposed to come out in Dec., isn't it? I don't suppose there's a chance of getting hold of a video copy anytime soon, is there?

I'll have a short piece on the Kurds in the Oct. LOOT.

Enclosed are a couple of other things I've done recently. The one of the Bay of Pigs might interest you especially, since we discussed that in detail. I tried to zap Bundy, which I think you will agree with, and I also got in what you mentioned once — the Zapata-Houston-Barbara J. connection. I really can't believe that aristocratic babe doesn't have a middle name. Georgie has two. Birth certificates must be easy to doctor. Nancy Reagan changed hers.

You are on p. 11 — hope I got it right.

I didn't know how to identify Gen. White and Gen. Decker, so I didn't. (White = Air Force Chief of Staff?)

I don't know yet when or if either of these will be published, so if you feel like making any suggestions/corrections, please do.

Enclosed also is a questionnaire I'm sending to everyone I can think of — no responses as yet.[14] I left Segal's name out of it because I thought the question might be easier to answer this way. If you know of anyone who would be willing and competent to respond, please pass it on.

It's all maddening, maddening, maddening.

I'll give my JFK assassination course again this semester, just to get madder.

I'm also trying to punch out a novel, maddening at times too but squeezing the words out is good therapy. The hardest thing is following it through. I keep starting over.

Any success getting Saigon Solution out?

We had a quiet visit with the folks in August but didn't get to Washington.

We're going to England for a week to buy diamonds — my wife's hobby. She resells them to her friends and makes a pretty good profit. Now that is a reasonable way to spend your time.

I'll make this a short one.

All the best,
Michael

1991.11.21 TO PROUTY

21 Nov. 1991

Dear Fletch,

Great to hear from you and will look forward to "the book" — is that a version of "Saigon Solution"? Does that mean you found a publisher for it?

Enclosed is another miniscule effort on my part to keep up with the news, i.e. debunking the lies.[15] Not much of this stuff I'm doing will be published unless I get it into a book. One good thing about teaching, though: a captive audience.

I'm about halfway through Sheehan's *Bright Shining Lie*. He puts Krulak in with Taylor and Harkins (vs. Vann) during those first years in their optimistic evaluation of the war, which NSAM 263 supposedly reflected. Sheehan's story (lie?) is that this overoptimism led to JFK's withdrawal plan, which actually started much earlier in the military, but which he would have reversed, as Johnson did, when he learned the truth. You say that Krulak was working with JFK behind the scenes toward withdrawal based not on optimism but the reverse. Is there evidence for that?

Everyone mentions JFK's TV interview in September when he said, "I don't agree with those who say we should pull out." Why did he say that if, as Kenneth O'Donnell says, he had decided to pull out in the spring of 63? And if he didn't change his mind until Oct., as others say (e.g. Peter Scott), what was O'Donnell talking about?

Sheehan also tells the story of Diem's murder, and like everybody else mentions nothing about him being called off the plane at the last minute. What is your source for that?

I'd like to write something on JFK's withdrawal plan, because I agree with you that it's the key — the biggest lie of all, after the Warren Report. The textbooks go through all kinds of gyrations to make it seem that Kennedy would have done the same thing Johnson did (escalate). No one mentions Peter Scott's essay in Vol. 5 of the PP, or your work. O'Donnell was just wrong, they say. The actual documentation should be collected and presented in readable form (Scott's essay is very difficult to follow). NSAM 273, for example — is that still secret? With what excuse, I wonder?

I read recently that the Turner film was shown in September on Arts and Entertainment cable. Wonder if it had any impact. I hope you're right that they've miscalculated on the Stone film and that it does have an impact. I'll come home for the revolution.

I've ordered *Plausible Denial*. You say Lane leaves you "thinking that the CIA was involved." Weren't they? You told me once it was MONGOOSE, or part of MONGOOSE. I know you distinguish between "the CIA" and "elements of the CIA," but does it really make any difference?

Best,
Michael

1992.01.11 TO CHOMSKY

11 Jan. 1992

Dear Noam,

Thanks for your letter — a tonic as always. I share your feelings completely. Maybe the deteriorating economy will wake people up. What I can't get used to is the big So what? People will listen and agree with you, and then say, "What does it matter? It's always been this way. What could we do about it, even if we wanted to?" Here I ask them, what would your parents (grandparents), who really had a reason to be scared, say if they could hear you? They get it, but it doesn't get <u>to</u> them. Nothing does.

I hoped the Stone film would knock a few people on their butts, but the critics are putting out a lot of cushions. I like Cockburn, but his essay in *The Nation* was just incredible. With friends like these...

JFK (which I haven't seen but I have a pretty good idea what's in it) is getting exactly the kind of hysterical reaction one sees to your books — when there is one. The difference here is, a big-time Hollywood is hard to ignore. The psychological strategy of our keepers, I suspect, is a bonfire of the vanities: let it burn itself out. The assassination will be a colder issue than ever in a few months. But maybe there is still a chance that it will seep into the subconscious of the less propagandized classes and percolate a bit.

I've just gotten started in computer networking (Association for Progressive Communications=Institute for Global Communications=Peace Net, etc.) which seems like a real potential grass-roots mass communication medium (no editors!), so I'm having fun sending up stuff I haven't been able to get published. Who knows, maybe the technology has gotten out of Big Brother's hand. I hope so.

Kassel is supposed to start a public access TV/radio channel on an experimental basis here this year — another ray of light, perhaps. If this is not too audacious a request, do you have any video/audio recordings you could contribute (i.e. for broadcast)?

I'm about halfway through *Deterring Democracy*. Do you collect reviews? If you do and at some point feel like sending them, I'd like to see them — sort of like watching gorillas shaking their cages.

Sincerely,
Michael

1992.02 X, Y AND JFK

[I wrote this sometime between January 11, 1992, when I wrote to Chomsky that I had not yet seen *JFK*, and February 2, 1992, when I enclosed this review in my letter. It was published three months later in *The Third Decade* May 1992, 8.4, 14-17.[16]]

Contrary to what the critics have been saying, there is far more fact than fiction in Oliver Stone's movie JFK, and its thesis — that the assassination was a coup d'état by the warmongers — is the most credible explanation of the facts, and the lack of them, to date.

It will be good to release the remaining classified documents, as ex-President Ford and the Warren Commission lawyers have now requested, but I doubt that they will add anything to what is already known, namely that the Warren Report is a pack of lies.

If the powers that be are so determined to get at the truth, why don't they just dig up the body, like they did old Zack Taylor last spring? If there isn't a fist-sized hole in the back of Kennedy's skull, the conspiracy theorists will have some explaining to do. This won't happen, though, or if it does, the skull will disappear at the crucial moment, just like the brain did, just like a dozen witnesses did, just like a mountain of other evidence did.

One could almost get nostalgic reading the reviews of JFK, watching all the old lies being dutifully trotted out again by the lapdog corporate press, which hasn't raised a paw to challenge the government's "lone nut" theory of history (extended to the murders of Robert Kennedy and Martin Luther King) for the past 28 years.

It is 1984+8, we must bear in mind, a difficult age to understand. Our current president, a spook, wages war on a former employee (Noriega) and on the reincarnation of Adolf Hitler (Saddam Hussein), killing tens of thousands but missing the demonic bull's-eye both times, watches while another spook (presumably for the other side), affectionately called Gorbi, ends the Cold War, and now our spook tells us (in his State of the Union address) that we won it, just like we won the Gulf War and yes, by God, the Vietnam War too! What's a Magic Bullet compared to this?

Some of the worst shots at Stone are coming from the left, I'm sorry to say, since I think Marx had some good ideas (unfortunately massively misapplied), though if pressed I will admit more readily to being a Thoreauvian conservative ("For government is an expedient by which men would fain [like to] succeed in letting one another alone" — *Civil Disobedience*).

In *The Nation* (Jan. 6/13, 1992, p. 7), for example, a magazine I usually agree with, Alexander Cockburn says, perfectly inanely, that "there was no change in policy" regarding Vietnam between the Kennedy and Johnson administrations. This is what the history books say, but the history books also say Oswald shot Kennedy, which makes it the second biggest lie of the century — No. 1 being the Warren Report. The main point of Stone's film is that Kennedy was killed because he had decided to pull out of Vietnam by the end of 1965, a documented fact (National Security Action Memorandum 263, signed on Oct. 11, 1963) which Cockburn, like his establishment colleagues, stubbornly ignores.

David Corn, another *Nation* columnist who even thinks he knows something about the CIA, weighed in two weeks later with his own diatribe against what he called Stone's "forcing and twisting facts into comic-book format" (*The Nation*, Jan. 27, p. 80), but doesn't name a single fact that Stone got wrong. He correctly recognizes Gen. Y as Edward G. Lansdale, the real-life Ugly American (in Lederer and Burdick's novel of the same name) and Quiet American (in Graham Greene's novel), Dirty Trickster par excellence, maker of US-puppet leaders (Magsaysay in the Philippines, Diem in South Vietnam), and Kennedy's own choice to head the CIA's Operation Mongoose, but none of this is "twisted" in the film. X says that after Mongoose was officially disbanded, at least part of it was secretly continued and turned on Kennedy himself. This is a theory, but it is not "twisting the facts." What Corn means is that he believes that Lansdale was a "creative and sometimes nutty guy" who had nothing to do with JFK's assassination and that "Mongoose was ended by the Cuban missile crisis in 1962." That is the government line, and could have come direct from the CIA public relations office. If Corn wants to swallow it, that's his problem.

There is a picture in Jim Garrison's book (*On the Trail of the Assassins*, Sheridan Square Press, 1988) of the three so-called tramps (one obscured), two so-called policemen, and a sixth man, walking away from the camera. None of these people, incredibly, have ever been identified, the most logical explanation for which is that Garrison is right and they are all government agents. Some claim the sixth man is Lansdale. Corn would call this "twisting the facts" too, probably. But what "facts"? They disappeared. What do you call that, and the thousand other flagrant examples of non-investigation (to put it mildly) in this case? I call it a coverup. We are not only entitled to speculate; we have no other choice.

X, Corn may like to know, in real life is Col. L. Fletcher Prouty, US Air Force, retired, who knows a hell of a lot more about the CIA and Lansdale (who died a few years ago) than he does. Those of us who know Prouty and his work have no trouble recognizing either him or Lansdale, whom he worked with on many occasions during his nine years at the Pentagon as liaison officer to the CIA (1955-64). Prouty's 1973 book *The Secret Team: The CIA and Its Allies in Control of the United States and the World* (Prentice-Hall) is even more relevant and insightful today than it was two decades ago. Everything that X says in the film Prouty has said elsewhere, in numerous articles and interviews, and he is widely quoted in intelligence and assassination literature. He wrote the appendix to Robert Groden and Harrison Livingstone's *High Treason* (Conservatory Press, 1989) and the introduction to Mark Lane's *Plausible Denial* (Thunder's Mouth Press, 1991). Strangely — or not so strangely — his second book has been ready and waiting for years, but he hasn't found a publisher with guts enough to put it out. Maybe the Stone film will change that.

I feel a strong affinity with Stone. He went to Vietnam, and I spent the war years in college and graduate school dodging the draft and hating the politicians who wanted me to go too. I especially hated their intellectual henchmen, like McGeorge Bundy and Rostow and Kissinger, who were supposed to represent reason but exuded only madness and destruction. The national security of the United States at stake in Vietnam? If that was joke, no one was laughing. If not, what was it? A "tragic error," the historical engineers tell us now, a well-intentioned mistake. But one thing I could never understand: How could they could have been so stupid? They came from Harvard and MIT (and, as I didn't realize at the time, CIA), and I couldn't even get into Harvard. I knew I wasn't smarter than they were. It was coming to grips with the assassination that answered this question for me. They weren't stupid, they were lying — maybe to themselves as well as to us, but they were lying.

That realization had the same effect on me as it did on Stone, from what I've read. The catalyst for him was reading Garrison's book in 1988. For me it was a British TV documentary called *The Men Who Killed Kennedy*, produced by Nigel Turner, which was broadcast in October of the same year in England and subsequently in 30 other countries — but not in the

United States until three years later (in Sept. 1991 on the A & E cable network). I saw it in November 1988 in Germany, where I live. I had never even been curious about the assassination, never read a single book about it, never heard the words "coup d'état" in connection with it before, but that film hit me like a freight train. It didn't mention Vietnam, but later, when I read in the assassination literature about Kennedy's withdrawal decision, my mind caught up with my gut. I knew what had hit me: the truth.

Prouty appears toward the end of the Turner film — a big, square-jawed, athletic-looking man with that steely glint in his eyes that earnest military men seem to acquire as an accoutrement to their uniform. My father and brother went to West Point, one uncle to Annapolis and another to the Coast Guard Academy, and I spent my childhood on Army posts, so I know what I'm talking about, and I suppose that also has something to do with the impression Prouty made on me: I know the type. I don't trust them or distrust them, but I can listen to them. Prouty struck me as honest, reasonable and courageous then, and that impression didn't change when I met him or during the two and a half years we have been corresponding. I wrote a nine-page review of the Turner film, quoting Prouty at length, because I felt his statement said it all. I still do:

> I think without any question it's what we called the use of hired gunmen. And this isn't new. In fact, this little manual here, which is called "the assassination manual for Latin America" [Clandestine Operations Manual for Central America], says that, talking about Latin America, "if possible, professional criminals will be hired to carry out specific, selective 'jobs' — "jobs" in quotes, which means murders. Well, if this manual for Latin America, printed within the last few years, and a government manual, says that, there's no question but that the application of the same techniques was dated back in Kennedy's time — in fact I know that from my

own experience. You know, I was in that business in those days. So, with that knowledge, you begin to realize that hired criminals, the way this book says, can be hired by anybody in power with sufficient money to pay them, but, more importantly, with sufficient power to operate the coverup ever after.

Because you see it's one thing to kill somebody; it's another thing to cover up the fact that you did it, or that you hired someone to do it. That's more difficult. So they used the device of the Warren Commission to cover up their hired killers. Now, who would hire the killers? And who has the power to put that Warren Commission report out over the top of the whole story? You see, you're dealing with a very high echelon of power. It doesn't necessarily reside in any government. It doesn't necessarily reside in any single corporate institution. But it seems to reside in a blend of the two. Otherwise, how could you have gotten people like the Chief Justice of the Supreme Court to participate in the coverup, the police in Dallas to participate in the coverup, etc. — and the media, all the media, not just one or two newspapers, but none of them will print the story that anybody other than Oswald killed the President with three bullets — something that's absolutely untrue.

I wasn't able to get my review published, but I sent copies to a number of people, including Stone, and now that I see the role that Prouty plays in *JFK* (he is not mentioned in Garrison's book), I like to think I had something to do with getting Stone and Prouty together. In any case, we're all in the same foxhole now.

Garrison, Prouty, and Stone are courageous men, and *JFK*, I hope, will prove to be a great public service. I am suspicious of Time Warner's motives for producing the film, however.

After all, Time-Life is the company that kept the Zapruder film locked away from public view for 12 years, and is hardly a bastion of dissent. So far, with the press feverishly toeing the "Get Stone" line, the impact seems negligible, if not negative. What if JFK turns out to be the assassination film to end all assassination films — and inquiry? What will we do when all the commotion dies down? Forget it? Back to business as usual? You can't say it any louder than Stone has said it, and if that doesn't do it, what will? A lot of people will be asking themselves that question.

On the other hand, the film speaks for a lot of people. According to a recent *Time*/CNN poll, 68% of the 73% of Americans who thought the assassination was a conspiracy (i.e. 49.6% of all Americans) said the CIA or the US military may have been involved (*Time*, Jan. 13, 1992, European edition, p. 40). That's 125 million Americans who think Stone may be right! Maybe that's the half that doesn't bother to vote. Certainly it is the half whose opinions are not reflected in the "responsible" press, since all of our "opinion leaders" are too propagandized to even think such thoughts, much less express them.

But what if some of those 125 million people get tired of just being cynical, and get mad? What about the vets — the victims — whose fates were sealed with Kennedy's? The Vietnam War gave 570 billion tax dollars (accounting for inflation) to the warmongers. What will the 24.5 million Americans now on food stamps think of that? We saw it once, in 1968, when Martin Luther King and Robert Kennedy were on the verge of forming a people's coalition that would have shaken the teeth out of the power elite. That's why they were killed. The revolution was decapitated. (Both murders, like that of the president, were conspiracies, despite Received Opinion to the contrary.) It could happen again.

1992.02.02 TO CHOMSKY

2 Feb. 1992

Dear Noam,

Enclosed is a review of the Stone film and a comment on some recent *Newsweek* hype.

I know that Prouty has associated himself, indirectly at least, with Liberty Lobby (so has Mark Lane, who defended them against H.L. Hunt), which is unfortunate, given the (not entirely undeserved) "fascist" reputation of that organization. However, I think the media campaign against them has more to do with their opposition to the Bush-Reagan regime (Gulf War, October Surprise, etc.) than with their reputed racism and anti-Semitism. Much of what *The Spotlight* (Liberty Lobby's newspaper) says is right in line with LOOT etc., even if they do support David Duke. I think people like Prouty and Lane end up more or less in their camp simply because it gives them a forum.

I suppose by saying a good word about Prouty, then, I'm taking a little risk, but what the heck. In the review I admit to "being" a "Thoreauvian conservative," the "conservative" part coming from you, i.e. in the true sense. I would have said "leftist Thoreauvian conservative," but don't think many people would make sense of that. "Anarchist" is another possibility, or as you said somewhere (in an interview, I think) "syndicoanarchist," but for most people the word evokes images of skinheads throwing Molotov cocktails. (Had an argument with my father-in-law recently about that: "Aber es gibt immer eine Regierung!").

JFK is getting more sensible reviews here (the worst one was in *Spiegel*) than what I've seen from the States. That is, the first paragraph or so will (predictably, as in the Gulf War) parrot the imported American Establishment line, but the rest often takes the film at least halfway seriously.

I don't think things like the assassinations and the origin of AIDS and the coverup of the truth about them should be subordinated to a structural analysis — by which I mean the sort of thing you do so well — or vice versa. They go hand in hand. One can say the capitalist system bred Vietnam which bred the assassination, but most people will understand more readily the other way around. I think it makes a big difference, given the natural inclination to move from the particular to the abstract.

With me, for example, despite opposing the war (Vietnam) and all that, I never really could believe the government was the enemy, and when I see how some of the "radicals" of the sixties have turned out, I don't think many of them really believed it either. That was the point of much confusion and some unhappiness. I don't want to be too dramatic about it, but the assassination thing freed me. *Der Groschen war gefallen*, as they say here ["the penny dropped"]. How often does that happen in a lifetime — once or twice (if you live long enough)?

Best regards,
Michael

[Chomsky replied to this promptly (March 3, 1992) and at length. I had touched a nerve. This was the beginning of our discussion of the withdrawal plan. In all this amounts to about 25 single-spaced pages on his part, much of which, if I were free to reproduce it here, would be familiar to readers of *Re-*

thinking Camelot (South End Press, 1993).[17] At one point (July 1, 1992) he said I had helped him "clarify the issues to myself, as I hope will show up in what I'm writing about this." This was a rather backhanded compliment, though, since by then it was clear that our views were radically opposed.

Chomsky said he knew Cockburn and Hitchens "very well" but had not seen the Stone film and did not intend to. He said he had read "a good bit" of the critical literature but had "no firm opinions" on the assassination and saw no "strong reason to believe that there was anything of political significance" in it, though he conceded it was possible.

On JFK's actual policies, Chomsky said he had been through the documentary record very carefully. Newman's book, he said, is a travesty, and despite his respect for Peter Dale Scott, whose essay suggesting a post-assassination policy reversal Chomsky included in Volume 5 of the 1972 Gravel edition of the Pentagon Papers, which he edited, he found Scott's argument "unpersuasive." Since then, he added, new evidence has left "little grounds for believing that there was a JFK-LBJ policy reversal."

There is no significant difference between NSAM 263 and 273, Chomsky said. JFK was fully committed to "victory" in Vietnam, that is, "battlefield success" and success "in imposing the rule of the terrorist client regime" the US had established in Saigon. Kennedy supported the coup against Diem, out of fear that he was planning a negotiated settlement "that would end the conflict without a US victory." Nevertheless, Kennedy approved (with NSAM 263) the McNamara-Taylor recommendations (for withdrawal) "on the 'optimistic' assumptions then prevailing."

Then, Chomsky said, after Diem was killed, the negative truth about the war began to get back to JFK, and "was presented at a high level for the first time at the Honolulu meeting." This resulted in McGeorge Bundy's draft of NSAM 273 (Nov. 21, 1963), whose differences from the final version (Nov. 26) are "trivial," despite Newman's argument to the contrary.

So whereas Newman argued for a significant change between the 273 draft, written for JFK, and the final version, written for LBJ, Chomsky was saying the difference is between 263 and the 273 draft. The Nov. 21 draft, Chomsky said, expressed the "essence of JFK's policy, but written after the factual assessment of the war had changed." In other words, if there is any significant difference between 263 and 273, it is attributable to Kennedy, not Johnson, because Bundy wrote the draft the day before Kennedy was shot.

Although it is possible that JFK would have followed a different path than LBJ, Chomsky said, there is little reason to think so. The best evidence for this thesis, he said, has been ignored: Douglas MacArthur's warnings against getting involved in a land war in Asia, by which Kennedy was "much influenced."

The anecdotal evidence that Kennedy told O'Donnell, Mansfield and Morse that he would withdraw from Vietnam, said Chomsky, lacks credibility, because "the JFK crowd" could be expected to "put the best spin" on anything concerning their icon. Moreover, even if he did tell them he would withdraw, he was more likely just telling them what they wanted to hear, "political animal" that he was.

There is little, Chomsky concludes, "that is convincing in the work that has attempted to show that JFK was changing course." Kennedy "was and remained a thug," and among other things escalated the war in Vietnam "from state terror to outright aggression."]

1992.03.19 TO CHOMSKY

March 19, 1992

Dear Noam,

Thanks very much for your last letter. I can't imagine how you find the time and energy to do all you do and also write letters to obscure admirers like me, but you said somewhere you work like a madman and I believe it. Anyway, you are truly a phenomenon and an inspiration.

Thanks too for the encouragement to continue my mini-LOOT thing, which I will do. I won't be able to research it carefully enough to do a very good job of it, but the point is just to give Big Brother some sass and encourage others (e.g. students) to do the same.

I guess I shouldn't speak so fast about German universities being "open." They've left me pretty much alone so far, but you never know. I was the only one in my department and one of a handful in the university (apart from the students) who said anything publicly against the Gulf War, and I guess people know my classes are pretty "open," but nobody has come down on me for that so far. I'm not exactly popular with the powers-that-be because I sued the state of Hesse ten years ago for a permanent contract, whereupon several of the other foreign lecturers did the same, fighting the professorial echelon and the administration all the way. There is a very nice federal law here that says if your function is permanent, your contract must be permanent, but I don't think the *Obrigkeit* [my employers] appreciated being forced to obey their own law by a bunch of mid-level foreigners. Still, the advantage of working in a bureaucracy (which is what universities are here) is that they tend to leave you alone, which makes up for being relatively powerless — no offense but a pretty good defense.

Re Cockburn, if he's a friend of yours he can't be all bad, but to be honest I am even more suspicious of him now, after reading his reply to letters from Zachary Sklar, Michael Parenti and Peter Scott in *The Nation* (3/9/92), which is even worse than his original article. He argues unfairly. I'll spare you the details, but just to take one example, after finally being forced by Scott et al. to discuss NSAM 263 (not even mentioned in the original article), he only mentions the 1,000-man withdrawal, not the plan to pull out all the troops by the end of 1965. *Time* magazine did exactly the same thing (2/3/92, box "Was It a Plot to Keep the US in Vietnam?"). There are other examples that are similar to the way *Time* and *Newsweek* do their thing, which is propaganda.

It's not just that I disagree. I disagree with you too on this (the first time ever, I believe!), but I certainly do not have the feeling you are being dishonest. I hope I'm wrong about Cockburn, and I probably am wrong to jump to conclusions, but it wasn't exactly reassuring to learn that he was living with Katherine Graham's daughter in 1979 when he was "asked," according to Deborah Davis (*Katherine the Great*), to attack Davis's book in the *Village Voice*. When I made the remark about his "strange bedfellows in the establishment," I didn't mean it literally, but it seems there's more truth in that than I thought.

Another blast, Davis says, came from David Ignatius of the *Washington Post*, and this name struck me too. As I think I wrote to you some time ago, I was impressed by a remark he made on C-Span in December 1990 when I happened to be watching. A caller said the primary reason we were defending Kuwait was economic and that the primary beneficiaries of the whole thing were everybody in the oil business except Iraq — a perfectly straightforward observation, and correct, in my opinion. Ignatius's response was that he didn't believe in conspiracy theories! I believe he also writes spy novels, which may indicate his true interests and loyalties.

Ok, that may be a little paranoid, but it is 1984 + 8, and the assassination, especially, does seem to bring out the smoke and mirrors, both inside and outside of people's minds. As you say in *Deterring Democracy*, it's unproductive to try to dig into people's minds to figure out why they say what they do or if they really believe it themselves or not. Still, one can't help wondering.

Now on to more substantive issues. I'm very glad to have your thoughts on this because I haven't seen anything in print you've done on it.

The political significance of the assassination is nil, of course, if the Warren Report is correct. If it is incorrect, as it seems to me the evidence overwhelmingly indicates, some version of the Garrison (coup d'état) theory <u>must</u> be correct, and the significance of that is clear. I say it must be correct because I see no possibility that anyone could have pulled off the coverup without the complicity of the government and the press. Not pro- or anti-Castro Cubans nor Russians nor the Mafia nor "renegade" US intelligence agents. None of these groups could have faked the autopsy, manipulated the Warren Commission, sabotaged the House investigation, etc. and managed the press non-coverage for more than a quarter of a century. However that complicity operates — by "manufacturing consent," conscious conspiracy, or (more likely) a combination of the two, it is real.

What Garrison's theory does not explain, but your propaganda model does, is the refusal or inability of the intelligentsia to take Garrison et al. seriously — a prime example of Orwell's problem and of education as the best form of propaganda in a "free" society.[18] Why else would 99% of elite opinion be so vehemently against the Stone film, when half the US population thought Garrison might be right (i.e. that the CIA or military were involved) — even before they saw the film? I suspect the even higher percentage — 73% according to *Time* — of the public who believe the assassination was a conspiracy would correspond to a much smaller figure among mainstream journalists and academics (both left and right), if a poll were taken just of them.[19]

Stone has at least informed the public and put the question on the table. How many people had even heard of NSAM 263 before the film? How many would have dared to talk about this "terrifying" hypothesis (and it is terrifying for most people, I think), even if they had heard of it? The film has at least made the subject discussable. I'm sure Time Warner is working a quite different agenda, counting on a burn-out effect (already apparent), but that is a different question.

Now the (putative) Vietnam connection. First I have to say that I haven't been able to get hold of Newman's book yet (one of the joys of living here — takes weeks and often months to get books), so I don't know what new evidence has come out, but I'll try to respond on the basis of what you say and the bits Cockburn refers to.

Taking it chronologically, Kennedy's public statements prior to October 1963, including the much-cited September TV interviews, are clearly subject to interpretation. Of course he was playing politics, since pulling out would be the unpopular course, both with the population in general and in his own administration. Rusk, McNamara, Johnson, Bundy, McCone of CIA — all the top people were against withdrawal. Cockburn and others have said the withdrawal plan was "political," as if Kennedy intended it to make him more popular, but how could it have? There was no political pressure for withdrawal, or at least less than there was for continued escalation.

The "McNamara-Taylor report," according to Fletcher Prouty, doesn't represent McNamara's opinion at all. It wasn't written by either him or Taylor, but back at the Pentagon, strictly according to Kennedy's wishes. They flew it to Honolulu and handed to McNamara and Taylor there for them to give to JFK as "their" report when they arrived in Washington. McNamara's true opinion was expressed to Johnson as president the morning after the assassination (Scott, p. 224-225), though it was no secret before then.

Prouty also says, by the way, that although JFK was for the coup against Diem, he planned to have him and Nhu evacuated by air to Europe immediately afterward. They were actually on the plane when for some reason they returned to the presidential palace and were later murdered in a military vehicle. I know there are different versions of this and I don't know where Prouty has his from, but by all accounts Kennedy was genuinely surprised when they were murdered. I don't mean to defend Kennedy here, but it looks to me like another CIA sabotage operation. CIA (and Rusk, Johnson, etc.) wanted to keep Diem, and when Kennedy insisted on his removal, they knew they would be blamed. Nixon later had Lucien Conein deliberately spread the word that JFK had been behind the murders (according to Jim Hougan, *Spooks*).

I see no reason to assume that Morse, Mansfield, Powers and O'Donnell lied about what Kennedy said to them privately, or that Kennedy lied to them. It makes sense — both the public dissembling and the private candor. Assuming, just for the sake of argument, that O'Donnell et al. are telling the truth, what else could Kennedy have done in the situation? He could not tell the world, "Ok, we failed, we're going home." Of course he was wrong to have us in Vietnam in the first place, but how could he admit it at that point? The only alternative was to declare the mission accomplished (not "victorious") and beat an orderly retreat, putting as good a face on the affair as possible: "We've done what we can, but it's their war."

The McNamara-Taylor report did not talk of "victory" (the word Cockburn repeatedly puts in their and JFK's mouth) but of "progress." Its "optimism" was in my opinion (and I gather in Newman's as well) a ploy under which to effect the pullout without it looking like complete abandonment of the South Vietnamese. Kennedy was also getting completely opposite reports from the field, i.e. pessimistic assessments, and the political situation was clearly bad — "deeply serious," as the White House statement said. Kennedy would have had to be a complete idiot to have thought the war was being "won" (in the sense that Johnson obviously wanted to win), but this is exactly what the "false optimism" argument implies. I know of no other cases where Kennedy, whatever else one might think of him, has been accused of being such a numbskull.

It is true that Kennedy's statements on Nov. 14 continue to present a belligerent front, but note that the first objective mentioned was "to bring Americans home," and none of these statements for public consumption can deny the overriding significance of the withdrawal plan implemented by NSAM 263. That was policy; the talk about "staying the course" was rhetoric. Again, what else could he have said?

All I know about the Honolulu meeting is what Scott says about it, based on references to it in the Pentagon Papers and the press at the time: the Accelerated Withdrawal Plan was confirmed. Are the documents related to that meeting still secret? What new information has been revealed to make you (or Newman) think Kennedy was not aware of the truth about the war before then?

I am skeptical of that Bundy draft of NSAM 273. You say he wrote it in Honolulu, Cockburn says the next day (Nov. 21) "back in Washington." I thought Bundy and virtually the entire Administration (except for JFK, LBJ, RFK and a couple of others) were still in Honolulu on the 22nd. The whereabouts of all these people at the critical moment is strange enough, but be that as it may, why would Bundy draft such an important document before he had even discussed the results of the Honolulu meeting with the president — especially if new information had been revealed there?

It is clearly foolish of Newman to try to find differences between that draft and 273, since they are almost identical. He should look at the big picture instead. We are talking about the possibility of a coup d'état. If it was a coup, it is even more likely that Bundy was in on it than Johnson, being No. 2 in the national security hierarchy (above the vice-president) — and this throughout the "transition." Of course Bundy would claim that there was no policy change, that Kennedy would have signed the same NSAM that Johnson signed, continued the war the same way Johnson did, etc.

And of course Johnson had to claim that Kennedy's withdrawal policy would continue, as formulated in paragraph 2 of NSAM 273. This is indeed the heart of the story: if Kennedy was killed (among other reasons) because of his withdrawal decision, every effort would have been made to conceal the fact that the successor to the throne disagreed with and reversed that decision. How convenient to have documents drafted both the day before the murder and two days afterward, neither of which JFK ever saw, much less approved, but which he supposedly would have signed and which supposedly show that there was a seamless continuation of policy!

What does it really mean to say, as Cockburn and others do, "there was no change in policy"? It means that both JFK and LBJ wanted and planned and implemented a policy to withdraw all US troops from Vietnam by the end of 1965. This is NSAM 263, confirmed by paragraph 2 of 273. Why is it never said this way? Because the inescapable conclusion is that Johnson not only reversed JFK's policy, he also his <u>own</u> policy. Saying "Johnson continued Kennedy's policy" sounds harmless enough, but if it is true it is only half the story. The other half is "...for a short time, then he reversed it." In other words, whether paragraph 2 of 273 is a lie or not, two things are incontrovertibly true:

1) Kennedy's plan was to withdraw all troops by the end of 1965.

2) Johnson reversed this policy.

Seen in this way, the differences between 263 and 273 are irrelevant. Whether Johnson reversed the (JFK's, or JFK's and LBJ's) withdrawal policy on Nov. 24 or a couple of weeks or months later, the fact remains that he reversed it.

The significant thing to me is that all the historians bend over backward to avoid acknowledging these facts, determined to make it appear that there was <u>no policy change, period</u>, which is patently false. Why?

Because there are three, not two, facts to consider — rather, to avoid considering:

1) Kennedy's plan was to withdraw all troops by the end of 1965.

2) Kennedy was murdered.

3) Johnson reversed this policy.

Once these facts are stated plainly — which is never done (except in the dissident assassination literature) — it is obvious why the historical engineers have struggled so long and hard to avoid doing so. The question then becomes inescapable: Is there a causal relationship between 1-3? Since the question is not permissible, 1 and 3 must be suppressed by all possible means. I've looked into this a bit and it is truly amazing what gyrations the "responsible" commentators go through to avoid making these simple and well-documented facts clear.

Questions are not proof, of course, but the point is that even the question must be avoided. It is not permissible, any more than it is permissible to ask, Is Washington the terrorist capital of the world?[20] Maybe for publicity-starved kooks like Garrison and war-crazed vets like Stone, but not for responsible journalists and historians.

If we had "won" the war, à la Gulf, maybe the truth could have been allowed to emerge. Then one could conceivably argue that "victory" was so important that Kennedy's assassination was necessary for "national security" reasons. But as things turned out, this excuse is impossible. Theoretically, one could still say, "Well, we thought the Vietnam War was so important that JFK had to be sacrificed," but it wouldn't work. In reality, it is impossible to admit the truth about the assassination because it violates the necessary illusion that such things don't happen in the USA. The irony is that exactly the same excuse is acceptable, as long as the president's assassination is omitted: "Well, we thought the Vietnam War was so important that 58,000 Americans and a couple of million Vietnamese had to be sacrificed." That is a perfectly acceptable truth, violating no illusions, since it is quite normal for us to sacrifice our own lives and other worthless entities for the good of the State — but not the life of a president.

You say the best evidence that JFK intended to withdraw is that he respected MacArthur's advice not to get involved in a land war in Asia. But that was rather early, wasn't it? JFK's initial escalation shows that he had something in mind — probably exactly what happened up to 1963, not full-scale war but counterinsurgency along the lines his hero Taylor recommended, using indigenous cannon fodder and mercenaries (as in Laos), with direct US participation limited to CIA and special forces. This conforms to what he told O'Donnell — that he would never send draftees to Vietnam. But certainly the best evidence — proof, in fact — of his withdrawal intention is NSAM 263.

I do not share the "Camelot" illusions, though one cannot help but observe that JFK was the last president to have any charisma and independence of mind whatsoever — neither of which are desirable qualities of leadership in a national security state. He did stand up to the Mafia and the CIA, which doesn't necessarily make him any less of a thug or less dangerous, but in fact it made him more dangerous — to his handlers. He bucked the Joint Chiefs and the CIA at the Bay of Pigs by refusing to send in the Navy and the Marines, and there was similar pressure to attack the Russian ships during the missile crisis. He defied them again ("them"=the military-industrial-intelligence-complex) with the Vietnam withdrawal decision. It was the Bay of Pigs all over again.

My theory about the Bay of Pigs, which I have written up in some detail based on a close reading of *Operation Zapata* (the minutes of the Taylor investigation), is that the CIA sabotaged it themselves.[21] (Sent this to CAIB along with some other stuff but they never even acknowledged.) The purpose was to put Kennedy in exactly the position he ended up in: send in the troops or face disaster. The scenario was repeated in Vietnam. The clandestine involvement had built up since at least 1954 and probably since 1945 (when Ho Chi Minh was still an ally), climaxing in the fall of 1963, when again it was: call it war or quits. Kennedy refused again, for the last time. These snafus don't occur any more. In the Gulf War, it was not necessary to maneuver Bush, CIA's own, into position; it was only a matter of getting congress into position, which was accomplished by Jan. 12: fight or be humiliated (after drawing a 500,000-man line in the sand and months of name-calling).

I have no inclination to defend Kennedy's record otherwise. He probably did what was expected of him on most occasions, but in that office you can't make too many mistakes. Witness Noriega, Saddam, etc., who also got out of line. Even Bush can make mistakes, like his hesitation about sending the troops into Iraq last April. Whatever the particularities were in that case, I doubt that it was a coincidence that Bush changed his mind the day after the *Times* published Gary Sick's *October Surprise* story (after ignoring the whole thing for years). In the end, JFK was a victim, just like the rest of us. He may have been a thug, but he was an inconvenient thug, and not enough of a thug for the people who really run the show. (I don't know who these people are but I'll bet McGeorge Bundy does.)

If others want to play up the significance of the test ban treaty, the rapprochement with Cuba and the Soviets, JFK's (albeit reluctant) commitment to civil rights, his opposition to Big Oil, the Federal Reserve, the Mafia, and the CIA, and so on, frankly I don't mind, because the arguments are going in the right direction. I doubt that any of those factors alone could have brought about the assassination and coverup, but the war was bigger than all of them put together. It's interesting to note that the *JFK* reviews (Cockburn being an exception in this respect) do their best to obscure this point, usually burying the Vietnam thing in the middle of a paragraph in the middle of the article among all the "other possible" reasons. There are no headlines that read: "Was JFK Killed Because He Wanted to Withdraw from Vietnam?" But this is the main message of the film, as most people who see it will confirm. It's that impermissible question again: ok for the movies but not for the papers. Damage control.

To change the subject just a bit, I must mention Michael Albert's terrible essay in *Z Magazine* (Jan. 1992) pitting Craig Hulet as an exemplar of "conspiracy theory" against you as one of "institutional" critique. I don't know anything about Hulet, but it's interesting that Cockburn mentions him too. I don't know Albert either, but this article is really a crock of do-do. *Time Newsweek*, Cockburn, Albert — they all form a united front against "conspiracy." Albert at least allows for the existence of "progressive and left conspiracy theory," which I guess is the category I would fall into, but I reject this dichotomy. I see a continuum, from the particular to the abstract, conspiracies as particular manifestations of -isms.

Not only is it a false dichotomy, it plays right into the hands of the CIA and their ilk, who would like nothing better than to see all "conspiracy theorists" branded as fascists, which is the usual implication (Cockburn's too). Why mention Craig Hulet (whoever this guy is) or Lyndon LaRouche (who some people, like Ramsey Clark, don't think is quite as crazy as he's made out to be), and not Peter Scott? (Cockburn, to his credit, does deal with Scott — by misrepresenting him — but more as a "fantasizer" than a "conspiracist.") The notion that "conspiracists" are fascists or even extremists is disproved by the great majority of Americans who think the assassination was a conspiracy and are not fascists or even extremists — yet, though they may be driven to fascism if their common sense understanding of the conspiratorial nature of government continues to be refuted by elite opinion. According to my dictionary, "conspiracy" and "government" are practically synonyms, and ordinary people seem to understand that much more easily than the better-propagandized elite. What governments do not plan bad things in secret? I see no contradiction between Jim Garrison and Noam Chomsky. Why can't they both be right?

The question is, why is what Scott calls "deep politics" and "parapolitics" (I guess to avoid saying "conspiracy theory") consistently "resisted by the establishment left (*The Nation*) in almost the same terms as the establishment center (the *New York Times*)"? Scott's answer is that the left writes out of "false despair," and, like the center, "out of false consciousness, to rationalize their disempowerment," but I don't see that that explains anything. (Garrison is more depressing than Cockburn, everybody rationalizes their disempowerment, and I have no idea what "false consciousness" is.) Cockburn's answer seems to be that if the conspiracists are right,

> Out the window goes any sensible analysis of institutions, economic trends and pressures, continuities in

corporate and class interest and all the other elements constituting the open secrets and agendas of American capitalism (*The Nation* 1/6-13/92:6).

which is so foolish I can't believe he means it. Why should Garrison, Scott et al. render Chomsky et al. (and Cockburn for that matter) invalid or superfluous? We don't need this confusion. Hasn't anybody thought of trying to consolidate the revolutionary (peaceful of course) elements in these supposedly disparate analyses rather than insisting on driving them farther apart than they really are? I see now why *Z Magazine* rejects my stuff; it violates the anti-conspiracy doctrine. But if that Albert article is their idea of "sensible analysis" I am unimpressed. Oh well, there's still the computer network (no editors!).

Best regards,
Michael

[Chomsky replied (May 21, 1992), again at length, that the "theory" that JFK was planning to withdraw from Vietnam was not credible, and that "the evidence to the contrary is quite compelling." The "theory" Chomsky was referring to is Scott's early theory, later elaborated by Newman, that there was a significant difference between JFK's NSAM 263 and LBJ's 273. But this Chomsky had already conceded, in his previous letter to me. The significant difference, he had said, was between 263 and the draft of 273, which was written by Bundy for JFK, and which was not significantly different from LBJ's 273. Newman, agreeing that the draft 273 was written for JFK, says it is significantly different from the 273 LBJ signed.

In the end, then, Chomsky was agreeing with Scott and Newman that 273 shows a policy change, but disagreeing with them that the change came with Johnson. Bundy's draft 273 proved that it came with Kennedy.

He went on to review "several types of evidence." The public record, he said, was clear, and everybody (including Scott and

Newman) agreed that "JFK was, publicly, an extreme hawk, until the very end, holding that withdrawal without victory is unthinkable and would be a disaster." He did not want to withdraw because "he knew that escalation was highly unpopular, both among the public and in the Senate," and that therefore, if he had wanted to withdraw, he would have said so publicly because "he would have received enormous support." Instead, he kept "using his bully pulpit to drive the general public in a more hawkish direction, as much as he could." The record makes clear "his unwillingness to withdraw without victory." If he had planned to withdraw, he "could have drawn on highly respected military authorities to back him up," such as MacArthur, Ridgeway, and Shoup.

The McNamara-Taylor report of Oct. 2, 1963, Chomsky said, concluded "that the military part of the war was going so well that if the 1964 battle plan succeeded, US forces could be withdrawn by the end of 1965." But all of this "was explicitly contingent on the success of the 1964 plan." By October 1963, JFK was concerned about the deteriorating political situation in Saigon and afraid that Diem and his brother Nhu would negotiate a settlement with the North, "which would lead to neutralization and force the US to withdraw." To this JFK was adamantly opposed, "because it would lead to withdrawal without victory." After the coup against Diem, negative facts about the progress of the war began to filter in, leading to the Honolulu meeting and the draft for NSAM 273, "adapted to the changing assessment."

If Kennedy had been planning to withdraw, "he surely had a great opportunity when the Diem family was negotiating with the North for a settlement." In that case his public utterances would have been different, there would be some trace in the internal record, and "he would have given prominence to the highest military brass who were strongly opposed to escalation, etc. None of this is the case."

Prouty, Chomsky said, is "utterly untrustworthy" and "a raving fascist," avoided by "serious journalists" such as Edward Epstein, "who does think there was an assassination conspiracy."

Oliver Stone had misinformed the public, spreading "fantasies about NSAM 263."

In sum, Chomsky said, it was clear "that no one with even a shred of rationality could have thought that getting rid of JFK had anything to do with the war in Vietnam." Maybe "right-wing nuts" thought so, but there was no evidence for it, just "belief and wish fulfillment." He lamented the "ugly name-calling and irrationality" that was causing "movement circles" to "tear themselves apart on this," when there were many more important issues to address.]

1992.06.18 TO CHOMSKY

June 18, 1992

Dear Noam,

Your letter arrived in the same mail (May 25) as Newman's book, which I've now read. I don't like being at an impasse with you on this, if we are, so I want to try to pin down as precisely as possible what we are disagreeing about.

I do not have access now to the new internal documentation you and he mention, so I can't evaluate that. On the whole, Newman's "deception within a deception" theory isn't much different from what occurred to me — that withdrawal on the basis of "mission accomplished" (not the same as victory) was a ploy on JFK's part, in order to withdraw without losing face and the 64 election. I agree, though, that if we discount O'Donnell et al., this is speculation, and Newman doesn't add anything to what we already know (or don't know) about what Kennedy himself thought.

He does seem to make a good case that Harkins and Taylor (and, less clearly, McNamara) were lying (i.e. lying about winning so Kennedy wouldn't pull out). This is different from the standard *Bright Shining Lie* à la Neil Sheehan (also the Pentagon Papers story), which says everybody at the top (except a few lower down the line like Vann), including Kennedy, actually believed they were winning.

I'm not convinced, though, that JFK could have or needed to have "deceived the deceivers." More plausible to me would be that Harkins, Taylor and McNamara were simply playing Kennedy's game — and probably reluctantly. If the top brass were really working against Kennedy, before the assassination, surely they could have thought up a more effective tactic to prevent withdrawal, such as staging a Tonkin-like "act of war" on US troops. In the context of a coup theory, if the military advisors felt they had been sorely misused (by being forced by JFK to lie about the true military situation), this would have added to their sense of moral indignation and made it easier for them to support a coup.

The two basic questions Newman addresses are: 1) Were the top brass really optimistic, and 2) Was Kennedy really optimistic? The standard answer (the "false optimism" hypothesis) is yes to both (e.g. PP Gravel, Vol. 2, 160-200). Newman says no to both.

I'm willing to leave both questions in abeyance, since it's not likely that we'll learn much more about what anybody "really" thought.

Still, before I go on, I have to comment on the "false optimism" argument. What it really means is stupidity. The top brass and/ or Kennedy were too dumb, naive, incompetent, indifferent, etc. — I'll just collapse this as "stupid" — to read the writing on the wall. We should note that this is the standard explanation for anything the US government does that threatens to be perceived as wrong. The whole war was a "tragic mistake," i.e. stupid. "Wise Men" and all, they were just too stupid to see what should have been obvious to any child — that US national security was never in danger in Vietnam, that it was an indigenous revolution, that the Saigon regime was hopelessly corrupt, that we shouldn't have been there, etc. Skipping up to the most recent war, we find the same explanations. Why did April Glaspie tell Saddam the US didn't care about his border disputes? Stupidity. Why didn't Bush at least try to get the foreigners out of Kuwait after the invasion, <u>before</u> sending in the troops (upon which Saddam took them hostage)? Stupidity. Why didn't they go on to take out Saddam Hussein? Stupidity. Why did they leave Saddam his helicopters and elite troops? Stupidity. Why did they get the Kurds to revolt and then abandon them? Stupidity.

No matter how skillfully the rhetoric may disguise it ("well-intentioned errors"), the "explanation" always boils down to plain old stupidity. (Well-intentioned stupidity is still stupidity.) I just don't buy it. I never thought I was smarter than McGeorge Bundy (to take my favorite hate-figure).

One alternative explanation is the propaganda model. I think it is valid and powerful, but it doesn't explain everything. For one thing, doesn't it too boil down to intellectual blindness and self-deception, and aren't those just fancy words for stupidity? Should I believe that McGeorge Bundy was so blind, propagandized, self-deceived — or stupid — that in 1963-64 he didn't know what I knew (at the age of 17-18), namely that Vietnam was (at least) a mistake?

The most obvious cases where the propaganda model fails are the assassinations. I suppose one might explain the execution of Fred Hampton (which you talked about in one of your books) in terms of the propaganda model. It's possible. Given the mindset of the Chicago police and the situation, it happened. But this will not do for JFK, RFK, and MLK — just to name the biggies. These were conspiracies, both the executions themselves and the subsequent coverups, and the evidence for high-level, long-term government complicity is overwhelming.

One could explain this complicity in terms of a propaganda model too, I suppose, i.e. if it was ultimately "well-intentioned." They did it for what they were convinced was the good of the country. But you could say the same about Hitler and anyone else. At this point, the notion of conspiracy disappears altogether, because the notion of right and wrong also disappears. If the "conspirators" are convinced that their goals are good and their means are justified, there is no conspiracy from their point of view. From our point of view, we can say they are (willing) victims of propaganda, but if we disagree with their idea of "good" we have to call it conspiracy (a plan by more than one person to do something bad).

To return to the question at hand, let us assume no more than what the paper record tells us, omitting all speculation about what anyone really believed and when, omitting Scott's thesis (that NSAM 273 confirming the withdrawal plan was a lie), omitting Newman's thesis (that the top brass were lying and Kennedy was pretending to believe them to justify withdrawal). We can also omit the question of the conditionality of withdrawal on continued battlefield success. You say the condition was crucial and explicit, but in the McNamara-Taylor recommendations implemented by NSAM 263 it is only implied ("we should be able..."), unless I've missed an if-clause. In any case, the importance you attach to this depends again on what you think people actually believed. If nobody really believed that there was any success in the first place, as Newman says, the question is irrelevant.

PP Gravel 2, 160-200 tells us that the withdrawal plan started in the summer of 1962, began wavering in December 1963 (p. 191-192, 276), and ended 27 by March 27 1964 at the very latest: "Thus ended de jure the policy of phase out and withdrawal and all the plans and programs oriented to it. Shortly, they would be cancelled out de facto" (p. 196).

This means that withdrawal was still policy on Nov. 22, and it changed under Johnson. Johnson reversed Kennedy's withdrawal plan. This — no more, no less — is fact. Do you agree?

I think the problem may be that we are coming at this from different directions. I think you are more concerned with making sure that JFK is not remade into a dove. I am more concerned with getting at the truth about the assassination. I guess I was wrong to say last time that I didn't mind if Stone et al. fall into the Camelot syndrome, because if it leads people closer to the truth about the assassination it would be in the right direction. There is no reason to compromise there, even for "strategic" reasons. You're quite right, of course, JFK was a hawk. But there are hawks and hawks. Hawks can have withdrawal policies. Reagan withdrew from Lebanon. Bush withdrew from Iraq. Nixon finally withdrew from Vietnam.

You might say that sure, the whole history of the war was based on a phony "withdrawal policy," which is true in a sense, but I refer again to the Pentagon Papers account. The withdrawal policy that ended by March 1964 was real and had nothing to do with Nixon's "secret plan" to end the war and eventual retreat.

There doesn't <u>have</u> to be a connection between the assassination and the withdrawal policy reversal. It is a theory, but a good one. I would hardly presume to remind you, of all people, that there is a difference between good theories and bad ones. The theory that Hinkley shot Reagan because he thought Reagan was a closet Leninist is a bad one. It's bad because there is no evidence for it and it explains nothing.

There is plenty of evidence, however, that the assassination and coverup was a government conspiracy, a coup d'état, without going into the Vietnam question. But if you add to all this the fact — which is all I am trying to establish here — that Johnson reversed Kennedy's withdrawal policy, you certainly have a basis to postulate that one reason for the assassination was to affect the policy change.

I think it would be more accurate to compare this theory with your propaganda model. It's not the fact that it can't be disproved that makes it a good theory. It's a good theory because it makes sense, explains more of the facts in a coherent way than other theories, etc.

That just about does it from my side for the essential point, but I'll go through your letter to make sure I've covered everything and in some cases to ask for information.

You say JFK knew that escalation was highly unpopular. What is the evidence for this? Certainly it was just the opposite among most of his own staff, and there must have been at least as many hawks as doves in Congress and in the population at large, inasmuch as anybody was even thinking seriously about it in 1963. (The first conversation I remember having about Vietnam was in the spring of 1963, when a friend asked me what I thought "we ought to do over there." All I could say then was "I don't know, what do you think?" but I was quite shocked when he said he thought we should "beat the shit out of 'em." I just thought, Why?)

I can't find any references in Newman to Shoup advising Kennedy to withdraw, or any at all to Ridgeway or MacArthur. I've read elsewhere that MacArthur advised JFK in 1961 never to get involved in a land war in Asia, but I didn't know either one advised him later on Vietnam.

What happened in Honolulu on Nov. 20 still seems a mystery, but I see no evidence whatsoever that the official withdrawal policy changed, whether the military reports had become more pessimistic or not. (Newman's argument is that the new pessimism only increased JFK's desire to withdraw, but let's ignore that.) The second paragraph of NSAM 273, both the Bundy draft and LBJ's version, confirms that the withdrawal policy was to continue.

If you consider the possibility of a coup d'état, the motives of people like Bundy, McNamara, etc., as well as Johnson, are highly suspect, to say the least, so there is no point in debating whether that Bundy draft was written "for Kennedy" or not. It doesn't matter.

I would feel like I am belaboring the obvious, except that it isn't. I mean, what should be obvious is not obvious at all to the people who should know. The standard accounts do not say what PP Gravel says quite clearly. They say the opposite. They say (like Cockburn) there was_no change of policy, meaning the policy of escalation. What should be "obvious," however, and what the PP say, is that there was no change in the policy of withdrawal until after Kennedy's death. There's a big difference. Almost no one says that Johnson continued Kennedy's withdrawal policy, and then reversed it. They say Johnson continued Kennedy's policy of escalation.

Here are a few examples I've collected, quite at random (emphasis added):

> ...President Kennedy...began the process of backing up American military aid with "advisers." At the time of his murder there were 23,000 [sic] of them in South Vietnam. President Johnson took the same view of the importance of Vietnam...(J.M. Roberts, *The Pelican History of the World,* 1980, p. 988-989).

> Although Johnson followed Kennedy's lead in sending more and more troops to Vietnam (it peaked at 542,000, in 1969), it was never enough to meet General Westmoreland's demands... (Paul Kennedy, *The Rise and Fall of the Great Powers,* 1987, p. 405).

> By October 1963, some 16,000 American troops were in Vietnam... Under President Johnson, the "advisors" kept increasing...

> Lyndon Johnson, who had campaigned in 1964 as a "peace candidate," inherited and expanded the Vietnam policy of his predecessor (Allan Nevins and Henry Steele Commager, *A Pocket History of the United States,* 1981, p. 565-566).

I haven't read Schlesinger's *RFK*, but you're right, he certainly doesn't mention the withdrawal plan in the earlier book. He buries a brief reference to the Oct. 2 White House statement in a context which makes it seem both insignificant and based on a misapprehension of the situation by McNamara, who

> ...thought that the political mess had not yet infected the military situation and, back in Washington, announced (in spite of a strong dissent from William Sullivan of Harriman's staff who accompanied the mission) that a thousand American troops could be withdrawn by the end of the year and that the major part of the American military task would be completed by the end of 1965.

> This announcement, however, was far less significant than McNamara's acceptance of the Lodge pressure program [on Diem] (*A Thousand Days*, 1965, p. 996).

Schlesinger does not indicate that this "far less significant" announcement was a statement of official policy, implemented nine days later by NSAM 263, confirmed at the Honolulu conference on Nov. 20, and (supposedly) reaffirmed by Johnson in NSAM 273.

Stanley Karnow, instead of citing the documents themselves, substitutes his own convoluted "analysis":

> ...what Kennedy wanted from McNamara and Taylor was a negative assessment of the military situation, so that he could justify the pressures being exerted on the Saigon regime. But Taylor and McNamara would only further complicate Kennedy's problems (*Vietnam*, 1983, p. 293).

This image of a recalcitrant McNamara and Taylor presenting a positive report when Kennedy expected a negative one is absurd, first because both McNamara and Taylor were in fact opposed to withdrawal, and second because if Kennedy had wanted a negative report, he would have had no trouble procuring one. Karnow goes on to say that McNamara and Taylor's true motivation for recommending the withdrawal of 1,000 troops by the end of the year was "to placate Harkins and the other optimists" (p. 293). First McNamara and Taylor are presented as defying the president's "true wishes," and then as deliberately misrepresenting the situation to "placate" the commanding general (without bothering to explain why troop withdrawals would be particularly placating to the general in charge of them). There is no mention of NSAM 263, and the reason is clear. If the recommendations were "riddled with contradictions and compromises" and contrary to the president's wishes, as Karnow says, how would he explain why the president implemented them?

Karnow also tells us why the recommendation to withdraw all US troops by 1965 was made: it was "a prophecy evidently made for domestic political consumption at Kennedy's insistence" (p. 294). But as I've mentioned, I know of no evidence that there was more public or political opposition to engagement than there was to disengagement (plenty of the latter even within the administration). Karnow has Kennedy wanting a negative report, getting a positive one, and then insisting on announcing it publicly for a political effect that would do him at least as much harm as good.

I could go on and on. Very rarely do we find a deviation from the standard myth, such as Richard Goodwin:

> In later years Johnson and others in his administration would assert that they were merely fulfilling the commitment of previous American presidents. The claim was untrue — even though it was made by men, like Bundy and McNamara, who were more anxious to serve the wishes of their new master than the memory of their dead one. During the first half of 1965 I attended meetings, participated in conversations, where the issues of escalation were discussed. Not once did any participant claim that we had to bomb or send combat

troops because of "previous commitments," that these steps were the inevitable extension of past policies. They were treated as difficult and serious decisions to be made solely on the basis of present conditions and perceptions. The claim of continuity was reserved for public justification; intended to conceal the fact that a major policy change was being made — that "their" war was becoming "our" war (*Remembering America*, 1988, p. 373).

Thanks to accounts like those of Schlesinger and Karnow, the general public has not even been aware that there was a withdrawal policy, much less that Johnson reversed it — despite the clear account in PP Gravel.

If the Stone film has informed people of this much, it has performed a public service.

You say JFK's most trusted advisers, though they were extreme hawks (agreed), proceeded haltingly and ambiguously toward committing US combat troops.[22] I don't see the point. Surely you don't mean to imply that the chiefs were doves. (I would be interested to see that quote from Shoup, but in any case 1965 was not 1963). Do you mean that if they had been in on a coup, they would have sent the Marines in immediately? That would have been too obvious. There had to be some transition period, some pretext that the military situation had changed, before the big commitment was made. It didn't take long, and there was plenty of time, once Johnson was in the White House. They didn't need Goldwater.[23] He also would have been too obvious a change. The goal was to establish and perpetuate precisely the myth that endures today — that "there was no change in policy."

This is the whole point I am trying to make. Once this myth is shattered, one way or another, the question of a connection between the policy change and the assassination is inevitable.

I quite agree that the JFK-Vietnam issue is narrow, if you define it as whether US imperialism should take the form of counterinsurgency (JFK's preference) or full-scale war. But that, for me, is not the issue at all.

The issue is whether the government is so corrupt, so powerful, and so much in control of our minds that it can murder (even) the president and keep it secret for more than a quarter of a century. It's not a matter of Kennedy as a person; his life was worth no more or less than anyone else's. I guess I'm thinking "strategically" again, but if the assassination was a coup, it is the most dramatic and powerful demonstration of the illegitimacy of the government, of the structures of the government, of the necessity for radical change that I can imagine. If anything like ideas can be the stuff of revolution, this is one, and I simply do not understand how you can deny the political significance of it. Do you believe the Warren Report, or even give it the benefit of the doubt? If you do in this case, where there is so much evidence to the contrary, how can you doubt their word about anything?

Re Prouty (haven't heard from him in a while), if he turns out to be a raving fascist I'll be more than a little embarrassed. What makes you say so? Maybe I've been overly impressed with his "insider" account, but he seems sincere. He was wrong to associate himself with Liberty Lobby, and he's no scholar, and maybe a raving conspiracist, but why "fascist"? I'm surprised that you say "serious journalists dismiss him," since we both know how much that is worth.

I think Epstein is the one who thinks the KGB did it, which is why I haven't read him. The best books I know on the assassination are Garrison's *On the Trail of the Assassins*, Jim Marrs' *Crossfire*, and Groden and Livingstone's *High Treason*. Prouty has a book coming out in the fall, but I haven't seen it.

You ask what makes me assume that JFK knew more of the truth about the war than McNamara, Taylor, Bundy, Hilsman, etc. I didn't mean to imply that. After reading Newman, I believe Taylor and Harkins, at least, knew the truth, and lied.

How much JFK knew about the true military situation, and when, what game he was playing, and whose side McNamara and Bundy, etc. were on, I suppose will go unanswered.

We do not need any of these answers, though, to make a rational connection between the assassination and the withdrawal policy reversal. It cannot be proved, but it is the best theory of the assassination I have heard. If that — the desire for rational explanation — is wish-fulfillment, then it is wish-fulfillment.

I don't see what "right-wing nuts" have to do with it one way or another.[24] Are you a right-wing nut if you "believe" (but cannot prove) that the CIA helped assassinate Allende, Lumumba, Trujillo, etc.?

The pro-war forces surrounding Kennedy were not "right-wing nuts," in the usual sense of the term. They were the Vice President, Bundy, McNamara, Rusk, McCone, the Joint Chiefs, etc. And, you will want to say, JFK too. But look at what we know. We know there was a withdrawal plan, and it was his plan. We cannot know if he would have carried it out, but we know that it was still his official policy on the day he was shot. What is irrational about suspecting that the pro-war forces would have assumed that he would do what he said he would do, that they feared he would do what he said he would do? Instead, we have a quasi-universal consensus that he would not have done what he said he was going to do [i.e., that he would have reversed the withdrawal policy, as Johnson did]. That is the point where the question of rationality, belief, and wish-fulfillment should be asked, in my opinion.

Kennedy was the only one of the bunch that we can say with certainty did support the withdrawal policy, because he was the one ultimately responsible for it. He is also the only one we can say did not support the policy reversal, because he was dead by the time it occurred.

Everything else is speculation. But the plain facts — the assassination and the policy reversal — suffice to support the hypothesis that Kennedy was killed in order to ensure that the withdrawal policy would be reversed and that the war, eventually worth $570 billion to the warmongers, would take place. The curious thing to me is how this not only rational but (one would think) obvious thesis has been suppressed in the mainstream. As I said last time, it strikes me as a perfect example of Orwell's problem.

I hope I've been able to hammer out some common ground, because frankly I'm surprised to find us (apparently) disagreeing on this. On the other hand, it confirms what I feel — that the assassination is the key to a lot of things, not only Vietnam. If it was just another US government-sponsored murder, I don't think we'd be talking about it at all.

With best regards,
Michael

1992.07.27 TO PROUTY

27 July 1992

Dear Fletch,

I just got back from spending two weeks in Miami Beach, where I thought of calling you, but it's been so long since our last exchange of letters that I didn't really feel comfortable about it. There's a lot to catch up on, so it's probably better to do it by letter anyway.

First, what's happened to your book? I saw it listed as "forthcoming" in a Tom Davis catalogue a few months ago but now it seems to have disappeared.

I see there was an assassination symposium in Chicago recently and there'll be another one in October in Dallas. Plan to go? I'd like to but I'm not sure it's worth the expense, and the October one comes when I have to teach, so I guess I won't make it.

I'm in touch with a couple of people here in Europe via Jerry Rose's *Third Decade* campaign to get the Warren Commission documents released, but for me it's just a way to contact people and keep from going stir-crazy with all these thoughts in my head and too many people saying, "Well, IF it's true it's terrible..." Either that or they yawn and wait for the next subject.

One of the guys I'm in contact with thinks JFK was done in by something called the Majestic 12 project. Eisenhower and

Nelsen Rockefeller supposedly set this up to keep secret a UFO-crash in 1947 or 48, which one alien survived (supposedly until 1952). The source for this is Maurice Chatelain, who headed the Apollo 11 moon landing communications division.

I've seen lots of references to you in the past months — in *The Spotlight*, *Neue Solidarität* (the German LaRouche newspaper), and of course in the reviews of *JFK* where the authors discovered who Mr. X was. Some were pretty nasty, particularly from the left. Associating yourself with that Liberty Lobby PAC seems to be proof enough for some that you are a raving fascist. Much of the left (*The Nation*, Z magazine) seems determined to brand all conspiracy theories as fascist, and some of the most respected leftist commentators (e.g. Alexander Cockburn) even deny that the assassination has any political significance at all. That's very confusing.

This same group (Cockburn et al.) insist that there was no policy reversal in Vietnam, that the only difference between JFK and LBJ was that the assumption that "we" were winning changed. The "condition" of withdrawal on "victory" never changed. I don't buy that, but I don't buy Newman's argument completely either (*JFK and Vietnam*). It seems impossible to know what JFK really thought, unless we accept O'Donnell and Mansfield's reports, which many simply refuse to do because they say they were biased.

Still, even if it was the assumption that victory was in sight that changed, which in turn caused the withdrawal policy to be abandoned, the fact remains that the policy changed after the assassination. Cockburn et al. argue that it didn't, because they define "policy" as "withdrawal conditional upon victory." Thus they say that the policy didn't change at all, just the condition. That seems to be the bottom line of this controversy. Those who are determined to see no connection between Vietnam and the assassination see it this way, and demand "proof" to the contrary. This attitude of course is indistinguishable from the government-media-propaganda line, and I find it very hard to take from people who claim to be (and are in most other cases) radical dissenters. I'm not going to say that they are part of the Grand Conspiracy, which is exactly what they would expect a Conspiracist to say, but it troubles me.

I have a copy of the film and also the book with the screenplay, notes, and discussion. Will be nice for a course if I can get the students interested. The impact has dwindled considerably. It's old news. On the whole I'm glad the film was made, simply because it makes the whole subject easier to talk about, but this reaction was predictable. An initial flare-up of controversy, then the whole thing dies down to an even quieter level than before. Ok, the worst has been said, and nothing can be proved. Next subject.

The LaRouche people have contacted me here about my Herrhausen article, but I'm not sure what they want. I'm leery of them too, I guess because of the propaganda branding them as fascists, which again comes from the left as well as from the mainstream. It's a good thing I'm not a joiner, I guess, but on the other hand it gets a little lonely out here. Not enough to become a LaRouchian, but I don't mind talking to them. At least they're out there, trying to cause trouble.

Which brings me back to the main theme: indifference. The Ross Perot scam will make a significant contribution. How will there ever be another third-party candidate after this? Either this was the purpose — to discourage all future third party candidacies — or somebody got something big on him he didn't want to get out. Or did he learn the truth about AIDS (as Reagan may have at Reykjavík in 1986) or something else and decide he didn't want to be the Head Trickster after all? He reminded me of what Peter Drucker said in your favorite book, The End of Economic Man, but I just might have voted for him, as an alternative to not voting at all. In any event, the result is more of the same: despair. JFK, all the other scandals — it all seems calculated to turn us into robots who accept the fact that nothing can be changed. Just work for our bread, eat it, pay our taxes, and make room for the next generation.

The process is far advanced. My first principle in teaching English (conversation) is that the student must want to say something before he can learn how to say it, or say it well or correctly (which is where I'm supposed to come in). It rarely works. Most of them do not want to say anything. Given the choice, they say nothing. Most of my job is trying to get them interested enough in something that they can be forced to say something — anything at all — which has nothing to do with the English language. Why they want to learn a foreign language so they can keep their mouths shut in it I don't know. Maybe one in twenty will have something to say — by which I mean a question, an inanity, a diatribe, anything. The rest are robots, speaking only when spoken to, their answers totally predictable. Strange, strange. But no different from the population at large, I suspect.

I try not to be discouraged, but it's hard. Approach it all as a student of mind control, I tell myself. And week after week, month after month, plus ca change, plus c'est la meme chose. It's not that nobody cares, I tell myself, it's just that they are confused, propagandized, controlled. Just like I was. I have to remember that, that I was the same way. Still, it's hard. And then when the few people that one does seem to be on the same wavelength with turn out to hate each other even more than the people and things they hate in common, it's worse.

I think I'll stop here and get this into an envelope before I work myself into a depression. Why couldn't I have a more tangible hobby, like gardening? My wife has the right idea. She buys and resells diamond rings as a hobby, which is mostly what we did in Miami. Makes a good profit at it and loves the work. I think we went to most of the pawn shops around Miami (lots). Life can be so simple. Guns by the ton in the pawn shops, and I admit I was fascinated, which is not so simple, now that I have (almost) convinced myself I am a pacifist. I even toyed with the idea of bringing one back, which is strange for a guy who says he is for strict gun control (one of the things I differ with *Spotlight* about, along with their support of David Duke, Le Pen, Clarence Thomas, flag-waving, etc.). Fortunately, German law is a lot stricter than Florida. I did go to a shooting range, though, feeling childish and scaring myself half to death at the same time, but there's no doubt about it, boys like guns. Vera's the least squeamish lady I know, but I couldn't get her to fire one. She likes diamonds. A larger truth there, I think.

Hope to hear from you soon and all about what's been happening in the wake of JFK, which I hope turns out to be more than what we read about in the papers.

Best regards,

Michael

P.S. I also picked up *High Treason 2*, Crenshaw's *JFK*, and the new edition of Weberman/Canfield's *Coup d'état in America*, and *Friends in High Places* (McCartney — a book you recommended some time ago) while I was in the US. I've started Livingstone's book. Seems to have had a serious falling-out with Groden, which is unfortunate, and he could have omitted all the blubber about Camelot, but I'll wait till the end to see if I'm more or less confused than I was when I started. Do you know a book called *Unholy Babylon* (Darwish and Alexander)? *War Crimes* (Ramsey Clark et al., Maisonneuve Press)? Ramsey Clark strikes me as an interesting guy, who obviously went through some kind of metamorphosis. He represents LaRouche, among other things. Know him?

1992.08.03 TO CHOMSKY

[In another long letter (July 1, 1992) Chomsky said he had finished about 100 pages of a manuscript (which I presume became *Rethinking Camelot*) attacking the "Schlesinger-Newman-Stone (etc.)" thesis that JFK "had a secret plan to withdraw." It would be hard, he said, "to find a historical thesis more utterly refuted by the evidence."

The argument is not really as complicated as it might seem. It hinges on the interpretation of the "McNamara-Taylor recommendations," which were based on their assessment that "the military campaign has made great progress and continues to progress" (*Pentagon Papers*, Bantam, 1971, p. 211). The second and third recommendations were that

> 2. A program be established to train Vietnamese so that essential functions now performed by U.S. military personnel can be carried out by Vietnamese by the end of 1965. It should be possible to withdraw the bulk of U.S. personnel by that time.
>
> 3. In accordance with the program to train progressively Vietnamese to take over military functions, the Defense Department should announce in the very near future presently prepared plans to withdraw 1000 U.S. military personnel by the end of 1963. This action should be explained in low key as an initial step in a long-term program to replace U.S. personnel with

trained Vietnamese without impairment of the war effort (pp. 211-212).

It is the phrase "without impairment of the war effort" in the last sentence that Chomsky insists is the "explicit condition."

I am trying to make the (simple, I thought) point that this was not a condition but an assumption. To say "My plan is to paint the living room without ruining the rug" is not the same as saying "If I can do it without ruining the rug, I will paint the living room." I was astounded by Chomsky's consistent refusal to acknowledge this point, since it is quite clear from a linguistic as well as common-sense point of view.]

Aug. 3, 1992

Dear Noam,

Your letter does help to clarify things, and I guess we've just about scraped bottom on this. Your position, at least, is clear, but I don't think I've made myself clear on a couple of points.

In sum, all I am saying, as far as "the record" goes, is what PP Gravel says: Johnson abandoned, i.e. reversed, the withdrawal policy by March 1964 (at the latest). You can say, as the PP also say, that policy changed because conditions and assumptions changed, but the fact remains that the policy changed, and it changed under Johnson, not Kennedy.

You say that the policy did not change, that it was "victory, then withdrawal" under both Kennedy and Johnson. I think this formulation skews the issue. This may be a question of what people call "semantics," but it is still important, since what the "facts" are always depends partly on how they are presented, and our discussion seems to be a good example of this.

What "withdrawal policy" are we talking about? I am talking about the one PP Gravel describes in 2:160-200. If you wish to say this policy did not change, you are using the term in a quite different way than the PP use it. The PP summary which

I quoted, and which you say is accurate, says: "Thus ended [by March 27, 1964] de jure the <u>policy</u> of phase out and withdrawal and all the <u>plans</u> and <u>programs</u> oriented to it (2:196)." The first indication of this change came the day after the assassination: "The only hint that something might be different from on-going <u>plans</u> came in a Secretary of Defense memo for the President three days prior to this NSC meeting [on Nov. 26]." Johnson "began to have a sense of uneasiness about Vietnam" in early December and initiated a "major <u>policy</u> review (2:191)."

The PP also support your point that the withdrawal plan was conditional on military success, but I think it is more accurate to say that it was based on the assumption of success. I don't read the condition in the McNamara-Taylor recommendations as explicitly as you do. There is a difference between saying "If we continue to win the war, we'll leave by 1966" vs. "The military campaign continues to make great progress. We should be able to leave by 1966." The latter is only implicitly conditional. I assume you take "without impairment of the war effort" in the third recommendation as the explicit condition, but I also see a difference between "We should be able to withdraw without impairment of the war effort" vs. "If it does not impair the war effort, we will withdraw." Under the latter formulation, the withdrawal decision has not been made, and there is no indication of what the decision will be. Under the former, which is what McNamara-Taylor say, the decision has been made, and the prediction is that the withdrawal will probably not impair the war effort.

That would be the only point I would insist on. One could argue further, though, if one wanted to stretch it, that the phrase "without impairment of the war effort" refers more to how the action "should be explained" to the public (i.e. "in low-key") than to a real condition: the public should get the impression that the war effort will not be impaired. This interpretation is not illogical, because propaganda purposes aside, how could the military (or Kennedy) really have thought that withdrawal would not impair the war effort? It would have to.

You say that there was "no policy change" and no withdrawal policy, only a "first victory, then withdrawal" policy (until Tet). But this formulation gives the word "withdrawal" such a general sense that it means virtually nothing. Everybody, in that sense, wanted to withdraw, just as everybody wanted peace. The same is true of "victory."

First of all, you use the word with much more insistence than Kennedy did. McNamara-Taylor speak repeatedly of "progress" and "success," but only in one place of "victory," where they feel immediately compelled to qualify it as "the reduction of the insurgency" (PP Gravel 2:757). Their recommended version of the White House statement defines this further as "reducing it to proportions manageable by the national security forces of the GVN, unassisted by the presence of U.S. military forces" (2:753). Kennedy omitted this qualification in the public statement, but he does not talk about "victory" either, nor about "winning," as Johnson did in NSAM 273.

Secondly, the question of what would constitute "victory" was the crux of the problem JFK and his successors faced throughout the war. A policy of defeat, of course, for any of them, would have been unthinkable. Therefore, all their policies had to be policies of victory, or at least appear to be so. What we are discussing is whether Kennedy came to the same conclusion about what would have to constitute "victory" as Johnson did. This question will probably remain unanswered, with arguments such as yours suggesting "Yes" and others (O'Donnell, Mansfield, etc.) suggesting "No." To say that Kennedy and Johnson both wanted victory, therefore, says little.

Whether this is "semantics" or not, we end up with two opposite versions of the "facts": there was/was not a withdrawal policy; it did/did not change; Johnson did/did not change it.

Why would you object to formulating your case in this way: JFK thought we were winning, so he planned to withdraw;

Johnson decided we were not winning, so he reversed the withdrawal policy. This would put the discussion on the level where it belongs — of speculation: Did JFK <u>really</u> think we were winning? Did he <u>really</u> want to withdraw? Did LBJ <u>really</u> want to continue the withdrawal policy? Did LBJ <u>really</u> change his mind about the war sometime between December 1963 and March 1964? Would JFK have changed his policy, as Johnson did? These questions can be discussed separately from the facts, plainly established in the PP, that there <u>was</u> a withdrawal policy, and Johnson reversed it.

What is the problem with saying that Johnson reversed the withdrawal policy because conditions changed? Your basic argument would still apply: JFK was a superhawk and would not have withdrawn without victory, and thus would have done the same thing Johnson did. But the argument, formulated in this way, is conjecture, and of course can be countered by conjecture. So what? But to insist that there <u>was</u> no withdrawal policy, or that if there was one it never changed, and that therefore Johnson did not reverse it, seems specious to me, frankly.

This is essentially the same problem I have with the other historians I quoted, with the significant difference that you are confronting the issue head-on. The tradition has been to avoid it. LBJ continued or expanded JFK's Vietnam policy, period. If the withdrawal plan is mentioned at all, it is glossed over. It is never stated plainly that Johnson reversed the withdrawal policy, or even that he reversed it because conditions changed. That plain truth is easily statable, and provable simply by citing the PP, but it does not happen.

True, it is happening now, and we have people like Schlesinger and Hilsman admitting it. That is Step 1, and these two even verge on Step 2, saying it is at least a "defensible premise" that JFK would have withdrawn completely. They draw the line at Step 3, calling the Garrison/Stone theory "palpable nonsense" (Hilsman) and "reckless, paranoid, really despicable fantasy, reminiscent of the wilder accusations of Joe McCarthy" (Schlesinger). Note that neither one makes the slightest attempt to justify his opinion in this regard, and that Schlesinger's hysterical reaction, implying that Stone is a fascist, is typical. This is what children do: "You're a creep!" says one kid. "You're a creep!" says the other. Stone is saying that the assassination was a fascist coup, so that makes him a fascist. This shows how hard the idea hits. "It was a fascist coup," says Stone. "What?" says Schlesinger. "And I didn't know it, still don't know it — or do you mean that I was in on it or went along with it? Why, that's despicable! Reckless! Paranoid! Why, you fascist, you!"

This is an interesting development, but not surprising. Neither JFK hagiography nor self-promotion explains it completely. Look at it through the propaganda model. If until now it has been impermissible to see the JFK-LBJ Vietnam policy as less than a perfect continuum, it's not surprising that opinions to the contrary have been few and far between. If it is now permissible, or becoming permissible, we would expect these opinions to multiply. Why would it be becoming permissible now? Because the truth will out, given time. The rush of conspiracy theories in the past few years, culminating in the Stone film, has resulted in too many people thinking impermissible thoughts. Damage control becomes necessary (a limited hangout, as the CIA calls it). Ok, LBJ reversed the withdrawal policy, and maybe JFK wouldn't have — though this is unknowable. But a connection with the assassination? Unthinkable, or, when thought, "reckless," "paranoid," "despicable," etc. — exactly Schlesinger's reaction. Which does not mean Schlesinger is in on the conspiracy, but merely a victim of propaganda, like everyone.

How else do you explain the fact that the overwhelming majority of historians have tried so hard to avoid saying that Johnson reversed the withdrawal policy, despite the clear evidence to the contrary in the PP? (The reasons in your case, I assume, are different.) As you say, this "fact" has been known all along. But it has not been presented this way, as I tried to illustrate. I'm sure if I had the energy I could make the point convincingly.

Just one more example: the NYT PP. I don't know why the NYT PP is generally referred to as an <u>edition</u> of the PP when it is only a summary by NYT reporters, with some documents added. The Gravel edition has the actual text, and is significantly different. The Gravel account gives 40 pages to the history of the withdrawal policy. The NYT reporters gloss over it in a way that cannot be simply to save space. NSAM 263 is not mentioned at all, and Kennedy's authorization of the McNamara-Taylor recommendations is mentioned only in passing, and inaccurately:

> [The report] asserted that the "bulk" of American troops could be withdrawn by the end of 1965. The two men proposed and — with the President's approval — announced that 1,000 Americans would be pulled out by the end of 1963 (p. 176).

That this "announcement" was in fact a White House foreign policy statement is cleverly disguised (McNamara made the announcement, but it was Kennedy speaking through him), along with the fact that the president also approved the more important recommendation — to withdraw all troops by 1966.

Earlier, the NYT reporter quotes a PP reference to the 1,000-man pullout (again ignoring the more significant total planned withdrawal by 1966) as "strange," "absurd," and "Micawberesque" (p. 113). Then he mentions a McNamara statement that

> ...the situation deteriorated so profoundly in the final five months of the Kennedy Administration...that the entire phase-out had to be formally dropped in early 1964.

The reporter's conclusion is that the PP account "presents the picture of an unbroken chain of decision-making from the final months of the Kennedy Administration into the early months of the Johnson Administration, whether in terms of the political view of the American stakes in Vietnam, the advisory build-up or the hidden growth of covert warfare against North Vietnam" (p. 114).

Notice how different this is from the actual (Gravel) account. It implies that the change in the withdrawal ("phase-out") policy began well within Kennedy's administration; Gravel says the change began in December 1963. The "unbroken chain of decision-making" and "advisory build-up" amounts to an emphatic statement that there never was a withdrawal plan, and that those 40 pages of the PP do not exist.

I think these differences are significant, particularly since the establishment line has followed the NYT version in this regard. Still, most historians should know that the Gravel edition presents a different picture, and one would not expect this kind of unanimity, if the propaganda imperatives were not at work. The Gravel account is simply ignored in this respect, except by the "wild men," who are in this case the "conspiracy buffs," though it does not require a conspiracy theory to state the facts as the Gravel PP state them.

Let me risk an analogy. Suppose Roosevelt had accepted his advisers recommendation not to drop the bomb, and made this policy by issuing a NSAM to that effect. "The war is going well and I don't want to kill <u>that</u> many Japs," he supposedly thought. He is murdered. Truman immediately orders a major review of the no-bomb policy and shortly thereafter, citing unforeseen developments in the progress of the war, drops the bomb.

Of course, the analogy is weak because we are talking about Japs as the victims instead of 58,000 of our own red-blooded, but still, would you be comfortable saying Truman's decision to drop the bomb was a matter of "tactics"? Would you say there was no policy change, that Truman did not reverse Roosevelt's decision, that Roosevelt and Truman in fact had the same policy about dropping the bomb? Would you insist on saying this, as opposed to saying "Truman reversed Roosevelt's no-bomb policy because conditions changed"?

Add to this fictive scenario that Roosevelt's murder occurred under very suspicious circumstances, much of the evidence (and lack of it) pointing to the military-industrial-intelligence establishment, who badly wanted the bomb dropped for various (the usual) reasons. Would it be unreasonable to suspect a connection between the smaller crime of the murder and the larger one of the dropping of the bomb?

You say (p. 9) that "if all of the claims about JFK's alleged policies and intentions collapse, then so does the interest of the assassination." That is partially true (not collapse but probably diminish), but so is the converse: If interest in the assassination collapses, so does the interest in JFK's Vietnam policy. Likewise, as the Stone movie shows, the more interest in the assassination, the more interest in Vietnam.

In my opinion, this is why the assassination coverup has been maintained so long. People may not care too much about the murder of a president, even if it was a coup, but they still care about Vietnam. This is why it has taken a quarter of a century for people (including me) to start thinking about the possible connection, and why it is so important for the establishment to denounce the Stone movie. The idea that the conspirators not only took over the government and killed JFK and dozens of witnesses is one thing; the idea that they killed 58,000 Americans is quite another.

In any case, the issues of the assassination and Vietnam will not be separated until the assassination is clarified — which may take a while. It is not possible to separate them by clarifying the question of what JFK <u>would have</u> done in Vietnam, because the answer is unknowable. We are left with the fact of the policy change, which is now, thanks to the movie, entering the realm of permissible knowledge, the fact of the assassination, the many facts (and lack of them) that implicate the government, and the many as yet unknown, but knowable, facts such as how big is the hole is the back of JFK's skull, which could be ascertained simply by exhuming the body. (They dug up Zachary Taylor last year, but they are not likely to dig up JFK until he is as important to us as Zachary Taylor is, i.e. not at all.)

You say it would be a good idea for those interested in the assassination to stay away from discussions of Vietnam, and I'm sure, unfortunately, that the ruling elite could not agree with you more.[25] But I think all voices should be heard. People can decide for themselves what is the truth, and should. If Stone, Prouty et al. get the facts wrong, it should be discussed. That's what we are doing, and if this shows anything it shows that it's not so easy. I don't mean to defend either one of these guys, but I don't think either deserves the names they have been called. Conjecture is one thing, but lying and distorting "facts" is another, and I don't see that they have done this. We are focusing in our discussion on one such "fact" presented in the film — that LBJ reversed JFK's withdrawal plan — which you deny is a fact. But the coup theory is clearly a theory, and I see nothing fraudulent, fascist, reckless, paranoid, despicable, or fantastic about it. Depressing, yes.

I am not particularly happy that I seem to share some of the ideas of people like Lyndon LaRouche, Liberty Lobby, John Judge, Fletch Prouty, Jim Garrison, Oliver Stone, etc. (not to put these in the same category). But I don't suppose that you are overjoyed, either, to be agreeing with 99% (guessing) of the establishment (and perhaps 10-20% of the population at large) that there is no reason to suspect a connection between the assassination and Vietnam, and that there is no evidence of conspiracy or political significance in the assassination.

I think it would be fair to bear in mind that since much of the left has taken the position, willy nilly, of the establishment on this issue, all the disadvantages of radical dissent are on the other side. It's even worse than usual, because here the dissenters must dissent to the dissenters (e.g., me to you) as well as to the establishment. I don't consider Newman's faculty status, Prouty's reputation among "serious researchers," or the imprimatur of the National Academy of Sciences as an indication of anything. Why should the latter be more credible than the Warren Commission — as in fact it isn't, since their well-funded findings were shown by a lone researcher (Gary Mack) to be invalid (see Jim Marrs, *Crossfire*). Certainly it's what people say that counts, not their rank in the system or their reputation, neither of which necessarily represents their degree of competence, honesty, or freedom from mind control.

Here's another way of looking at it. Suppose there was as much uncertainty in 1963 among certain powerful elements about what JFK would do in Vietnam as there is now about what he <u>would</u> have done. If the war was important enough to them, this uncertainty could have been enough to bring about the coup. This has to be taken into account too: ultimately we are dealing with the question not so much of JFK's actual intentions but of how those intentions were <u>perceived</u> by the (possible) coup plotters.

Going through your letter, I find that most of the points you make that I would quarrel with are covered by what I've already said. My objections would disappear if you said "Assumptions changed, therefore policy changed" instead of "Assumptions changed, but policy didn't." There is plenty of room for argument about the assumptions, but we seem to be arguing — perhaps unnecessarily — about the facts. If you can point to new evidence that Kennedy changed his assumptions about the war after Oct. 11 (or after Nov. 1 or 20 for that matter), that would support the thesis that he <u>might</u> have changed his withdrawal policy, but it would still be speculation, and it would not change the fact (i.e. what I consider a fact but you don't) that he did not change his policy, and Johnson did.

At one point, in apparent contradiction to much of the rest of what you say, you put it just this way (p. 8): "As assessments of the precondition changed, so did policy." That is, if you mean Johnson's assessments, and Johnson's policy. In any case, you do acknowledge here that policy did change.

You say (p. 1), that the Schlesinger-Newman-Stone thesis is that JFK "had a secret plan to withdraw." This might apply to Newman, who says JFK was pretending to agree with Harkins et al. that the war was going well so that he could withdraw, but not to Stone or Schlesinger, who merely acknowledge that JFK planned to withdraw. It was no secret. NSAM 263 was secret to the public, but not to insiders, the White House statement on Oct. 2 was not secret, and neither were the press reports at the time, as you point out.

You say (p. 3) "If JFK had had the slightest intention to withdraw..." But what does NSAM 263 express if not his intention to withdraw? You say it expresses "virtually nothing," that it "authorizes" the McNamara-Taylor recommendations, but that "there is no commitment to implementing anything." What, then, would constitute such a commitment, in your view?

Then you say JFK was "reluctant to make the commitment to withdrawal recommended by his advisers," which implies that he did make the commitment — again a contradiction.

You say (next paragraph), apparently referring to the White House statement (or to NSAM 263?), that JFK "insisted on weakening" the recommendations and "dissociating himself from any time scale." But the time scale ("end of this year" and "end of 1965") is explicitly mentioned in both the public statement and in the recommendations authorized by NSAM 263.

You say (same paragraph) that the withdrawal plan, which JFK "weakened," "had been drawn up by the JCS." Do you mean to imply that the JCS (or McNamara or Taylor) were less hawkish than Kennedy? Do you think that they would have drawn up anything that Kennedy didn't want to have? Do you think, if it were not for JFK's more hawkish influence, that McNamara and Taylor would have produced an even stronger case for withdrawal? You say (p. 4) that the internal record does not show that JFK was "more reluctant than his advisers to move towards withdrawal," implying that everybody but Kennedy was anxious to withdraw. This is precisely opposite to all the accounts I have read, which indicate that almost all of his advisers were urging him to escalate and against withdrawal. Taylor said Kennedy was the only man reluctant to send in ground forces. The initiative for withdrawal (based on success) came from JFK, not McNamara or Taylor. I think we saw exactly what McNamara and Taylor wanted after the assassination. The only puzzling thing might be that McNamara and Taylor recommended withdrawal at all, but it is not puzzling if we consider that on Oct. 2, 1963, they were still working for Kennedy.

You say (p. 3) that NSAM 273 differs slightly from the McNamara-Taylor recommendations because by then there were different factual assumptions. These assumptions, however, and the changes in them, are not evident in the document. What is evident, and explicit, is that the withdrawal policy should continue. Whether there was a change in factual assumptions or not, there was no change in policy.

The Bundy draft complicates matters, for the very reasons you mention. The appearance of this document now is very convenient, much too convenient. After all, the CIA has known about the Scott thesis for twenty years. Now Schlesinger pops up, saying just what Scott said, that 273 constitutes a reversal of JFK's withdrawal policy. Together with the argument that Bundy wrote the draft on Nov. 21 "for Kennedy," the conclusion is that JFK reversed his own withdrawal policy the day before the assassination! Of course, this makes a fool (and/or a tool) of Schlesinger, but I doubt that he cares.

In my opinion, the Bundy draft is either a plant (inauthentic), or, if he did actually write it on Nov. 21, he wrote it for Johnson. If it was a coup, Bundy was in on it for sure.

By the way, you know who called off the air strikes at the Bay of Pigs, don't you — nine hours after Kennedy had given his official approval? Why did Bundy refer Cabell and Bissell to Rusk, who was completely outside the chain of command in this operation? Why did Cabell and Bissell then refuse to talk directly with JFK about what they knew perfectly well — as did Bundy — would ensure the failure of the invasion? They did not hesitate to talk directly with him at other points in the operation, when it was not crucial. Bundy is a very clever fellow, and the cleverest thing he did was not getting fired along with Dulles, Cabell and Bissell. The Dulles brothers, Cabell brothers (Earle was mayor of Dallas when JFK was shot, controlled the motorcade route, etc.), the Bundy brothers (McGeorge was Bissell's student at Yale) — all of them CIA all the way.

As far as I'm concerned, the Bundy draft is totally irrelevant to our discussion. Kennedy didn't see it and didn't approve it. You can take it as evidence that JFK did not change his mind about withdrawal (para. 2), that he did (para. 6), or that Johnson did, or did not. All the possibilities are open. This is how the CIA likes to have things. But I for one am not going to waste a second thinking about what Bundy might have been thinking when he supposedly wrote something that Kennedy never saw, and I certainly won't accept it as evidence for what Kennedy might have thought. This particular lying genocidal fascist scumbag is still alive, so if anybody is interested in his views they can ask him. I wouldn't bother.

As for establishing "the record," I have already conceded that 263 and 273 do not differ regarding the withdrawal policy, which you agree with. Where we disagree is, you say it never changed, or not until after Tet, and I agree with the PP that

Johnson changed it between Dec. 1963 and March 1964. (And it changed again after Tet, of course.)

There seems to be no reliable documentary record of the Honolulu meeting, and as far as I know there is no indication that Kennedy knew any more about what happened there than we do, and no evidence that he changed his mind about how the war was going, before or after Honolulu, or after Oct. 11, or after Nov. 1. More to the point, there is no evidence that he changed his policy.

You say it was assumed by NSAM 273 that the GVN was solidly behind the war after the Nov. 1 coup. Johnson, Rusk, McNamara et al. had been against the coup, however, because they saw no viable alternative to Diem. What made them change their minds?

What you see as the second assumption contradicts the first. If the GVN were now ready to fight, the military situation would have been more favorable, not less. In any case, I don't see either of these assumptions in NSAM 273.

I agree with you that some of Kennedy's public statements contradict his policy. That is quite normal. I also agree that a president who wanted to get out and didn't care about losing face or maintaining the support of his own administration, the military, the ruling elite, and the conservative elements in Congress and the population at large, would have acted differently. But as you say, JFK was a political animal. He could not ignore these things. His problem was to get out under the pretext of success, if not victory. That was still possible in 1963, when only about 50 Americans had died in Vietnam.

When I said that Stone deserves credit for informing people about the withdrawal plan, I meant the general public today. Despite the press reports at the time, and despite the PP (Gravel, but not NYT), the consensus of historians has been that JFK got us into Vietnam, and Johnson got us in deeper. I'm sure that if you had taken a survey of college students before the film came out, you would have found that almost all of them thought this, but almost none of them knew about JFK's withdrawal plan — unless they had read some of the assassination literature.

If you disagree with Newman's conclusion that the top brass were lying about the war, how do you explain his numerous examples of negative reports from the field that were deliberately suppressed? This deception need not have been as elaborate as you say, or elaborate at all. All you need are a few key people to keep the screws on, and I can't think of any organization where this should be easier than in the military or (especially) the CIA. If a lot of people were optimistic, it doesn't mean they all knew the truth, or were in a position to know the truth, or had any reason (or the guts) to doubt what their superiors and colleagues were saying. It's easy to spread lies from the top. Look at the Warren Commission. For every "authority" who lies, there can be thousands or millions who assume it is the gospel truth. This applies to Vietnam as well as to the assassination. The "huge edifice of deception," as you call it, does not mean everybody is lying, just that everybody is deceived. Even within the Warren Commission, most members may have been merely deceived, with just a few (Dulles, Ford, Warren) the deceivers. Accepting, believing and repeating lies doesn't make people liars.

My point about "stupidity" was not that this explains anything: just the contrary. This is what the public is often left with as an "explanation," though of course it is expressed differently. Glaspie was not "stupid," she made an "unfortunate mistake." Vietnam was an "unfortunate mistake." That, in plain language, means stupidity. I don't know what the Arab leaders knew about Saddam's plans, but with 200,000 Iraqi soldiers poised to invade Kuwait, for Glaspie to say the US doesn't care about Arab border disputes was stupid — assuming the US (and I'm sure Glaspie was saying exactly what Washington told her to say) did not want Saddam to invade. I believe Bush wanted exactly that. Saddam was sandbagged.

When I said I knew that Vietnam was a "mistake" in 1963-64, I meant I felt then the way most people do now. This is, again, what we are asked to believe: that bright guys like Bundy make mistakes. But as I said, what always bothered me was that I never believed I was smarter than somebody like Bundy. The result was extended puzzlement.

I don't feel that way now. Of course Vietnam was not a mistake. Of course Bundy wasn't stupid. They accomplished exactly what you say — and don't forget the $570 billion for the warmongers, the domestic economic stimulus, the war as a distraction from the civil rights movement, and (to get real nasty) the reduction of the Third World population at home and in Southeast Asia.

No, planners are not stupid. What I meant was, the establishment's historical explanations, i.e. propaganda, lead us to that conclusion, if we are willing to call things by their right name. This is a dead end, a conundrum, unless we go one further step and realize that they are not only not stupid, they are not on our side. As long as we are prisoners of the propaganda that the government is on our side, i.e. "well-intentioned," we must accept that they do stupid things (if we do any thinking at all), though we know they are not stupid. Once disabused of this, what we have been forced to view as mistakes and stupidity, i.e. the established version of history, appears quite differently.

What I meant about the propaganda model was simply that it makes sense, and is a good theory, even though it can't be proved. I said that because you compared the Garrison/Stone theory to a theory that Hinkley shot Reagan because he thought Reagan was a closet Leninist. You said they could be said to be equally good theories because neither can be disproved. But a theory is not good because it cannot be disproved, e.g. the propaganda model/theory. Furthermore, if a good theory is one that provides the best explanation for the most facts (and lack of facts, including evidence withheld, destroyed and manipulated), then the coup theory of the assassination is a good one.

You say there isn't a shred of evidence for this theory, that it is remote from the factual record and would have required phenomenal discipline of thousands of people. I think just the opposite is true on all points. We needn't get into the morass of details on the assassination; there are plenty of books on that. But I see no place where it deviates from the "factual record," inasmuch as there is one, including the fact we are discussing here: that Johnson reversed the withdrawal policy. I don't think thousands of people were actively involved in the murder — maybe a couple of dozen. The propaganda model takes care of the rest. Take the people present at the autopsy, for example — although they have not all been identified. Nearly all of them, even Humes at one point — have described wounds quite different from those shown in the official photos and X-rays, at least the ones that have been published. This means the latter are fakes, as many of the medical personnel have unequivocally said. Who could have done that? Not most of the people present at the autopsy. And so it goes. It doesn't take many people to manipulate others, just the right ones. Fear, intimidation, propaganda, false sense of duty, ideological blindness, etc. do the rest. Everything you say about the propaganda model applies here. Nevertheless, over the years, people have come forward, and much evidence has come out.

Aren't you applying a much more restrictive standard for evidence in this case than in others? The Church committee turned up no evidence that the CIA had ever assassinated anyone or been involved in any assassination plots other than the one to kill Castro, but does this mean there was no evidence? Is there more evidence for US government involvement in the assassinations of Diem, Lumumba, Trujillo, Allende, etc. than in the case of Kennedy? On the larger scale, what evidence is there that US foreign policy is guided by economic and not humanitarian interests? What evidence is there that the US was not fighting for the freedom of the South Vietnamese, or the freedom of the Kuwaitis?

In all of these cases, arguments are based on "evidence," but what makes this evidence so much better than the evidence in the JFK assassination that theories in one case are considered tenable and in the other untenable? Suppose the National Academy of Sciences concluded that there is no evidence that the US is an imperialistic country or that Washington is the terrorist capital of the world, as you have written.[26] Would that settle the matter and relegate all such claims to the realm of pure speculation? You say in reference to the JFK/coup theory that "all counterevidence can be eliminated simply by appeal to the assumption" — I guess meaning the assumption that the theory is correct. Isn't this how all theories are investigated and tested? How do you investigate and test the theory (or assumption) that the Vietnam War was a war of aggression by the US against the South Vietnamese people for global strategic and economic reasons? Do you not eliminate the counterevidence by appeal to the assumption? Do you really think there is more evidence for this than for the theory that the assassination was a conspiracy, or for the coup theory?

Of course I would like to have what you've written on the withdrawal thesis, if you care to send it. In the end I guess we'll just have to agree to disagree. No harm done. I understand your position, but frankly I find it inconsistent with your thinking on other subjects. I can understand the need to excise the Camelot blubber and debunk the "JFK-as-dove" mythology, but the withdrawal plan doesn't make JFK a dove any more than Reagan's withdrawal from Lebanon makes Reagan a dove. One could argue that no president, by definition, as commander-in-chief of the armed forces, can be a dove. However, "the man who escalated international terrorism to outright aggression" (p. 1), i.e. counterinsurgency to war (commitment of US combat troops), in Vietnam was not Kennedy; it was Johnson.

I admit that my interest in the withdrawal policy reversal follows from my interest in the assassination. I don't care about Kennedy's historical image and have no illusions about the sublimity of leaders. But I did not mean to suggest that "assassination theorists should separate themselves from consideration of JFK's secret plans" (p. 9). Why should they? Assassination theorists need not be Camelot enthusiasts (though many are, regrettably), and they need not be concerned with secret plans, since the withdrawal plan was not secret.

Your position on the assassination(s) puzzles me. I agree that the assassinations of Hampton and King are politically significant, but why is that of King only "possibly so" and that of the Kennedys not at all? The two great popular movements of the sixties, civil rights and antiwar, were historically intertwined, and in terms of their political impact remained a combined threat to the establishment beyond their ideological split. The largest common denominator was the war. King was killed not long after he (finally) came out against it, RFK likewise. It's not difficult to imagine the enormity of the threat posed to the ruling elite by MLK, with blacks and the poor behind him, and RFK, with the white middle-class antiwar movement rallying behind him (after McCarthy chickened out), both at the height of their popularity in the summer of 68.

One may say that the "Wise Men" had already decided to start winding down the war by then, but it wasn't just the war that was at stake. I don't want to get into another discussion over whether RFK would have ended the war any quicker than Nixon did (!), but from my recollection of the temper of the times, and confirmed by everything I've read, if I had been one of the 1% running the country at that time I would have been scared to death. Scared that the war would end too soon and too abruptly, scared that the truth about it (that it never should have occurred) would come out too fast, scared that the truth about the JFK assassination would come out, scared that too many people might get the idea they really can change the government if they get together, scared that that pushy bleeding-heart knee-jerk liberal phony little Kennedy brother might give that Commie bimbo King the idea that niggers are people too, etc. — in short, that all hell would break loose. I know that the record shows that Johnson did much more for blacks than either Kennedy did, but that is not the way they were perceived. Nobody doubted that Johnson was a racist; there was some doubt (justified or not), even among many blacks, about the Kennedys. For keeping blacks in place, i.e. running in place behind the carrots that new legislation offered them, Johnson was a safer bet than the Kennedys, and I'm sure this was the consensus not only among Texas oilmen.

To demonstrate or even claim the political significance of <u>any</u> of the assassinations, one has to get into conspiracy theory. It has become clear to me that the left traditionally eschews conspiracy theories, and it is true that fascists have abused such theories in the past (and continue to do so). So what? I am not going to eschew Marxist arguments because Erich Honecker uses them (or used them). The claim that there is an ideological difference between "institutional" and "conspiracy" theories (re. Michael Albert's recent *Z* magazine article) is not only wrong, but counterproductive. They can and should be part of the same analysis.

On the question of "evidence," it should be obvious that if we are content to wait for the government to indict itself, and in the case of JFK to declare itself illegitimate, which is exactly what we expect if we depend on investigations like the Warren Commission and the House committee, we'll wait forever — just as long as we'll have to wait for some president to declare Washington the terrorist capital of the world. Nor can we wait for the truth to be revealed in a court of law (but see Mark Lane's *Plausible Denial*), by a congressional committee, or by the National Academy of Sciences. When the politics becomes important enough, there is no science, only scientists, no matter how respectable they may be. The Magic Bullet theory is proof enough of that.

This doesn't mean the "evidence doesn't mean a lot" (p. 9), or that it doesn't exist. It is massive.[27] I don't see how anyone can read much of the assassination literature and come to the conclusion that there is no evidence of conspiracy and no evidence of government complicity, which seems to be your position. Obviously, if you believe that, there is no reason to be interested in the question (p. 10) if the government is so corrupt (and the population, particularly the journalistic and academic elite, so propagandized) that it can murder the president (and Fred Hampton, MLK, RFK, etc.) and keep it secret for decades.

Note, however, that what the government and the mainstream media may keep as an official secret need not always be, and in this case is not, a secret to the majority of the population. Opinion polls have consistently shown that in contradistinction to the journalistic and academic elite, most Americans believe the JFK assassination (and probably the RFK and MLK assassinations, though I have seen any figures on these) was a conspiracy. According to a *Time*/CNN poll before the Stone film, half the population thinks the military or the CIA might have been involved. Compare this with the press coverage of the film. It is the best example I can cite of the gulf between common sense and manufactured elite consent — a point you have made on other issues many times.

By now I think it's clear that the Stone movie will have no lasting effect or political impact, whether one approves of it or not. I would like to see people on the streets demanding answers, but instead of that we see Ford and Nixon "demanding" the release of the classified files, which of course will reveal nothing except perhaps further disinformation to cloud the trail and keep the "buffs" busy. I suppose it will take a catastrophe at least equal to Vietnam to reach the critical mass of 1968 again, and our job is to prepare ourselves and others for that.

Not a very encouraging note to end on, but all I see is apathy, people waiting for the fire to reach their butts. I guess there's nothing new about that.

I'm glad my letters have been helpful to you. Yours have been a big help to me too, and I am very grateful and flattered that you have taken the time and effort to write them.

With best regards,
Michael

1992.09.08 TO PROUTY

8 Sept. 1992

Dear Fletch,

I was delighted to hear from you, as always. Let's see, where to start. That German publisher. I tried to call them, but there's no listing for Eastis Verlag, Rastatt. I talked to a woman at Agis Verlag in Baden Baden, which is nearby, and she looked it up in her catalogues and couldn't find anything. I wanted to offer my services if they need any help with the translation. I couldn't actually do it, but I might be able to help. I hope it's not a phony BND/CIA company that just bought the rights to keep the book off the shelves. I haven't forgotten what you told me about *The Secret Team*. Next time you talk to your American publisher, see if you can get their phone number or address.

Anyway, I hope you can write back and tell me the book has appeared in English, at least. I'm looking forward to reading it.

I'm sorry to hear about your health problems. I hope the prosthetic device works out. I wouldn't worry about the weight loss, though. It's probably the best thing you could do for your heart.

Thanks for the encouraging words. Next time I'm in the States I will call.

I won't go to the Dallas conference either. I agree with you. I know all about the Magic Bullet that I need to know. If I did go it would be just for companionship. Yes, let's get on with reality. Trouble is, I'm not sure what that is. Where do we go from here? That should be the question at these conferences. We know what happened. The question now is what to do about it. You know what that makes us? Revolutionaries. I guess we both became revolutionaries in middle age — you from 1963 (?), me from 1988. Kind of a strange feeling, to get older and older and more and more radical. I always thought it was supposed to go the other way.

Sure I'd like to see your stuff on MJ 12. Love to have that UFO tape too. If they have Magic Bullets, why not UFOs?

I'm working my way through *JFK: The Book of the Film* now. I'm very impressed. They did a great job with the research notes. I've never seen a movie so carefully documented. Yet this is the film the critics are calling "dancing with facts." It's crazy. But we're used to that.

I was considerably less impressed with Livingstone's *High Treason 2*. It's the most poorly written and disorganized book I've ever read. The critique of Stone is ludicrous — just sour grapes, I imagine. The adulation of Kennedy is disgusting. I suppose there's some useful testimony in there, if you can sort out the contradictions, but on the whole it's a mess. Too bad. Carroll and Graf should never have let it out the way it is. That's what editors are supposed to be good for.

Richard Crenshaw's little book (written with Gary Shaw) is good.

I've also been through Richard E. Sprague's *Taking of America 1-2-3*, which is very interesting. I didn't know there was so much photographic evidence, much of which he seems to have himself. I wonder what he's done with it? All that stuff that is in private hands should certainly be published.

I've gotten halfway through Peter Scott's *Dallas Conspiracy*. I wonder why that was never published.

Re the tramps, who have now supposedly been identified, does anybody really believe that? Too bad you can't get that friend of yours who also identified Lansdale to say so publicly. What about the policemen in the photos? They should have been identifiable. If they were federal agents, as Garrison says, that should have been demonstrable, one would think.

I got a letter a few weeks ago from a group of researchers in Texas who say they've proved that it would have been possible to escape through the sewer system after shooting through the drain opening on the street. That angle would explain the motion of Kennedy's head in the Zapruder film better than a shot from the grassy knoll.

The "association" with Liberty Lobby I was thinking of was their inclusion of you as a supporter of their PAC. That's the way it was presented anyway. If it's any consolation to you, I have seen no evidence whatsoever to support the name-calling.

You mention Cockburn, Newman, Wicker, Ford, Belin, and Lardner. Do you put them all in the same box? The last three, for my money, are CIA agents. I wouldn't be surprised if Wicker is on the payroll too. Newman's book is flawed as far as his basic theory is concerned — that JFK was pretending to believe Harkins et al. I see no support for that. Maybe I misread, but I thought he made a good case for Harkins and Taylor (and, less clearly, McNamara) lying. How else can you explain their deliberate suppression of the negative field reports, of which Newman gives many examples? What's your beef against him?

Cockburn is my special peeve. I know we shouldn't get personal, but what can you think of somebody who lived with Katherine Graham's daughter? I spent some time analyzing his critique of the Stone film, and I think he fights dirty, which makes me more suspicious. What bothers me is, apparently he relied for his research (and perhaps his conclusions) on Noam Chomsky. I've corresponded pretty intensively with Chomsky on this withdrawal plan thing, and his position on that, as well as on the assassination in general, continues to puzzle me, but I respect him a lot. To tell you the truth, this gets me in the gut. It's what I've been thinking about most lately.

What you say about Bundy's draft of 273 makes sense, and it's just what I suspected: either it's a plant (inauthentic), or he wrote it for LBJ. He wouldn't have drafted it without even discussing what went on in Honolulu with JFK first, and I know of no evidence that JFK knew any more about Honolulu than I do, which is virtually nothing. Newman and others who claim to have read the newly declassified materials say the news about the war was bad. Scott says the Accelerated Withdrawal Plan was confirmed. It could have gone either way: 1) the war was going well, so continue to withdraw; 2) the war was going badly, so continue to withdraw; or 3) the war was going badly, so escalate. Apparently there is still no reliable first-hand record of what went on at that conference, but as far as I know there is no evidence either that JFK changed his policy after Oct. 11. That's the crucial point, so what does it matter what happened in Honolulu?

Bundy's draft, appearing now, gives us a situation exactly as I imagine the CIA likes it: all possibilities open. Put 263, the draft of 273, and 273 together, and you have the following possibilities:

1. LBJ continued JFK's withdrawal policy (para. 2).

2. LBJ reversed JFK's withdrawal policy (para. 6-8); Schlesinger now agrees with Scott that this is the case.

3. JFK continued his own withdrawal policy (para. 2).

4. JFK reversed his own withdrawal policy (para. 6-8); I wonder what Schlesinger would say to this?

3 and 4 presume Bundy's draft reflects JFK's thoughts.

In other words, either JFK or LBJ did or did not reverse the withdrawal policy. Doesn't this sound like CIA garbage to you? It's the same thing they've tried to do with every piece of evidence in the assassination. (Livingstone's book being an exemplary contribution to the confusion.) A plethora of possibilities. The more the better.

All excellent points that you make, and I hope they're in your book. As far as I'm concerned, Bundy was in on it, from the Bay of Pigs on. Did you ever read that paper I sent you called "The Bay of Pigs Revisited"? I know you think differently about it, but I think I showed, just by a close reading of *Operation Zapata*, that the CIA (Bundy included) deliberately sabotaged it. The purpose would have been to put JFK April 1961 just where he was again in November 1963: give us war or face disaster. He chose disaster twice, and the second time it took him down too.

Bundy must have been the key operative throughout. I was right about him from the start. I hated him, for some reason, more than the others, from the beginning. It's all very simple, in retrospect. Anybody that smart who could say the national security of the US was at stake in South Vietnam had to be lying. It took me 25 years to realize it, though. That's enough.

I do not trust the LaRouche people. They call me here periodically, but they just want me to renew my subscription. I won't. I don't like personality cults. They do some good work, but I haven't seen anything by LaRouche (I admit I haven't read much) that strikes me as the work of a genius. He seems to be a political prisoner, but there are a lot of those.

I am more interested in Ramsey Clark. I guess I should try and contact him. Have you seen the volume he put together on Gulf War war crimes (*War Crimes*, Maisonneuve Press, 1992)? If the ex-Attorney General of the US says the US committed war crimes in Iraq, it means a lot. He has also been active in the LaRouche case. This is the kind of guy we should cultivate — dissenters from the establishment, people who've fallen (or jumped) out of the nest, so to speak. You are one. Gary Sick is another one, Barbara Honegger. There must be a lot of them, lesser lights perhaps, people who've never spoken out. Of course they are discredited as quickly and thoroughly as possible, but the pattern to this can be exposed. I think that should be our strategy, to nurture these disaffected "government servants" and encourage more.

Best wishes,
Michael

1992.12.24 TO Z MAGAZINE

[Z did not publish this, but I sent a copy to Chomsky in my letter of Dec. 25, 1992, and it appeared in slightly different form in *The Third Decade* ("Chomsky on JFK and Vietnam," 9.6:8-10, 1993). This was the article that caught Vince Salandria's attention and led to my joining his correspondence group.

Dec. 24, 1992

Dear Z,

Noam Chomsky's argument against what he calls the "withdrawal thesis" ("Vain Hopes, False Dreams," *Z*, Oct. 1992) contains a number of logical errors.

It may be true that some biographers and assassination researchers are JFK "hagiographers," but one need not deny that Kennedy was as ruthless a cold warrior as any other president to acknowledge that he had decided to withdraw from Vietnam.

Reagan's decision to withdraw from Lebanon doesn't make him a secret dove, either.

The withdrawal "thesis" is not a thesis but a fact, amply documented in the Gravel edition of the *Pentagon Papers* ("Phased Withdrawal of U.S. Forces, 1962-1964," Vol. 2, pp. 160- 200). Since Chomsky himself co-edited Vol. 5, I am surprised that he fails to mention that this PP account states clearly that "the policy of phase out and withdrawal and all the plans and programs oriented to it" ended "de jure" in March 1964 (p. 196). It is also clear from the PP that the change in the withdrawal policy occurred after the assassination:

> The only hint that something might be different from on-going plans came in a Secretary of Defense memo for the President three days prior to this NSC meeting [on Nov. 26]....In early December, the President [Johnson] began to have, if not second thoughts, at least a sense of uneasiness about Vietnam. In discussions with his advisors, he set in motion what he hoped would be a major policy review... (p. 196).

There can be no question, then, if we stick to the record, that Kennedy had decided and planned to pull out, had begun to implement those plans, and that Johnson subsequently reversed them.

The thesis which Chomsky is actually arguing against is his own formulation: "withdrawal without victory." It is true that the withdrawal plan was predicated on the assumption of military success, but the world's most famous linguist, should not have to be reminded that an assumption is not a condition. There is a difference between saying "The military campaign is progressing well, and we should be able to withdraw by the end of 1965," which is how I read the McNamara-Taylor report and Kennedy's confirmation of it in NSAM 263, and "If we win the war, we will withdraw," which is how Chomsky reads the same documents.

We do not know what Kennedy may have secretly wanted or what he would have done if he had lived. Whether he really believed the war was going well, as the record indicates, or privately knew it was not, as John Newman contends (in JFK and Vietnam, NY: Warner Books, 1992), is also unknowable. What we do know, from the record, Chomsky notwithstanding, is that Johnson reversed the withdrawal policy sometime between December 1963 and March 1964.

The point is crucial. If one manages to say, as Chomsky and others (Michael Albert, Alexander Cockburn in *The Nation*) do, that in truth there was no change in policy, that in truth there never was a withdrawal policy but only a withdrawal policy conditional on victory (until after Tet), and that therefore Johnson and Nixon simply continued what Kennedy started, then the question of the relation of the policy change (since there wasn't one) to the assassination does not arise.

If, however, one states the facts correctly, the question is unavoidable. Exactly when Johnson reversed the policy, and whether he did so because conditions changed, or because perceptions of conditions changed, or for whatever reason, is beside the point. Why do Chomsky et al. avoid the straightforward formulation which is nothing but a summary of the PP account: JFK thought we were winning, so he planned to withdraw; Johnson decided that we weren't, so he killed the plan. The reason is clear. Once you admit that there was a radical policy change in the months following the assassination, whether that change was a reaction to a (presumed) change in conditions or not, you must ask if the change was related to the assassination, unless you are a fool. Then, like it or not, you are into conspiracy theory.

Chomsky, uncharacteristically, is telling us the same thing the government, the mass media, and Establishment historians have been telling us for almost thirty years — that the assassination had no political significance. The withdrawal plan was never a secret, but the overwhelming majority of historians have simply ignored those forty pages in the Gravel PP (also carefully circumscribed in the *New York Times* edition of the PP), treating the Kennedy-Johnson Vietnam policy as a seamless continuum, exactly as Chomsky does.

Conspiracy does not explain this degree of unanimity of opinion in the face of facts clearly to the contrary, but Chomsky's own propaganda model does (see Chomsky and Edward S. Herman, *Manufacturing Consent*, NY: Pantheon, 1988). One variation of this model, as Michael Albert has made clear in this magazine, is that conspiracy theory is incompatible with "institutional" or "structural" theory. That the distinction is spurious, and counterproductive for progressive goals, becomes clear with one example. The CIA (Operations, at least) is by definition a conspiracy, and at the same time a structural part of the US government, i.e. an <u>institutionalized conspiracy</u>. When Garrison, Stone et al. say the President was removed by the military-industrial-intelligence complex because he was getting in the way of their war plans (or was perceived to be getting in the way), what could be more "structural"?

If the withdrawal policy reversal is now entering the realm of permissible knowledge (e.g. Schlesinger, Hilsman), some version of the propaganda model, which includes truths and half-truths as well as lies, will explain this too, just as it will explain why CIA (Colby) endorses a book by an Army intelligence officer (Newman) that apparently supports the coup d'état theory, and why a film such as JFK was produced by the world's biggest propaganda machine (Time Warner). As always, the realm of permissible knowledge is infused with smoke and mirrors.

Which brings me to the document Chomsky attaches so much importance to, the Bundy draft of NSAM 273, supposedly showing that Johnson's Vietnam policy was virtually identical to Kennedy's. Bundy, as National Security Adviser, was the highest common denominator in the intelligence community in the Kennedy- Johnson transition — above even CIA, and far above Johnson. Whatever the nation's darkest secrets were on November 22, 1963, it was Bundy who filled Johnson in on them, not vice versa. Now, after a quarter of a century, just as Garrison, Stone et al. are bringing the question of the relation between the assassination and Vietnam to a head, a Bundy document appears that ostensibly proves (for Chomsky) that there was no change in policy. How convenient.

But in fact the Bundy draft can be seen as supporting any one of several contradictory analyses, which I'm sure is exactly the way the smoke and mirrors artists at Langley like to have things. If you take NSAM 273 and the Bundy draft at face value, as Chomsky does, they prove there was no change in the withdrawal policy, as explicitly stated in paragraph 2. If you take that as a lie, and the other paragraphs (6-8) as an implicit reversal of the withdrawal policy, as Peter Scott and Arthur Schlesinger do, they prove that either Kennedy reversed his own policy, or Johnson reversed it, depending on whether you believe Bundy wrote the draft for Kennedy or for Johnson (meaning, in the latter case, that Bundy was part of the coup). To this must be added the question of the authenticity of the Bundy draft (worth asking, considering the circumstances), and the question (unanswerable) of whether Kennedy would have approved it, since he never saw it or discussed it with Bundy.

Here again, Chomsky is fighting a straw man. One need not prove that Johnson reversed the policy with NSAM 273 to prove that he reversed it. All we need for the latter is the PP and all the documents, including Bundy's draft, taken at face value, which prove that withdrawal was official U.S. policy in November 1963, and that Johnson began abandoning that policy the following month. Chomsky's Camelot debunking, on target as it may be in some respects, cannot obscure this fact, and should not distract us from the enormously important question that Garrison, Stone and many others are asking.

Sincerely,
Michael Morrissey

1992.12.25 TO CHOMSKY

25 Dec. 1992

Dear Noam,

This may seem a strange thing to be doing on Christmas day, but I sent the enclosed letter off to Z yesterday,[28] and we are driving to Prague tomorrow for a few days' change of scenery, so I figured I might as well get this off today.

I don't think they'll print the letter since it's a bit late — I didn't get the copy of your article until a few days ago, sent by a former student who subscribes to Z — and probably too long. Of course I had the manuscript copy you sent me, but I didn't know where it would appear.

On re-reading I see that I've made at least one mistake. You do of course mention the PP account, but not the parts I quote, which I think are the point. Otherwise, as far as I can tell, it's a fair reading of what you say and of the points I made back in August. I realize that it's strong, but I feel strongly about the issue. In my last letter I said we'd have to agree to disagree, but I am finding that difficult. If it were anybody else but you — and I mean anybody — it wouldn't bother me so much. As it is, I can't help feeling that one of us is very wrong on a crucial issue, and that does stick in the gut.

Sincerely,
Michael

1993.01.08 TO PROUTY

8 Jan. 1993

Dear Fletch,

Enclosed is a letter to *Z* magazine responding to Chomsky's article in same.[29] I'll send it if you like. He says more or less the same thing he has been saying to me privately. If anybody else had said it, it wouldn't bother me so much, but coming from him, it sticks in the gut. My letter is too long and probably too late to be printed, but I sent it to Chomsky too. I hope this doesn't mean the end of our correspondence, but I can't let the point rest. It's too important.

Any more on the German translation mix-up? I'm also anxious to hear what has resulted from the talk shows, book reviews (if any), etc.

Fascinating to read more of your biography. I'm not clear on the main point, though. You say you doubt if "such a thing had never crossed your mind before 1963." What exactly do you mean? That the assassination was a conspiracy? That it was an inside job? A coup? Related to Vietnam? Obviously, since you smelled something fishy when you saw that prefabricated news story on Oswald in New Zealand, you must have suspected something. What? Then you had virtually no thoughts at all about it until 1975, when the truth dawned upon you full-blown? That must have been quite a shock. What did Fensterwald say in his letter, or what was it about the prospect of writing in Gallery that caused such a radical insight?

Don't misunderstand me. I'm not doubting you. I'm trying to get at something which, as you say, may be impossible to reconstruct in hindsight, but I think it is worth trying. I find it hard to understand how you could have evolved from a military intelligence officer to the man you are today without at some point experiencing a real crisis. (I had a crisis and I had been pretty disaffected ever since they tried to kick my butt into the army.)

This is a real mystery to me, and I keep digging at it because I think it's important. Whatever it is that causes people's heads to turn around, it is not black and white, and it's not information alone, nor reason alone. You seem to be saying that this never happened to you. After New Zealand, whatever you thought then, you just put it out of your mind until 1975, when in the process of brainstorming about things to write for *Gallery*, it just occurred to you that the US government had been overthrown by a warmongering secret group of fascists, aided and abetted by people in the institutions you had been intimately associated with (military and CIA) for many years. Didn't it occur to you, at least at that point, to discuss your suspicions with your friends and former colleagues, who, after all, would have been much better positioned to have an inkling of what was really going on than most people?

There must have been a process of discovery, of change. Those are the times, I believe, when we grow, when we are really alive. The rest of the time we are just plodding down the same old ruts we stay in for years — decades, a lifetime. That's why I think it's important.

I think I've shot my little wad on JFK and Vietnam. Either Chomsky or I am very wrong. He is a mystery to me too, solely because of his position on this issue. Can you imagine what the situation would be if Chomsky et al. agreed with me and you and Garrison and Stone etc.? The fact is that much of what Chomsky writes is exactly in line with what *The Spotlight* writes, though he would be appalled to hear it, as I suppose *Spotlight* would be too. Some things just have to stay mysterious, I guess. You can see in the letter that I see no usefulness either in trying to sort out the contradictions re. Newman, Schlesinger, Colby, etc.

But I am curious about your remark that Newman/NSA are spreading disinformation. Just what is this disinformation, as you see it, and cui bono?

I'm going to end this here, because if I put off getting it in the mail to you any longer it may be another two months. The delay is not lack of interest, I assure you, but time necessary to get things straight enough in my mind to write. Your letters are very important to me.

Do try to get hold of the October *Z* and read some Chomsky in other issues (he writes for them pretty regularly). His style is turgid and difficult, but I would be very interested to know what you think. (He does not think much of you, but that's neither here nor there. He may not think much of me anymore, either.)

In the meantime I will continue reading your book. I'm taking my time, letting it rock around in my brain. I know most of the content anyway. I'll get back to you on it. It's a book that should be discussed forever, or thrown away. I am not throwing it away.

I've also whipped through Norman Mailer's monstrous *Harlot's Ghost*, turning the pages faster and faster until I finally reached the end, where he seems to be implying that Harlot (who seems patterned after Angleton) masterminded the assassination, perhaps for the Russians. What a bunch of crap. Did he add the Russian gambit just to get it through the publishers, I wonder, or is he really that stupid? How can anyone write so much much much about so little little little.

Also have the *JFK Assassination: The Garrison Tapes* video through Liberty Library, where you appear. Good flick.

Well, I said I'd get this in the mail and I will. Take care.

Michael

1993.01.18 TO PROUTY

18 Jan. 1993

Dear Fletch,

Enclosed is a copy of Chomsky's reply to my letter to *Z*, which as I told you I also sent to him. He's a pretty hard nut to crack. I'd be interested in your opinion of our exchange. I also include his *Z* article, in case you haven't been able to get hold of it, and the first page of another article, which could have come straight from *The Spotlight*, to illustrate my point that the so-called "extreme" left and right have much more in common than they have differences.

Please keep C's letter to yourself. I have become super-sensitive on this point since that unpleasant experience with Livingstone. (He showed Weisburg one of my letters in which I quote Weisburg's nasty remarks about Marrs, Garrison et al., whereupon Weisburg blew his stack.)

I guess I've shot my wad on this. There are a lot of things I could respond to, but this is not our first exchange and I don't think I can make the general point any clearer. I still think I'm right, but C's insistence depresses me, partly because he thinks I'm full of crap, but even more because I think he is.

Best,
Michael

1993.01.23 TO CHOMSKY

[Chomsky responded (Jan. 7, 1993) that my letter to Z made it "even clearer that we've left the bounds of rational discussion." My "effort to distinguish 'assumption of military success' from 'condition for withdrawal," he said, was "entirely without merit. If plans are made on the assumption of success, and the assumption proves wrong, it is logical to expect the plans to change." The argument that the withdrawal plan would have been carried out anyway, "even with the explicit assumption on which they were based withdrawn, is too outlandish to merit consideration." I was "now really grasping at straws," which was not surprising, he said, given the "overwhelming evidence" against my position. "NSAM 263, like the rest of the documentary record, is explicit about the condition of victory."

The "M-thesis" (mine) – that the withdrawal plan was based on the assumption of military success – is "uncontroversially true, and completely – totally – without interest." The "C-thesis" – that JFK planned to withdraw without victory – has been "refuted across the board and without exception." Kennedy was committed to "victory" in Vietnam, went along with the withdrawal plan only "reluctantly" and "on the explicit presumption of victory."

What Chomsky was calling the "C-thesis" he should have called the "N-thesis," since he meant Newman's thesis, but the confusion is understandable considering that it is really Chomsky's thesis, too, in the sense that this is the one he is determined to refute.

"On this," Chomsky said, "we seem to agree, except that (for reasons that are unclear) you think the M-thesis is important. It is not." Everyone, including the hawks, was "looking forward to withdrawal by the end of '65 on the presumption of victory." JFK too, he said. I had failed to make clear why these "uncontroversial matters" were of any interest at all.]

23 Jan. 1993

Dear Noam,

Thanks for giving it one more try. I'll make this as short as possible, since I guess we're both tired of it.

As for the rhetoric, I'm sorry if I overdid it. I didn't mean to sneer.

I think we can simplify, and agree, finally, on the facts, although you find them uninteresting.

As for the "C-thesis" — that JFK planned to withdraw without victory — the one you wish to refute, we can drop it. I am not defending it.

The "M-thesis" — that JFK planned to withdraw on the assumption of military success — is a fact, as you say (not a "thesis"):

> It is surely true, and uncontroversial, that when McNamara, Bundy, and the other planners realized that their assumptions were false, they withdrew the plans [for withdrawal] based on those assumptions, and that LBJ followed their advice (dragging his feet all the way.

We should also be able to agree that it is equally true and uncontroversial that this change in plans — and of the assumptions — took place after the assassination. As far as I know, NSAM 263 is the last document that directly attests to JFK's plans — and assumptions — regarding the war, and there is no evidence that his plans or assumptions changed after that.

We thus have:

> 1. a president (JFK) who thought he was winning a war (with a total of 50 or so casualties) and could therefore end it
>
> 2. his murder
>
> 3. a new president (LBJ) who began to doubt the success of the war within days of the murder of his predecessor and reversed the withdrawal policy within days, weeks, or months (take your pick).

You take these facts, if I understand you now, as uncontroversially true, uninteresting, and — though you did not use the word — coincidental, at least until proven otherwise. Here we disagree. I am content to leave it at that.

We can also agree that the policy reversal has been treated as unimportant in Establishment propaganda (with, as you say, some exceptions) and by "historians of the war, independent of their political persuasion." You say they are right, that "they treat the withdrawal plans as without much importance, for a simple reason: they were without much importance." Here too we disagree.

I say they are behaving in full accordance with the (dominant, but not the only) propaganda model (PM 1) that dictates: "No Vietnam policy change between JFK and LBJ." As for the apparent exceptions, Hilsman and Schlesinger, I have no quarrel with your pre- and post-Tet analysis. Post-Tet, in order to accommodate the Schlesingers and Hilsmans who wish to dissociate themselves with the US defeat, PM 1 can be modified to PM 2 (though PM 1 remains dominant): "LBJ reversed JFK's policy, and JFK might have acted differently" — but God forbid that this should imply any connection with the assassination (note Schlesinger's hysterical insistence on this point).[30]

PM 2 will be extended in due time to PM 3 — that powerful, but "renegade," elements in the CIA and elsewhere were behind the assassination. Eventually, the passage of time will allow the arrival of PM 4, which will be a version of the coup d'état theory (which now has the status of a paranoid pipe dream), with the difference that by then the world will be assumed to be (and may be) a completely different (i.e., reformed) place, and nobody will give a damn about Vietnam. Do you notice anyone getting upset now at the suggestions (treated seriously even by *Newsweek*) that Churchill and Roosevelt had prior knowledge of the attack on Pearl Harbor and chose to let it happen for strategic reasons?[31]

Of course I am talking here about the dominant PMs shared by the elite, not necessarily by the general population, among whom PM 4 is already well established. This is a striking demonstration of the degree of control exercised by the ruling class, regardless of which PM you consider closer to the truth. Half the population thinks the assassination may have been a coup d'état (PM 4), with Vietnam as a direct consequence, the message is flashed across the silver screen to millions — and nothing happens. The lesson is clear: they have us by the balls. Result: further resignation. The Stone film may have been a bit of a gamble by Time Warner, the biggest propaganda machine in history, but it was well calculated, and it worked. The coup theory has been effectively laid to rest, at least for the time being, and the more general point has been made again, with emphasis: it doesn't matter at all what "the people" think. This particular PM, that we are powerless, is of course a total lie, but it is firmly entrenched, and the end effect of the Stone film, unfortunately, is to entrench it further.

You ask how I would answer your questions about Schlesinger. To the extent that it is worthwhile trying to dig into people's individual psyches, we do not have to assume that he was either lying or ignorant, pre- or post-Tet. He believed what he was supposed to believe, according to PM 1 or PM 2, as one evolved into the other. The third alternative — that there was no withdrawal plan, even one based on the assumption of military success ("victory" if you like) — can be eliminated, as I hope we can finally agree.

Schlesinger's behavior is a fine example of the propaganda model at work, applying more readily to academic elites than to the less "educated" population, who are much slower to conform.

I wrote to Schlesinger recently, by the way, to ask him about the phone call Rusk supposedly made to Kennedy the night before the Bay of Pigs invasion, since the account in *A Thousand Days* implies that he was there (at Glen Ora) when the call came. His reply was that he did not have the time to refresh his memory of those events. These are the words of a man whose memory of critical events he (may have) personally witnessed is not directly accessible, even to himself. He must "refresh" them. How would he go about this, even if he wished to? This is a man, neither a liar nor an ignoramus, who has consistently done what has been expected of him, and what he expects of himself, according to the evolving models of permissible thought which he submits to. I don't think I need to explain further. You wrote the book.

One more time on the Bundy draft business: 1) Stone started working on <u>JFK</u> long before the declassification (at least summer 1989); 2) that particular aspect/version of the coup theory (that 273 reversed 263) has been around since 1972 (Scott); 3) it doesn't matter anyway (my point).

Finally, I agree that it is difficult to conceive of a coup being carried out under the noses of so many people (about 220 million). But it would not have required nearly as many conspirators as you imagine. Just look at Schlesinger. He was close to the action, and I don't think he was a conspirator, a liar, or a fool, either then, when he conformed to PM 1, or now, when he conforms to PM 2. Why should <u>anyone</u> have thought differently? That takes care of 99.9 % of everybody involved. As for the rest, the conspirators themselves (e.g., for my money, Bundy), surely you don't expect them to have left a paper trail, or to confess. A historical first? So what? So was the holocaust, the moon landing, the capitalization of the Soviet Union, etc. Who would have imagined...?

I'd better stop, before that adjective comes to your mind again, if it hasn't already.

Maybe a change of subject is in order. Have you done anything on Somalia and Bosnia? I think the goal (of Washington) is war, as usual, preferably with Germany and the other Europeans heavily involved. Good for the economies and UN (US) hegemony. Somalia was preparation (public relations) for the coming war in Yugoslavia, and more to come. Have you read a book called *Report from Iron Mountain*, by Leonard Lewin (Dial, 1967)? Makes it all depressingly clear.

Best regards,
Michael

1993.01.25 TO PROUTY

25 Jan. 1993

Dear Fletch,

Enclosed is a copy of my reply to N.C. There are a lot of things I could have attacked him on, but this is not our first exchange and I prefer to leave it at a point where we can at least agree on the "facts," however trivial they may seem to him. The bit on "propaganda models" refers to Chomsky and Edward Herman, *Manufacturing Consent,* Pantheon, 1988. Note that I mentioned Lewin. I won't dare mention you to him again, since I know what his reaction would be. I find this quite sad. I have the greatest respect and admiration for you both, yet you seem to be on opposite sides of some sort of fence. Strange. I think you are both right. Am I schizoid?

Best regards,
Michael

1993.04.05 TO CHOMSKY

[On the Bundy draft 273, Chomsky pointed out that it was declassified in January 1991, "before Stone's film, at a time when there was little interest in Garrison's version" of the assassination. In other words, it could not be a false document, as I had suggested, created to detract from the film's thesis, because it was declassified 11 months before the film was released.

It was clear to me, however, that government agencies would certainly have known about the film before January 1991. Furthermore, as I had said, the draft 273 doesn't matter, because it can be interpreted as significantly different from LBJ's 273 (Newman), or not significantly different (Chomsky), also argue about whether the draft 273, written one day before the assassination and not signed (or, presumably, read) by JFK, was really by Bundy for LBJ, which would mean that Bundy knew that JFK would be killed.

What I was trying (in vain) to get Chomsky to admit was both the draft and the final version of 273 explicitly (Paragraph 2) continued JFK's withdrawal policy as stated in 263. The official changes in policy, clearly reversing the withdrawal policy in favor of escalation, came in the first few months of LBJ's administration. And that is the entire point: the change came after the assassination. Whatever the differences between 263 and draft 273, or draft 273 and final 273, the withdrawal policy did not officially change according to those documents; it changed according to documents issued later. In other words, I was trying to say, the whole discussion about the differences between 263, the draft of 273, and the final 273 is.]

April 5, 1993

Dear Noam,

First I must try again to make clear to you that my motivation for persisting on this point has nothing to do with hero-worship, despite your comments about "millenarian movements," etc.[32] The coup theory, to which our discussion is directly connected, is in my opinion the most powerful intellectual force for potential revolutionary change that is likely to come along. Discussions of yet another example of despicable US policy, however often repeated and well footnoted, are nothing compared to this. If any idea can mobilize significant numbers of people and lead to radical change, this is the one. Otherwise we'll have to wait for the next big war, depression or other catastrophe. I don't think I am exaggerating. Suppose you, for example, agreed with me. Add the thousands (literally — no need for modesty) that would follow your lead to the millions — half the US population, according to the polls — who already think Garrison/Stone may be right, and what do you think would happen? If ever there was a chance for peaceful revolution, this is it, and I see the chance slipping by. The point is not to chase down individual culprits, as the anti-conspiracy theorists contend. The point is to use this most dramatic example to expose and destroy the <u>structure</u> of secret government and the inherent collusion of the national security state with the anti-democratic capitalist forces which combined to make the coup, the war, and the continuing coverup possible.

My motivation is therefore quite simply that if I can change your mind on this point, I feel I would be doing a service to what I presume is our mutual cause. JFK hagiography has absolutely nothing to do with it.

I suppose you think that besides having messianic illusions I have been overly influenced by Fletch Prouty, since I think I mentioned that I correspond with him (and met him a couple of years ago at his home). I'm not interested in defending him, but I honestly see nothing in his latest book or the previous one, or in his letters, that remotely justifies calling him a "raving fascist" or a "fraud." He is short on footnotes, yes, and his view of the world is depressing (if that's what you meant), but — appalled as you will be to hear it — not fundamentally different from yours (or mine), in my opinion. For example, you wrote in *Z* last July-August:

> Another objective [of "the corporate sector, its political agents, and ideological servants"] is to establish a de facto world government insulated from popular awareness or interference, devoted to the task of ensuring that the world's human and material resources are freely available to the Transnational Corporations and international banks that are to control the global system.

Prouty could have written that. You call it the "corporate sector"; he calls it the High Cabal. Others call it the "ruling class," the "power elite," the "military-industrial-intelligence complex," etc. What's the difference?

You think Prouty is a raving fascist fraud, he thinks you're "on the payroll" (CIA), and I think you're both wrong — about each other — and both right about a lot else. Which leaves me in the middle of nowhere, I guess, but that's my problem.

Re. your "facts":

1. What you call "Thesis I" and "IA" do not exist. They are <u>facts</u> — namely, NSAM 263 and the three McNamara-Taylor recommendations it approves. These recommendations were not "basic policy" but Kennedy's <u>last</u> specific policy directive regarding Vietnam.[33]

2. There is no indication in NSAM 263 that Kennedy was "hesitant" or had "reservations" about the recommendations

he implemented. Your speculation as to Kennedy's reason for not formally announcing the 1000-man withdrawal does not amount to a "reservation," even if it is correct.[34]

3. I cannot believe you fail to see a significant difference between:

> a) Mary is doing well in school. She should graduate on schedule.

> b) If Mary continues to do well in school, she will graduate on schedule.[35]

a) is analogous with McNamara-Taylor, containing a prediction and an assumption, or, if you like, an implicit condition. In a), graduation is assumed to be probable. In b), which contains an explicit condition, graduation is neither probable nor improbable. You refer to McNamara-Taylor as if it were analogous to b), implying that withdrawal was assumed to be neither probable nor improbable. This is simply not true, and misleading. The implication of NSAM 263 and the McNamara-Taylor recommendations was that withdrawal by the end of 1965 was probable.

The phrase "without impairment of the war effort," which you attach great significance to, means, from the point of view of the people who made the statement (McNamara, Taylor, and JFK, confirming them), "without impairment of the effort by the South Vietnamese government, with US assistance, to suppress the Viet Cong insurgency." This was the official definition of "victory."[36] When Kennedy issued NSAM 263, no such impairment was foreseen, and "victory" was in sight — probable — by the end of 1965.

All speculation as to how Kennedy may have really seen the situation is irrelevant to establishing the facts. My opinion is that he must have seen the writing on the wall, and was creating a context for withdrawal that would allow a "victory" of sorts regardless of the true military situation. You will disagree, but again I remind you that Bush withdrew from the Gulf after declaring a "victory" that was unconvincing to many, and Reagan withdrew from Lebanon without declaring anything at all. You insist that Kennedy would not have accepted any "victory" short of what Johnson and Nixon vainly pursued, but this is just as speculative as my opinion (and that of O'Donnell, Powers, Mansfield, etc.) that he would have.

4. The facts of the withdrawal plan are of marginal interest to you because you misstate them, in my opinion.[37] The point is not that JFK would withdraw if victory was assured. The point is that he was withdrawing because victory was, if not assured, probable. This is the fact which has been ignored or misrepresented by most "serious historians," including the New York Times edition of the Pentagon Papers. The Gravel edition makes it clear, but it is incompatible with most secondary accounts, including yours.

5. The entire Oct. 2 White House statement was attributed to McNamara and Taylor, not just the 1000-man withdrawal.[38] Again, you can speculate as to Kennedy's reasons for putting it this way, but it does not mean he "dragged his feet" or was "hesitant" or "not entirely convinced" of their recommendations, which he approved three days later and officially implemented, secretly, by NSAM 263 on Oct. 11. This is your interpretation. My interpretation is that Kennedy wanted the withdrawal to look as much like a sound military strategy as possible so as to contain the backlash of the hawks in his own administration, in congress, and in the public at large. He failed, as the events of November 22 showed.

I would be interested to see your documentation of JFK's "distancing himself from the withdrawal plans publicly announced by the military, and refusing to commit himself to them" after Oct. 11.[39] He certainly committed himself to them with NSAM 263, and as I've said, I know of no evidence whatsoever that Kennedy himself changed his assessment of the war, much less his withdrawal plans, after Oct. 11. If such evidence exists, I will reconsider my position, but it would have to be directly attributable to JFK, on a par NSAM 263.[40]

I see no reason to reject Thesis II — that JFK intended to withdraw short of "victory." This, unlike what you call Thesis I and IA, is indeed a thesis, but none of the "evidence" you have reviewed undermines it. There can be no evidence of JFK's secret intentions or of what he would have done. The closest we can come to "evidence" in this case is what O'Donnell et al. said Kennedy told them he would do, and it supports Thesis II.

You accuse me of continually switching from Thesis II to Thesis IA.[41] The truth is that you are continually switching from the plain facts, which you insist on calling a "thesis" and dismiss as "uninteresting," to Thesis II. Then you say, in effect, "Either you defend Thesis II, or our correspondence is a waste of time"! This is quite unfair. I believe Thesis II is correct, but I am trying to get to first base first, which is to get you to accept the facts as they are. You do not accept the facts as they are if you continue to insist that "there was no policy reversal." You can't have it both ways. You want to say: Of course the withdrawal policy was reversed, but this is totally uninteresting; the only thing that is interesting and important is that it wasn't really a policy reversal. It is you who are playing a word game. If not, you would be willing to state your position thus (as I have been urging you to do): LBJ did reverse JFK's withdrawal policy, but it was because conditions changed; their basic policy of victory remained the same. I suggest you ask yourself again why you find this formulation unacceptable.

6. Optimism may have declined after Diem's assassination on Nov. 1, but again, I know of no evidence that JFK changed his assessment of the war or his withdrawal policy after NSAM 263.[42] On the contrary, whatever one thinks of the Bundy draft and NSAM 273 itself, both confirm the policy announced on Oct. 2. I agree with Scott and (now) Schlesinger, who say

Paragraph 2 of NSAM 273 is a lie, and I think Bundy wrote the draft for Johnson, but I need not insist on either point for the purpose of our discussion.[43]

7. Agreed that it was clear from late December that the withdrawal plan was doomed.[44] Note too, however, that Johnson began to have "doubts" about it in early December (according to PP Gravel), that is, within days of the assassination. The fact that JFK's advisers sensed no departure from JFK's policy — assuming we can know what they "sensed" at the time — is of no significance. NSAM 273 <u>stated</u> that there was no departure. In order to "sense" a departure, in contradiction to stated policy, one would have to have been psychologically willing and able to deal with the implications: that the new president was a liar and that the murder of the old one may have been a coup. People have trouble enough dealing with those implications now. How many do you think could have managed it then? Remember too that we are talking about military and government careerists, who are not generally noteworthy for their independence of mind, and this "sense of departure," given the implications, would require them to be revolutionaries.

This is also the answer to your argument that no conspiracy of such grand proportions could have occurred.[45] How do you think the lie that US national security was at stake in Vietnam was propagated and maintained? That was not a deliberate lie, and thus not a conspiracy, for the great majority, even at the upper echelons. Lies work not because most people are liars but because most people believe them, if they support, rather than challenge, the general political mythology ("All Americans are on the same side," "American policy is always well-intentioned," "If there was a scandal the free press would expose it," "A coup d'état is impossible in America," etc.). Conspiracies, which are conglomerations of lies, work for the same reason. The number of actual conspirators does not have to be — cannot be — large. What is necessary for a conspiracy to obtain grand proportions, while initiated and maintained at the center by a relatively small number of knowing participants (liars), is that the capacity of the human mind to shift "paradigms," as Thomas Kuhn calls them, or propaganda models, as you call them, be quite limited ("Orwell's problem").

Schlesinger is a case in point. I believe I answered your question, but to repeat, the answer is: None Of The Above. I don't believe Schlesinger contends there was a "secret plan" to end the war. He is merely admitting the truth that he failed to recognize in 1965 — that LBJ reversed the withdrawal policy. He knew there was a public plan to end American participation in the war, and a secret implementation of that plan (NSAM 263), but he failed to "sense" LBJ's reversal of the policy because it clashed with the imperative propaganda of the time, which was that there was "no change in policy." When the war had been clearly lost and it became permissible to blame Johnson and Nixon for it, and simultaneously exonerate JFK and, by implication, himself, his sense of reality changed accordingly. If he goes beyond that, now, and speculates as to what JFK would have done, that is also permissible now, but it remains speculation, just as your contention to the contrary is speculation. Schlesinger was not lying, in 1965 or now. He knew the "facts," then and now — just as I think you and I know them, despite our discussion. The only thing that has changed, in Schlesinger's case, is that he no longer feels compelled (unconsciously) to maintain the myth that there was no policy reversal. He now permits himself to recognize that there was a policy reversal, but at the same time he does not permit himself to recognize its possible connection with the assassination. Since the latter position is obviously naive, he must defend it with the kind of hysterical name-calling he resorts to in his review of the Stone film, without even attempting justification.

Schlesinger's current position, though naive, is more tenable than yours, in my opinion. If he is driven by JFK hagiography, perhaps you are driven by an exaggerated anti-hagiographical reaction to the Cameloters (and a particular antipathy towards JFK?), and a general aversion to conspiracy theories. You simply cannot change the fact that JFK's assessment of the war and consequent plan to withdraw remained in place and on the record as his policy until it was reversed by Johnson sometime between Nov. 22 and March 1964 (at the latest). You can call it "Thesis IA" and "uninteresting" — though admittedly true — on the one hand, then dispute it by insisting there was "no policy change," and then accuse me of being irrational, playing word games, evading the issue, "shifting theses," etc., but with all respect, aren't you putting the shoe on the wrong foot?

Sincerely,
Michael

1993.06.18 TO PROUTY

June 18, 1993

Dear Fletch,

Sorry for the long delay. Enclosed are corrections to the "book" I've self-published (mainly for students), which I sent off to you surface mail at the end of May, so you should be getting it about now.[46] Not very impressive, I know, but I had to get it out somehow. I'm still working on a novel format, which would probably be more publishable.

I've also sent a copy to Noam Chomsky (and a few other people). His position on the pullout business, as you know, has really bugged me, and I can't seem to get beyond it. That's another reason why I had to get it out. I've been putting some of it through the electronic nets and gotten some feedback, but not much.

Please do me a favor, if for no other reason, and read Chomsky's *Rethinking Camelot*, which just came out. I don't have it yet, but through the letters I've got a pretty good idea what's in it. Some passages about you, too, apparently. You mention Epstein, Berlet, etc. (haven't seen the Epstein *Atlantic* article), but they are lightweights. Chomsky is the one to take seriously. It would be well worth your time to counter his arguments in as much detail as possible. I've done my best (recounted in my book), but he's a damn hard nut to crack. I'm sure you could add some things.

I'll be honest: I've got myself between a rock and a hard place. The two people who have most influenced my thinking in the past few years are Fletch Prouty and Noam Chomsky, both of whom I respect and admire greatly. Trouble is, each thinks the other is a fraud. I think they're both wrong, about each other, and both right (and in fact in total agreement) about most other things. That puts me in a hell of a position, especially since all three of us are 180° from the mainstream. The geometry gets very confusing.

I think Chomsky is wrong on JFK and Vietnam, as I have been at pains to demonstrate to him. I think I won the argument, but obviously he doesn't agree. I can't believe he's "on the payroll," though I admit that if anyone else argued as badly as I think he is arguing on this point, I would be suspicious.

There is another explanation, which I have tried (without being too blunt about it) to make clear to him. One of his best contributions (e.g., *Manufacturing Consent*) is the idea that academic and journalistic elites are generally more propagandized than less "educated" folk. What he fails to see is that this — his own theory — also applies to himself. He has his own "propaganda model," and it simply does not allow the notion of conspiracy to play a significant role. That is a traditional leftist stance, shared by people like Alexander Cockburn and the late I. F. Stone, but certainly not by everyone on the left (Michael Parenti, etc.).

It's hard for me to accept that Chomsky can be so doctrinaire, but as he would admit himself, intelligence and scholarly credentials are no antidote to propaganda, more likely the contrary. I have said the same thing about Arthur Schlesinger. In fact, I see them quite similarly on the withdrawal matter. Neither can allow the coup thesis to penetrate. Schlesinger allows the policy reversal to penetrate, but as a result must reject the coup thesis all the more irrationally and hysterically. Chomsky knows the policy reversal leads directly to the coup thesis, so he rejects the policy reversal — equally irrationally, in my opinion.

Chomsky wasn't very responsive to my prodding on the AIDS question, either. Like the coup thesis, it requires serious consideration of a conspiracy factor, which he won't allow. The question is, why won't he allow it? As I said, I can't believe this block in his thinking is deliberate. He has been far too critical, and sensibly critical, of the government and what he calls the "corporate sector" to be secretly on their side. I just can't imagine that. He must be sincere. Why else would he bother writing to somebody like me, for example, if he weren't?

No, I think it is the idea itself — the notion of the coup. It is just too powerful. It would require a total reorientation. In the end, I think he would end up in the same place, but there would be a journey in between, an emotional journey. You see, that's why I keep bugging you about your own bio. I was looking for the crucial moment, the thing, the time, whatever, when the ice broke. Apparently there was no single event in your case that you can point to and say, "That's when I changed my mind." Since there was such a single event (seeing the Turner film) in my own case, I guess I expect the same in others, though I suppose there's no reason why it should be that way.

However, since I did go through a quite dramatic (all in my head, of course) experience of change, I know that there is a "before" and "after," and I know that this specific idea — of the coup — can do it, because it did it to me. I don't want this to sound so egocentric, but really, if it weren't for that I could never understand what it means to change one's mind. And if I couldn't understand that, I couldn't understand what it means not to change. Nobody could have convinced me, before November 1988, that I was a thoroughly propagandized victim of mind control. Chomsky could not have convinced me. I don't know if you could have. All I know is, I saw a film on TV and it happened.

In other words, I guess it should not surprise me that I cannot convince Chomsky that he too is a victim of mind control, and that this — the coup — is the crucial point. As I keep saying, I don't think it is entirely a matter of reason — which of course makes it hard to discuss. Anyway, it does bother me, nevertheless, simply because I respect Chomsky so much. It's like somebody trying to be a good Catholic and at the same time explain to the Pope that though he's right about most things he's wrong about this one thing, which he considers trivial but you consider an essential point of faith. (Chomsky would wreak havoc with this analogy, since he thinks — wrongly — that my obsession with JFK has something to do with "messianic" illusions anyway.)

I'm not inclined to continue my correspondence with Chomsky on this point (the withdrawal policy reversal, which he says didn't happen), but I'm not giving up. It's too important. I'll get his book and see if there's anything new. I'd like to send my book to Peter Scott, Michael Parenti (do you happen to have their addresses?), and maybe a couple of other people like that, because I think the argument with Chomsky would interest them too. Maybe a bunch of us should get together and do a book of articles refuting him. You might say this would be paying him too much attention, but I think not. He is extremely influential.

I've renewed, with some hesitation, my *Spotlight* subscription. Some of their stuff is way off my line, and weird, but they've got guts and do treat things that others won't touch. I see the mainstream has picked up on the ADL "foreign agent" thing recently, one of *Spotlight's* recurrent themes. But to publish some guy's unjustified claim that the Trade Center bomb was a nuclear device is just plain stupid. Why didn't they go there with a Geiger counter and check it out? The way it's written, it might be good for ideas sometimes, but it's totally useless as a source. Chomsky learned that lesson early: the more "extreme" you are, left or right, the more careful you've got to be about documentation. Unless *Spotlight* is content with the label "neo-fascist," they should tighten up their act. "America First," the "holocaust lie," "gun-grabbers," "ministate Israel," and such phrases should not be thrown around either, if they want to be taken seriously. I remember reading, for example, an assertion that the figure of 6 million holocaust victims has been questioned even by "establishment" historians — but no names, no references. One guy says he can prove no gas chambers existed because there isn't enough physical residue of the chemicals on the walls. Again, just plain stupid, if they want anybody to listen who isn't already convinced (I certainly am not). Where is the argumentation, the dialogue, the debate? Reference to the book the guy wrote who made the claim, repeated in the newspaper, is hardly what I would call documentation. Ditto the business about the Bilderbergers, the CFR and the Trilateral Commission running the world (for the Rothschild and Rockefeller families). Interesting, the first time you read it, but it gets old very fast. They need a lot more depth.

I won't go into your fine letter of last January now. You'll have enough from me to read when you get my book (parts of which you've already seen). We agree, I think, virtually 100%. My problem and concern is convincing Chomsky et al., or, if that's impossible, at least shoring up the counter-case. What we need is a full-scale, nitty-gritty debate. I suppose you could be right that Chomsky et al. just write what they know will get published (a weaker version of the "on the payroll" theory), but I don't believe it, about him anyway.

Just one thing I have to mention, re-reading your letter, about Newman. You say "the 'cui bono' is the essential belief that the government must keep alive the idea that JFK never did intend to keep us out of the Vietnam War." Yes, I agree completely, but this doesn't jive with your suspicions about Newman. Newman, after all, is saying that JFK did want to withdraw. I am suspicious of Newman too, simply because William Colby praised the book, but I don't see your point about Newman working for NSA. You said in your letter you had not read his book, so maybe you meant simply that he could have been spying on Stone. But he did write a book, and the book says JFK wanted to pull out.

I would speculate somewhat differently. Suppose Newman was a patsy — ignorant of the material, as you say, and recruited to write the book (as well as spy on Stone) for Colby and his ilk. The cui bono may be in the disastrous reception the book encountered from people like Cockburn and Chomsky. Newman's more specific thesis is that JFK had a secret plan to withdraw — pretending to go along with the optimistic view of McNamara/Taylor, but secretly agreeing with the pessimistic views he was also apparently getting; so his real, secret plan, according to Newman, was to withdraw to prevent defeat under the guise of withdrawing after "mission accomplished," as per McNamara/Taylor. I tend to agree with Newman, because I don't think JFK was a bloody fool, but I can't prove it, nor do I think Newman proves it. But that may be just the point. Since he cannot prove it, it opens the door to Chomsky et al. to attack him and the "withdrawal thesis," as if Newman's version of it (a "secret plan") was the only one. This is exactly the quarrel I had with Chomsky, as you will see.

I just wonder if Colby & Co. didn't foresee this. In other words, they may have gotten Newman to write an unconvincing book they knew would be discredited, in order to discredit the whole idea of JFK wanting to withdraw — which, despite Chomsky, and as I told him over and over again (in vain), is not a "thesis" but a fact. So you have the film, containing a legitimate and credible thesis, a book (by somebody associated with the film) exaggerating the thesis to the point where it can be discredited and rejected by respected elements of the left, and the public caught somewhere in between. Result: limbo. This is where they want us, not knowing what to think or what the facts are.

Even Chomsky and I, who are presumably on the same side and both sincere, cannot agree on the simple and basic fact of the policy reversal. Newman's book may have been a planned ingredient in generating this destructive dispute (which involves many more people than just Chomsky and me).

Or do I give Colby and Co. too much credit? I don't think so. CIA may be just one claw of the beast, but they're not stupid. Guys like Colby and Bush and Bundy weren't recruited from Yale and Harvard for nothing. It doesn't really matter who makes the grand strategy, does it? We have to keep our eyes on what we can see, and when I see Colby lauding Newman, I know something must be wrong.

Of course, I'm wondering how your book has been doing in the meantime, if you heard any more about the German version, reviews, talk shows, or other feedback. Hope you're ok healthwise. We take off for the US via Bangkok, Hongkong, Singapore, and Sidney on July 27 — one of those "have to get it out of your system" trips. I've been there, actually, except for Sidney, but my wife hasn't and it will be nice to go back after — God, 18 years now!

With very best wishes,
Michael

1993.07.26 TO PROUTY

July 26, 1993

Dear Fletch,

We're leaving tomorrow on a longish trip (Far East, Australia, US), so I'll get this off today. Be back Sept. 2.

First, thanks for all the interesting and helpful material. Also for the encouraging words regarding my own little effort.

It is always fascinating to hear the anecdotes of your personal history. I still think you should do an autobiography, telling everything from the inside out. People like Chomsky, who are totally impersonal and rely on scholarship and footnotes, and who have ready access to research facilities (and grad students to help them!), will always have the edge on people like us, who are perhaps less well equipped and less willing to play that game.

I sent him a copy of my book, by the way, and he was "shocked" that I included one of his letters and passages from others. This shocked me, because I don't think I quoted him as saying anything he hasn't also said in print. So I'll have to leave that part out if I do another version.

I took out my replies to him, though, and put them in the form of an "Open Letter to Noam Chomsky," which I sent through the e-nets. The response has been disappointing so far, but I have heard from a couple of people, and I was glad to learn they are as puzzled by his position on these issues (assassination and withdrawal plan) as I am.

The trouble with the "information highway," as I saw the computer networks (Internet) referred to recently, is that it all comes and goes so fast.

I also put the chapter on the Bay of Pigs on the nets, and got zero response. I guess that's even more ancient history than Vietnam for most people. I haven't had anyone even try to refute my argument that the CIA (Dulles, Bissell and Cabell, at least, in cahoots with Mc Bundy) sabotaged it. The internal evidence (from the Taylor memos = *Operation Zapata*) seems quite clear to me. There is no other way to explain the systematically inconsistent behavior of Bissell and Cabell — refusing to talk to JFK directly at the crucial moments, and doing so when it was too late, for example. I can't go for your suggestion that JFK just let it happen to let the CIA dig their own grave. He would not have inflicted that public humiliation on himself purposely. My theory fits much better into the larger "make war" scenario (as you see it too), with the CIA trying to do in Cuba what they finally managed in Vietnam.

I've had better luck in the e-nets with the AIDS topic. I put that chapter out too a few weeks ago, and have gotten a good response from people (microbiologists) who, of course, disagree but seem to know what they're talking about. I'm answering them and forwarding their comments to Segal, who writes back to me in German, and I translate and send it through the nets. This is a fast, cheap and effective way to reach people, provided you hit the right nets and newsboards and catch some interest. I send the stuff from my end to several boards (where anybody can read it), as well as to the half-dozen or so individuals who have logged into the debate.

The interchange has become voluminous, but I'll send it to you later (it will peter out soon enough, no doubt) if you're interested. At the moment I'm in pursuit of one guy who has admitted that even according to the published literature, it was probably possible to make HIV in the lab in 1980! That's only 2 years off Segal's scenario (1978), and this guy (a grad student and very naive, I'm afraid), cannot believe the government could have been doing anything earlier, secretly. It's interesting to hear what these guys have to say, but I'm afraid that even if I manage to convince one of them that theories of artificial origin must be taken seriously, I won't hear from him again. He would be afraid to be on the record — even an electronic record — as giving credence to such wild, paranoid and (especially) un-American nonsense. He would fear for his career, and probably be right to do so. All I can hope for is to get the scientist in these guys to prevail long enough that maybe we can all learn something.

Segal is 82, and his health correspondingly fragile, so I can't expect too much from him (like running back and forth to the library to check references). He's still feisty, though, and holds his own — an amazing feat when you consider that virtually the entire "scientific community" is against him. I'm afraid that when he is no longer around there will be absolutely no one willing and able to challenge the so-called "science" of all this. I can't, unless I go back to school and become a microbiologist, which I don't plan to do. This is discouraging. Normally, all an "expert" has to do, if he is challenged at all, is cite a few references. Case closed. You're wrong, since you can't follow the technical literature.

On the other hand, my experience with Chomsky, though negative, has been enlightening and encouraging in some respects. It has taught me that no one, absolutely no one, is beyond propaganda and mind control. I still respect scholarship and science, but nothing that emerges from the mouth of a human being can be taken for granted. Everything deserves to be questioned, no matter who says it. There is only one brain you can rely on, and should rely on: your own. This sounds like some sort of Boy Scout homily, but the reality is that we spend most of our time thinking what other people want us to (they, in turn, thinking what others want them to think, etc.).

I guess I'm getting crotchety. The other day I went to a meeting of people at the university who were supposedly interested in "doing" something about the current situation in Germany (racism, constitutional changes, the army joining the World Police Force, etc.). I left early, because I couldn't listen to their monologues anymore, and you're not supposed to interrupt with questions like "But what IS 'structural violence' and 'the violence of scholarship'?"

Speaking of suggestions, I read the other day that some assassination researchers asked to autopsy Connally's body to extract the bullet fragments, which would prove the Magic Bullet story a lie (as if we needed more proof), but I haven't heard any more about it so I guess their request was denied. They could dig up JFK too and check out the back of the skull, but needless to say, that won't be done either.

I don't want to bore you with my introspections, but I may be reaching the point where I don't feel like "making the case" for anything anymore. That's also partly a product of my Chomsky experience — I'm sure you're getting tired of hearing that name. But I would not have expected anyone to be more reasonable than Chomsky, and yet, ironically, I credit him now with being the person who convinced me that reason and facts are not enough. If people have a wall inside their brain, facts and reason won't knock it down. Another elementary conclusion, I suppose, but they seem to be the ones that are hardest to come to.

I hope you're ok healthwise. Do you ever hear from Stone? I sort of hoped that at some point after the film, somebody would come forward, at least privately, to you or Stone and whisper in your ear that yes, you got it right (or almost right, or wrong), and say it in a way that would remove all doubt, so that you or he could pass it on by word of mouth at least to other people, like me. Has anything remotely like that happened? I guess this is almost like a childish fantasy on my part, since, when I really think about it, what good would it be? Suppose I by some fluke landed at a cocktail party with McGeorge Bundy or David Rockefeller, and he got plastered and actually said it — the names of the guys on the High Cabal, the name of the Martian who lives in the basement of the White House and runs everything... whatever. Would I really be any better off than I am now? Maybe it would be much worse, actually knowing the details and not being able to do anything about it. I don't know.

On the other hand, I can't get rid of this anger at being deprived of a knowledge of reality that I feel I and everyone else has a right to. Life has enough fundamental mysteries, for god's sake, without us being teased and tortured by the mysteries of human conspiracies on such a grand scale (another reason why people don't like to think about them). Medieval peasants didn't have such problems — though they had others and I admit I prefer mine to theirs. A little knowledge is a dangerous, and frustrating, thing — to come to another elementary conclusion. I'm afraid that if I had McGeorge Bundy to myself for a few hours I would shake his teeth out until he told me what he knows.

I finally got the address of Philip Agee, who lives in Hamburg. I knew he lived in Germany but didn't know just where. I've sent him the book and a letter asking if we could meet sometime. I said I wanted to see how his view of reality compared with mine (the current state of which is pretty much shown in the book). If I do see him, of course I'll ask him what he thinks of you, Chomsky, Segal, etc. I'll probably be disappointed, but again, I have this fantasy that somebody with his experience might be able to sharpen the outlines. Of course, the opposite could happen as well, but there just aren't a heck of a lot of people you can talk with about these things, and I'll take what I can get.

Enough for now. Have to get into a traveling mood. Again, thanks for your mailings. I'll be re-reading it all and will get back to you on it.

Best regards,
Michael

1993.09 CHOMSKY ON JFK AND VIETNAM

This was published in *The Third Decade* 1993, 9.6, 8-10.

Noam Chomsky has been described, justifiably, as the leading American (leftist) dissident, and his argument against what he calls the "withdrawal thesis" (see "Vain Hopes, False Dreams," Z, Oct. 1992) is a serious challenge to those who believe Kennedy was killed because he was planning to withdraw from Vietnam.

Although I have the greatest admiration for Chomsky and agree with him on most other issues, I think he is dead wrong here, and his argument is flawed. First of all, although it may be true that some biographers and assassination researchers are JFK "hagiographers," as Chomsky puts, one need not deny that Kennedy was as ruthless a cold warrior as any other president to acknowledge that he had decided to withdraw from Vietnam. Reagan's decision to withdraw from Lebanon doesn't make him a secret dove, either.

Secondly, the withdrawal "thesis" is not a thesis but a fact, amply documented in the Gravel edition of the *Pentagon Papers* ("Phased Withdrawal of U.S. Forces, 1962-1964," Vol. 2, pp. 160-200). Since Chomsky himself co-edited Vol. 5, I am surprised that avoids mentioning that this PP account states clearly that "the policy of phase out and withdrawal and all the plans and programs oriented to it" ended "de jure" in March 1964 (p. 198; my emphasis). It is also clear from the PP that the change in the withdrawal policy occurred after the assassination:

> The only hint that something might be different from on-going plans came in a Secretary of Defense memo for the President three days prior to this NSC meeting [on Nov. 26]....In early December, the President [Johnson] began to have, if not second thoughts, at least a sense of uneasiness about Vietnam. In discussions with his advisors, he set in motion what he hoped would be a major policy review... (p. 191).

There can be no question, then, if we stick to the record, as Chomsky rightly insists we do, that Kennedy had decided and planned to pull out, had begun to implement those plans, and that Johnson subsequently reversed them.

The thesis which Chomsky is actually arguing against is his own formulation: that JFK wanted "withdrawal without victory." This is wordplay, but important wordplay. It is true that the withdrawal plan was predicated on the assumption of military success, but Chomsky, who is also the world's most famous linguist, should not have to be reminded that an assumption is not a condition. There is a difference between saying "The military campaign is progressing well, and we should be able to withdraw by the end of 1965," which is how I read the McNamara-Taylor report and Kennedy's confirmation of it in NSAM 263, and "If we win the war, we will withdraw," which is how Chomsky reads the same documents.

We do not know what Kennedy may have secretly wanted or what he would have done if he had lived. Whether he really believed the war was going well, as the record indicates, or privately knew it was not, as John Newman contends (in *JFK and Vietnam*, NY: Warner Books, 1992), is also unknowable.

What we do know, from the record, Chomsky notwithstanding, is that Johnson reversed the withdrawal policy sometime between December 1963 and March 1964.

The point is crucial. If one manages to say, as Chomsky and others (Michael Albert in *Z*, Alexander Cockburn in *The Nation*) do, that in truth there was no change in policy, that in fact there never was a withdrawal policy but only a withdrawal policy conditional on victory (until after Tet), and that therefore Johnson and Nixon simply continued what Kennedy started, then the question of the relation of the policy change (since there wasn't one) to the assassination does not arise.

If, however, one states the facts correctly, the question is unavoidable. Exactly when Johnson reversed the policy, and whether he did so because conditions changed, or because perceptions of conditions changed, or for whatever reason, is beside the point. Why do Chomsky et al. avoid the straightforward formulation which is nothing but a summary of the PP account? PP: JFK thought we were winning, so he planned to withdraw; Johnson decided that we weren't, so he killed the plan.

The reason is clear. Once you admit that there was a radical policy change in the months following the assassination, whether that change was a reaction to a (presumed) change in conditions or not, you must ask if the change was related to the assassination, unless you are a fool. Then, like it or not, you are into conspiracy theory — which is anathema to the leftist intellectual tradition that Chomsky represents.

Thus Chomsky, uncharacteristically, is telling us the same thing the government, the mass media, and Establishment historians have been telling us for almost thirty years — that the assassination had no political significance. The withdrawal plan was never a secret, but the overwhelming majority of historians have simply ignored those forty pages in the Gravel PP (also carefully circumscribed in the New York Times edition of the PP), treating the Kennedy-Johnson Vietnam policy as a seamless continuum, exactly as Chomsky does.

Conspiracy does not explain this degree of unanimity of opinion in the face of facts clearly to the contrary, but Chomsky's own propaganda model does (see Chomsky and Edward S. Herman, *Manufacturing Consent*, Pantheon, 1988). One variation of this model, as Michael Albert has made clear in recent articles in this magazine, is that conspiracy theory is incompatible with "institutional" or "structural" theory. That this distinction is spurious, and counterproductive for progressive goals, becomes clear with one example. The CIA (Operations, at least) is by definition a conspiracy, and at the same time a structural part of the US government, i.e. an institutionalized conspiracy. When Garrison, Stone et al. say the President was removed by the military-industrial-intelligence complex because he was getting in the way of their war plans (or was perceived to be getting in the way), what could be more "structural"?

If the withdrawal policy reversal is now entering the realm of permissible knowledge (e.g. Arthur Schlesinger, Roger Hilsman), some version of the propaganda model, which includes truths and half-truths as well as lies, will explain this too, just as it will explain why CIA (Colby) endorses a book by an Army intelligence officer (Newman) that apparently supports the coup d'état theory, and why a film such as JFK was produced by the world's biggest propaganda machine (Time Warner). As always, the realm of permissible knowledge is infused with smoke and mirrors.

Which brings me to the document Chomsky attaches so much importance to, the Bundy draft of NSAM 273, supposedly showing that Johnson's Vietnam policy was virtually identical to Kennedy's. Bundy, as National Security Adviser, was the highest common denominator in the intelligence community in the Kennedy-Johnson transition — above even CIA, and far above Johnson. Whatever the nation's darkest secrets were on November 22, 1963, it was Bundy who filled Johnson in on them, not vice versa. Now, after a quarter of a century, just as Garrison, Stone et al. are bringing the question of the relation between the assassination and Vietnam to a head, a Bundy document appears that ostensibly proves (for Chomsky) that there was no change in policy. How convenient.

In fact the Bundy draft can be seen as supporting any one of several contradictory analyses, which I'm sure is exactly the way the smoke and mirrors artists at Langley like to have things. If you take NSAM 273 and the Bundy draft at face value, as Chomsky does, they prove there was no change in the withdrawal policy, as explicitly stated in paragraph 2. If you take that as a lie, and the other paragraphs (6-8) as an implicit reversal of the withdrawal policy, as Peter Scott and Arthur Schlesinger do, they prove that either Kennedy reversed his own policy, or Johnson reversed it, depending on whether you believe Bundy wrote the draft for Kennedy or for Johnson (meaning, in the latter case, that Bundy was part of the coup). To this must be added the question of the authenticity of the Bundy draft (worth asking, considering the circumstances), and the question (unanswerable) of whether Kennedy would have approved it, since he never saw it or discussed it with Bundy.

Here again, Chomsky is beating a straw man. One need not prove that Johnson reversed the policy with NSAM 273 to prove that he reversed it. All we need for the latter is the PP and all the documents, including Bundy's draft, taken at face value, which prove that withdrawal was official U.S. policy in November 1963, and that Johnson began abandoning that policy the following month. Chomsky's Camelot debunking, on target as it may be in some respects, cannot obscure this fact, and should not distract us from the enormously important question that Garrison, Stone and many others are asking.

1993.10.28 TO PROUTY

Oct. 28, 1993

Dear Fletch,

I've been slow in writing again, for which I apologize, but further procrastination is impossible! I think I've just this morning made a discovery, and after all the help and hints you've given me, I have to get this off to you today.

Going back to your July letter, you make an excellent point about the M-T report being JFK's opinion, certainly if Bundy's draft of 273 is to be considered his opinion. I think, though, that the 273 draft was LBJ's opinion, not JFK's, because Bundy was one of the primary coup plotters.

I fail to see the significance of the main point of your letter, though — that there was "no war and no military in Vietnam before 1965." Whether the "personnel" were under military or CIA command, they were under JFK's command in either case. Why is that "the underlying problem"?

You say that the CIA does not wage war, that it may get involved in covert activity, but not warfare. If by that you mean CIA officers do not necessarily take up rifles, ok, but neither do politicians, and certainly politicians wage war. Surely the CIA was waging war in Laos in the 60s and Angola in the 70s, as well as in Vietnam throughout the whole period.

If you mean that the CIA prefers to wage war covertly (through mercenaries and proxy armies), again ok. CIA starts the wars, fires them up, and when the fire is hot enough to keep itself going, the military kicks in, with all the economic consequences of that. The latter are of course the primary motivation for having the war in the first place, CIA being the agent of what you call the High Cabal, or Big Business.

If you are saying that NSAM 55-57 threatened to take away CIA's ability to perform this function for the High Cabal, that is, to start wars, that makes sense to me. But I'm not sure that's what you're saying.

I still cannot, for the life of me, see any sense in your theory that JFK let the Bay of Pigs fail in order to let the CIA destroy itself. First, that failure hurt JFK at least as much as it hurt CIA. Second, it did not destroy the CIA, or even come close to it. Nor did NSAM 55-57. The CIA was no weaker in 1963, as far as I know, than it was in 1961. It is inconceivable that JFK would have done himself that much damage on purpose, especially when it had no other visible effect.

Nor do I understand why you don't agree with me on the Bay of Pigs. I think my argument that the CIA sabotaged it is pretty solid, based as it is solely on the internal evidence contained in *Operation Zapata*. The behavior of Cabell and Bissell is systematically contradictory. It cannot be accidental. Over the course of those four days, the pattern is clear: when action is crucial to success, they do not contact JFK; when it is not, they do. The pattern is repeated twice. It fits the larger "CIA makes (initiates) wars" theory perfectly, and also the scenario that unfolded in the latter part of 1963. I've rewritten that chapter of the book to make it clearer and will send if you like.

I've started rewriting the book as a semi-autobiographical novel. Hard to imagine, I guess, but maybe I'll have a better chance of finding a publisher that way. I hate to say it, but I'm afraid footnotes, and even logic, don't help all that much when people's minds are made up in concrete. Something more subtle, more insidious (dare I say subversive?) is necessary.

Having thus expressed my own disillusionment with foot-notes, I hesitate to ask you this, but is there any way you can substantiate your account of the murder of Diem? You say on p. 273-4 of your book that Krulak knew about it. Did he tell you? Did he tell anyone else, or write about it? Who else knew? What were those "carefully worded phrases" in the cable traffic that you say gave Lodge his instructions for getting Diem out of Saigon?

By the way, I met Philip Agee and his wife in Hamburg a few weeks ago. He's in the US now on a speaking tour. He's had a rough time, and I don't doubt his sincerity. He's not as skep-tical of conspiracy theories as Chomsky, but still skeptical. He sees no "invisible hand." What can I say?

Best regards,
Michael

1994.01.29 TO PROUTY

Jan. 29, 1994

Dear Fletch,

It was great to hear from you again. I'm glad your health is good. Also glad your book finally came out in German. I haven't seen it yet but will look for it.

Your friend Peter MacKenzie did write to me and sent a copy of his article, which was very good. I hope we can continue to correspond. I suggested we establish email contact, and try to include you and some other people. Are you into that?

I enclose a copy of my Bay of Pigs article as it came out in the last issue of *The Fourth Decade*. I know you've seen it before, but I've rewritten it slightly and it may be clearer. You say you'd agree with me "if it could be shown that the CIA chose to work through Bundy." Well, Dulles admits that the D-2 air strikes (which he refers to as a "plot," interestingly) were partly CIA's plan and partly Bundy's.

It was interesting to see how the other journals rejected it. *CovertAction Quarterly* finally answered, with somebody named Phillip Smith saying:

> We regret that we are unable to use your manuscript. While your take on CIA motivations surrounding the Bay of Pigs is interesting, it is unsupported by any documents, interviews, etc. other than the one source

you cite. And the speculative leap between Bay of Pigs and the JFK assassination is indeed breathtaking. Furthermore, CAQ is, as a rule, less interested in historical articles than in contemporary features that rely on substantive investigative journalism.

Now, this is not sour grapes. I'm used to manuscript rejections. But the "one source" I cite happens to be the only official one. Did they want me to take the lies of Dulles, Bissel, etc. into account? True, I limited my sources to this one document, which is not kosher, normally, but 1) it is the only one I trust, and 2) it suffices to make my case. And no one, so far, has denied that I made the case! That should be all that counts. Strange, don't you think?

Here's what Erwin Marquit, editor of *Nature, Society, and Thought* (a new Marxist journal, recommended to me by Michael Parenti, who liked my article and thought CAQ should publish it) said:

> Despite the interesting material contained in it, we find that its subject matter is appropriate for a journal that is less theoretical than ours. We would expect a historical paper on a subject for which a body of scholarly literature already exists to reflect critically the existence of this literature in the development of its arguments....I should add that your introduction of the controversial question of CIA involvement in the Kennedy assassination would certainly raise objections from the referees. This is really a separate topic that is an inappropriate add-on to the discussion."

Again, not a word about whether I made the case or not. If I made the case on the basis of that one official source, the rest of the "body of scholarly literature" is irrelevant. But for Marquit, in any event, the connection with the assassination is too "controversial," and not "theoretical" enough.

Ecco Academia. It makes me want to puke.

Have you read Gaeton Fonzi's *The Last Investigation*? That should remove whatever doubt remains about the CIA being behind the assassination (at the operational level). A good book, a mine of information, and most importantly, totally credible. I was surprised, though, at Fonzi's negative comments about Gonzalez, because I had thought of Gonzalez as the only guy left in Congress with any guts or sense of justice (Bush impeachment initiative, BCCI investigation). His attack on Richard Sprague doesn't fit this image. Strange. I would also have liked more discussion of the acoustic evidence, especially of the so-called refutation of it after the report came out.

Here is what Chomsky said to me at one point:

> [Assassination theories] are in a realm where evidence doesn't mean a lot, because of the ground rules, which make them immune from refutation. Thus if we begin by assuming conspiracies and lying of cosmic proportions, all counterevidence can be eliminated simply by appeal to the assumption. Thus when the National Academy of Sciences refutes by careful experiment the one reason offered by the House Committee to question the Warren Report, we can simply conclude that the scientists are in on the conspiracy. Anyone who knows them personally knows that this is laughable, but the ground rules are constructed so that counterevidence is self-refuting.

Thus, for Chomsky, the Maverick Defier of Institutions and Established Thought, the HSCA and the National Academy of Sciences are the final word on the matter.

It is also interesting that the only assassination researcher Chomsky ever mentioned to me was Edward Epstein, whom many consider as transparent a CIA operative as George Lardner. Epstein, for Chomsky, is a "serious journalist." You, on the other hand, are "utterly untrustworthy" and even "a raving fascist." I tried a couple of times to get Chomsky to justify this name-calling, but he did not respond.

Nuff said, perhaps. But while I'm at it, we should bear in mind that Chomsky's early linguistic work was funded, at least in part, by the military. His mathematical, mechanical approach to language was (and perhaps still is) ideally suited to machine translation and whatever other military applications might be dreamed up. I'm sure that MIT is one of the most important, if not the most important, connecting points between academia and military intelligence and technology. It strains the imagination just a little to think that someone like Chomsky would have been tolerated on the faculty so long, if he were really what he purports to be — namely, the No. 1 radical dissident in the country, who calls Washington the "terrorist capital of the world." It doesn't fit.

I recently joined an email discussion list with a bunch of Vietnam veterans (about 300). The first thing I learned was that all discussion of the JFK assassination is forbidden by the list owner (manager). So a few weeks ago I sent the following out back channel (to individuals rather than to the list itself) to about twenty people on the list:

> The question I am pursuing is whether you think it is possible, from your experience with weapons, that a bullet fired from an elevated position (6th floor) a couple of hundred yards away to JFK's right rear could have caused the motion of JFK's head that is clearly visible in the Zapruder film, namely: violently and instantaneously backward, upward, and to his left. (Blood, brain matter, and a large skull fragment were also blown to the rear of the limousine.) The Warren Commission claimed that Oswald's bullet, striking the head at the cowlick at a downwards angle from the right rear and emerging from the right side of the head, caused the head to move violently upwards to the left rear.

One person answered the question as follows, and I would like to know what you think of his answer:

> Head jerks in the direction the round came from is normal. Action-reaction dictates it. Remember that the round goes all the way through. So not all the energy is dissipated in the target head. The energy that is dissipated therein, and the energy still left in the round as it exits is the action. The reaction goes in the other direction, of course. The entry wound, being much smaller, has a much smaller reaction, so the head (or most any small loose object proportionate to the size of the round) is jerked in the direction of the gunman. One of the most solid arguments against a second gunman actually hitting the Pres. If the other gunman missed, well, evidence is inconclusive in either direction. You can prove this to yourself with a 9mm and a watermelon. Works every time. I know it works on heads from personal experience.

I will try the watermelon experiment as soon as I have the opportunity, but I must say this goes against my common sense. The only shooting I've done is with a 9mm pistol at a firing range, and I don't remember the target moving forward at impact. Maybe the watermelon will behave differently. I will find out.

My second problem with this person's explanation is that I don't think I've heard it before. I believe the government ballistics experts explained the backwards motion of the head as a muscular reaction, which of course would not apply to watermelons.

I asked him if he could describe the personal experience he is recollecting. I wonder if even in Vietnam there were many opportunities to observe carefully exactly what happens when someone is shot in the head. Remember that I am talking about the moment of impact and immediately thereafter, not what happens to the body afterwards, when due to the inertia of the last position or motion it may fall in one direction or the other.

> I realize that this is a gruesome topic, and I would not ask about it if it were not so important. But I value your opinion at least as much as that of the Warren Commission's so-called "experts" (more, in fact). So if you do have an opinion based on experience, I'd be very grateful if you'd share it with me — or perhaps you can send this query on to others who might be able to respond.

I got no response whatever to this query. Zilch. I guess I really will have to try it out myself. (I think a cantaloupe would be better than a watermelon.)

Then a couple of days ago I posted what may be my last contribution to the list (it's called VWAR-L). It may be of interest to you:

> I've been following the posts on guilt and victimization and would like to add my two cents. I live in Germany. I know no German veterans of World War II who have "syndromes" from that war. Why? I think it is because hardly anyone here is still struggling with the illusion they may have had at the time, namely, that it was a good idea. Those who still have such illusions (and there are some, of course) probably keep quiet or join neo-Nazi groups. But the vast majority of veterans and civilians accepted their defeat and their victimization by the Nazis long ago. They had no choice.

> America also lost its war in Vietnam, but the difference is this: our government has not changed. It is still essentially the same as it was then. It has never accepted or admitted defeat, and has never allowed us — the veterans and the people in general — to "cleanse" ourselves of that war by denouncing and reforming the

enormously powerful political and economic forces that made it happen. That's why the Vietnam War, in a sense, is still going on, and why emotions on this list still run high. The Germans could put it behind them. We cannot.

Not long ago another non-vet on the list who is a psychiatrist and works with vets wrote:

> Loss of self-respect is damn near universal among survivors of severe, prolonged trauma under conditions from which there is no way to leave. Concentration camp survivors, incest survivors (remember, that's both men and women), battered women, survivors of political torture, of abusive cults, all experience this.

The incest analogy is interesting. Father rapes son and has son rape little brother. So son becomes both victim and perpetrator. But if son is to be healed, isn't the first thing he has to do is recognize himself as victim and perpetrator, and the second thing to recognize the father as the *primary* perpetrator and the only one truly to blame? What role does the son's subsequent relationship with his father play in the (possible) healing process? Should the son be enraged at his father, hate him, denounce him, indict him, see him punished, prevented from doing it again, and (possibly) rehabilitated? Or should the son just accept his victimization by his father as bad luck, and try to make the best of it?

In the case of the Vietnam War, father was Uncle Sam. Has he ever been called properly to task by the victims of his crimes, or by anyone else? Has he admitted his guilt? Has he been punished? Has he been rehabilitated? Quite obviously not. When Bush announced "our" triumph over the "Vietnam syndrome" at the end of the Gulf War, he did not mean that Uncle Sam had seen the error of his ways, but just the opposite. Nothing much has changed. I wonder if this is what lies at the heart of much of the psychological problems of Vietnam vets, as opposed to vets of other wars.

I would not be surprised if, say, VVAW (Vietnam Veterans Against the War) vets are more at ease with themselves, in general, than other Vietnam vets, because as political activists they have been able to use their sense of victimization to fight for others, and thus overcome it to some extent. Those who have not been able to identify the US government as the primary perpetrator and victimizer, and thus cannot express their rage in a meaningful way (through political opposition), are inclined to direct their rage towards themselves and others (e.g., "long-haired Commie protestors") who are equally blameless. Note the great interest on this list in "soldier morality" at My Lai, etc. The far more important question is why any US soldier was there or anywhere else in Vietnam in the first place. Not asking it, or not continuing to ask it, or pretending that it has been answered, is simply letting Uncle Sam off the hook (where he belongs) and continuing to blame the victims (ourselves).

The veterans of WWII (on both sides) were able to begin their post-war lives in a political culture they felt a part of. The Americans won the war, and did not feel they had been screwed by their own government, so they did not have that estrangement to deal with. The Germans lost WWII, as we lost in Vietnam, and had every reason to think they had been screwed by the Nazis, just as Vietnam vets have every reason to think they were screwed by their government. But when the Germans lost their war, they also got rid of the government that was responsible for their suffering and the suffering they had been forced to cause others. They had a chance to start again, and re-integrate themselves into a new and rehabilitated culture.

Nothing analogous to that has happened in the United States since Vietnam. What we got instead was a Watergate here, a few confessions ("limited hangouts") by the CIA there. We've never gotten the whole story, never even been able to bang on the table and shout our rage and denounce the bastards (except in private ways), much less reformed the government. Many of the individuals who can rightly be accused of genocide against both the Vietnamese and our own citizens are still around, and still in positions of power. More importantly, the structures of privilege and power and greed are the same now as they were then. If there had been a revolution in 1968, with veterans and other "victims" (having turned their victimization into activism and leadership) leading the way, I suspect there would be a lot less "stress syndromes" today. But the revolution was decapitated (RFK, MLK), the same way a recalcitrant Administration (JFK) was decapitated that had threatened to deprive the warmongers of their $570 billion war. How can any Vietnam vet "adjust" to such a situation without becoming an outraged political dissident?

My suggestion for thought, then, is that much of these presumably psychological problems are really political, and need to be dealt with politically. That is partly what I imagined I might be able to contribute to on VWAR-L. The psychiatrist also wrote:

> What about the rest of us, who are not combat vets? Do we have anything to give, or should we just unsub and get out of the way? I believe we *do* have something to offer. If we can be trustworthy listeners I think it matters a lot. But what does it mean to be trustworthy as a listener?

But my question here is, how can trust be built up just by listening and commiserating? How can someone trust me if he can't see me for what I am? (That's why I took a deep breath and plunged into the list as "Draft Dodger," etc.) And how can I trust him, if all I do is say "Uh huh" and "Amen" (however compassionately) to whatever he says? Maybe that's what shrinks are supposed to do, but I have my reservations, and in any case, I am not a shrink. It can also have negative consequences, which I've noticed occasionally on the list from some who seem to believe their "baptism of fire" gave them a halo.

Haven't gotten any reaction to this yet, either. I think they're ignoring me and hoping I will go away (which I probably will soon). I mention it not only because of the direct JFK-Vietnam connection, but also because I think it relates to the inability of people to connect with the larger truth about the assassination(s). The key may be in this notion of recognizing one's own victimization before one can recognize that of others. I know it was true in my case. It was the recognition that I had been a victim of mind control (and perhaps still am, in some way that I have not yet recognized) that changed me. That was the key.

Victimization requires a perpetrator, and failing to find one outside oneself, one tends to take on that role oneself. I suspect this is true of all of us, not only combat veterans. But if the true perpetrator can be identified, one can resist the debilitating feelings of helplessness and hopelessness by fighting back at the perpetrator. Thus recognition of the truth and politicization go hand in hand.

Sounds simple, but it obviously ain't. Where is the perpetrator (enemy), and how can we/should we fight him/them, especially when so many of our fellows deny that a crime has even been committed? But who said it should be easy?

By the way, at least one person on VWAR-L has read your books and is an admirer. His name is ***, a college student (non-vet) at Franklin Marshall in Pennsylvania, and very sharp. One of the things we have discussed (back channel) is finding out who could have been the person who ordered the army unit in Texas to stand down instead of coming to Dallas. These things must be traceable, within the chain of command. Who could have given that order? Same question with regard to the Cabinet's being sent to Hawaii and Japan. Why do these points remain mysteries? I suppose one could begin by telephoning the people involved, if they are still around, and there may be documents, but that sort of detective work is beyond me, given my situation.

History will look back on this whole period and see the most important question as this: How can so many people not have known? It's some consolation to know we tried, and that we are way ahead of Chomsky and his ilk, despite their arrogance and prestige.

Best wishes,
Michael

1994.05 RETHINKING CHOMSKY

[This review of Noam Chomsky, *Rethinking Camelot* (South End Press,1993) was published in *The Fourth Decade* May 1994, 1.4, 22-23.]

Rethinking Camelot is Noam Chomsky's worst book. I don't think it merits a detailed review, but we should be clear about the stand that "America's leading intellectual dissident," as he is often called, has taken on the assassination. It is not significantly different from that of the Warren Commission or the majority of Establishment journalists and government apologists, and diametrically opposed to the view "widely held in the grassroots movements and among left intellectuals" (p. 37) and in fact to the view of the majority of the population.

For Chomsky, the only theories of the assassination "of any general interest are those that assume a massive cover-up, and a high-level conspiracy that required that operation." These he rejects out of hand because "There is not a phrase in the voluminous internal record hinting at any thought of such a notion," and because the cover-up "would have to involve not only much of the government and the media, but a good part of the historical, scientific, and medical professions. An achievement so immense would be utterly without precedent or even remote analogue."

These arguments can be as glibly dismissed as Chomsky presents them. It is simply foolish to expect the conspirators to have left a paper trail, much less in the "internal record," or that part of it that has become public. It is equally foolish to confuse the notion of conspiracy and cover-up with the much more broadly applicable phenomenon of "manufacturing consent," to use Chomsky's own expression. You don't have to be a liar to believe or accept or perpetuate lies. This is exactly what Chomsky himself and Edward Herman say about the media, and it applies to the "historical, scientific, and medical professions" as well:

> Most biased choices in the media arise from the preselection of right-thinking people, internalized preconceptions, and the adaptation of personnel to the constraints of ownership, organization, market, and political power. Censorship is largely self-censorship, by reporters and commentators who adjust to the realities of source and media organizational requirements and by people at higher levels within media organizations who are chosen to implement, and have usually internalized, the constraints imposed by proprietary and other market and governmental centers of power (*Manufacturing Consent*, NY: Pantheon, 1988, p. xii).

Nevertheless, Chomsky admits that a "high-level conspiracy" theory makes sense if "coupled with the thesis that JFK was undertaking radical policy changes, or perceived to be by policy insiders." *Rethinking Camelot* is devoted to refuting this thesis.

I've addressed this subject before ("Chomsky on JFK and Vietnam," *The Third Decade*, Vol. 9, No. 6, pp. 8-10), so I won't repeat myself. But two things should be clear. First, Chomsky has loaded the deck. The theory that Kennedy was secretly planning to withdraw from Vietnam regardless of how the military situation developed is not the only one that supports a conspiracy view of the assassination. This is John Newman's highly speculative argument in *JFK and Vietnam* (Warner

Books, 1992), which is so easy to refute that one wonders if it was not created for this purpose. Why else would the CIA, in the form of ex-Director Colby, praise the work of Newman, an Army intelligence officer, as "brilliant" and "meticulously researched" (jacket blurb)? In any case, accepting the fact that we cannot know what JFK's secret intentions were or what he would have done, the fact that he was planning to withdraw by the end of 1965 is irrefutable.

Secondly, it should be clear that Chomsky's view of the relation, that is, non-relation, of the assassination to subsequent policy changes is essentially the same as Arthur Schlesinger's. They are both coincidence theorists. Schlesinger says Johnson reversed the withdrawal plan on Nov. 26 with NSAM 273, but the idea that this had anything to do with the assassination "is reckless, paranoid, really despicable fantasy, reminiscent of the wilder accusations of Joe McCarthy" (*Wall Street Journal*, Jan. 10, 1992). The assassination and the policy reversal, in other words, were coincidences.

I suspect Chomsky knows he would appear foolishly naive if he presented his position this way, so he has constructed a tortured and sophistic argument that "there was no policy reversal" in the first place, which, if true, would obviate the question of its relation to the assassination. A neat trick if you can pull it off, and Chomsky gives it a good try, but in the end he fails. In fact, he undermines his own position by making it even clearer than it has been that the reversal of the assessment of the military situation in Vietnam, which caused the reversal of the withdrawal policy, occurred very shortly after the assassination, and that the source of this new appraisal was the intelligence agencies:

> The first report prepared for LBJ (November 23) opened with this "Summary Assessment": "The outlook is hopeful. There is better assurance than under Diem that the war can be won. We are pulling out 1,000

American troops by the end of 1963." ... The next day, however, CIA director John McCone informed the President that the CIA now regarded the situation as "somewhat more serious" than had been thought, with "a continuing increase in Viet Cong activity since the first of November" (the coup). Subsequent reports only deepened the gloom (p. 91).

By late December, McNamara was reporting a "sharply changed assessment" to the President (p. 92).

The only difference between this and Schlesinger's view is that Chomsky says the assessment of the military situation changed first, and then the policy changed. So what? The point is that both things changed <u>after</u> the assassination. The President is murdered, and immediately afterward the military assessment changes radically and the withdrawal policy changes accordingly. It matters not a whit if the policy reversal occurred with NSAM 273, as Schlesinger says, or began in early December and ended <u>de jure</u> in March 1964, as the Gravel *Pentagon Papers* clearly say (Vol. 2, pp. 191, 196).

Nor does it matter what JFK's secret intentions may have been. It is more important to note that according to Chomsky's own account, whose accuracy I do not doubt, the source of the radically changed assessment that began two days after the assassination was the CIA and the other intelligence agencies. Furthermore, this change in assessment was <u>retrospective</u>, dating the deterioration of the military situation from Nov. 1 or earlier. Why did it take the intelligence agencies a month or more to suddenly realize, two days after the assassination, that they had been losing the war instead of winning it?

This question may be insignificant to coincidence theorists like Schlesinger and Chomsky, but not to me. *Rethinking Camelot* has shown me — sadly, because I have been an admirer — that Chomsky needs to do some serious rethinking of his position, and that I need to do some rethinking of Mr. Chomsky.

1994.09.17 TO PROUTY

Sept. 17, 1994

Dear Fletch,

We haven't exchanged letters for quite some time now, so I hope this finds you in good health and spirits. I am fine.

The main reason I'm writing now is I'm wondering if you're going to the Coalition on Political Assassinations conference in Washington Oct. 7-10 (Sheraton on Woodley Rd.). They asked me to give a talk on my Bay of Pigs article, so being a sucker for flattery, I couldn't refuse. It'll cost me a bundle but I haven't been to any of these conferences before, and it's a chance to meet people and who knows, maybe they'll stir something up. Anyway, if you're there I'll see you, I trust, and if not I'll give you a call.

My theory, as you know, is similar to what you imply in JFK, and I see on re-reading that you also use the word "sabotage," referring to Bundy's role. I concentrate more on Cabell and Bissell's specific actions, but I suspect strongly that Bundy was in on it too.

Have you read Harold Weisberg's book *Case Open*? Try to read, I should say, because it is absolutely unreadable. It is the worst book I have ever seen. What bothers me most is not that it makes Weisberg look like a petty, vindictive, functionally illiterate chicken farmer (which is an accurate enough impression), but that the editors at Carol and Graf actually published it this way. They didn't even bother to correct the punctuation, much less disentangle the syntax. I have never seen such a thing before. It looks like they didn't even read the thing, just keyboarded it in straight from the manuscript, no editing at all. I'm seriously asking myself if this was not on purpose, to make Posner look good and Weisberg, the so-called "dean of assassination researchers," and by virtue of association all other assassination researchers, look atrocious. That's the effect, anyway, and I can't believe that any publisher would allow that to happen unintentionally.

Not much has been happening on my end in the way of "assassination research." I'm not one, really. I've been participating in a round table correspondence with a group centered around (i.e., he distributes our letters) Vince Salandria. You've probably heard of him — one of the earliest debunkers of the Warren Report. One guy in the group, Chris Sharrett (whose name also crops up occasionally in the literature), does a slide/lecture presentation on the assassination, which I haven't seen but I may get into doing something similar myself. One gets tired of relying solely on the written word. I'll continue writing, of course, but doing an occasional "show" like this may prove recreational, and it's all for the cause.

See you — or talk to you — I hope in Washington soon.

With best wishes,
Michael Morrissey

1994.10.20 TO JOHN NEWMAN

[I sent this to a dozen COPA board members after the first meeting in Washington in October 1994., and also to Chomsky.]

An Open Letter to John Newman

Oct. 20, 1994

Dear John,

I sent a letter a couple of days ago to John Judge and Gary Aguilar (but intended for all members of the governing board) urging the creation of an electronic network (mailing list) whereby we could continue the public discussion that began at the conference. Until we have such a mechanism, I'm sending this by snail mail to a few people who might be interested (and whose addresses I happen to have), and of course I'm hoping there will be some feedback. An e-mailing list will make this kind of exchange much simpler — and cheaper.

This will be a bit confrontational, but I hope you will understand that I don't mean it personally or disrespectfully. The first question concerns your intelligence background. Can you say anything to make those of us who suspect high-level government complicity in the assassinations (about half the general population, in fact) less suspicious of someone like yourself, who after spending 20 years in military intelligence now purports to lead the fight for "full disclosure"? As a former intelligence officer, are you not still bound by secrecy oaths that would prevent you from revealing or publishing material that some intelligence agency or other deems damaging to "national security"? If you do not do so now, if you overstep the bounds can you not be forced to submit everything you write and say for clearance by intelligence officials? Is it not logical to suspect that a former intelligence officer might still be working for the government? Would it not be ideal for the government to have one of its own leading an assault on government secrecy, so that this assault could be steered in less harmful directions than might otherwise be the case? Is it not also possible that a 20-year intelligence veteran might be more easily convinced than others that playing such a role is fully compatible with notions of "patriotic service"?

I'll give you an example of the kind of remark that does not allay these suspicions. You said during your talk on Oswald's 201 file something to the effect that at the end of this investigation we might find "not an institutional conspiracy, but perhaps a conspiracy on the part of some elements within the Agency." Why do you think so? What makes you think a crime and coverup as massive as the JFK assassination is more likely to have been carried out by a few individuals rather than by an institution such as the CIA? To me, this "renegade CIA" theory is as implausible as the Lone Nut theory — just one more propaganda model or phase of the coverup. Peter Scott's phase analysis (*Deep Politics and the Death of JFK*, Univ. of Calif., 1993, p. 38) can be extended as follows:

Phase 1: The KGB (or Castro) did it.

Phase 2: Oswald did it.

Phase 3: The Mafia (+ anti-Castro Cubans) did it.

Phase 4: Renegade CIA agents (+ Mafia + Cubans) did it.

Phase 5: The CIA (+ their allies in the rest of the government and society at large) did it.

The government and the mass media now seem to be somewhere between Phase 2 and Phase 3. Phase 4 is waiting in the wings, and it seems from your remark that you expect its entrance soon, perhaps as the result of your own work.

Phase 5, which in my opinion is the truth, will be further postponed until enough time has passed that the future government will be able to plausibly dissociate itself from the powers-that-were in 1963. There are signs already that the CIA as an institution may be on the way out, and if that happens it will make Phase 5 easier to introduce. The public will be all too readily convinced that bygones are bygones and that their current government and institutions have nothing to do with those that presided over the coup d'état in 1963.

But we would do well to remember the words of Gen. Walter Bedell Smith, one of the first directors of the CIA, who told the investigative committee appointed by Kennedy to investigate the Bay of Pigs operation:

> When you are at war, Cold War if you like, you must have an amoral agency which can operate secretly and which does not have to give press conferences...I think that so much publicity has been given to CIA that the covert work might have to be put under another roof...It's time we take the bucket of slop and put another cover over it (*Operation Zapata*, Frederick, MD: University Publications of America, 1981, pp. 276-277).

So they were considering putting the shit bucket elsewhere already in 1961. Who knows where it was in 1963, or where it is now, or how many buckets there are? This is why the term "CIA" should be taken as a metaphor for the larger secret criminal networks of power that pervade not only the government but also private enterprise. But you have to start somewhere, and since at least according to the overt structure of the government the CIA is the <u>central</u> shit bucket, that seems the best place to start.

The CIA is, after all, an <u>institutionalized</u> conspiracy. The Directorate of Operations (formerly "Plans") is by any reasonable definition the Department of Conspiracy ("two or more people planning secretly to do bad or illegal things"). It is part of an institution in the executive branch of the government, which makes both the CIA and the government, to some extent, institutionalized conspiracies. As are all governments, for what governments do not secretly plan to do bad or illegal things at some time or other? So much for the false and counterproductive distinction between "structural" or "institutional" analysis vs. "conspiracy" theory (e.g., Michael Albert, Z magazine), as Michael Parenti eloquently pointed out at the conference. So much, too, or so one would hope, for your apparent willingness to exonerate an institution which is by definition conspiratorial, while looking for "renegades" within that institution.

To put it a little differently, do you really think that "renegades" within the CIA could have pulled off the public execution of the president and controlled the official investigations and press coverage forever after? To modify that a bit, do you think "renegades" could have done it and then been protected forever after by government officials, institutions, and virtually the entire "free press" — merely because all these people made individual decisions to cover their asses concerning some aspect of the matter they inadvertently participated in?

To see how much this strains the credulity of any but the Truest Believers in the purity and goodness of the US government, try substituting "KGB" for "CIA." Does it sound reasonable to suspect "renegade" KGB agents of pulling off the assassination and the coverup, and at the same time to exonerate the KGB as an institution, and the Soviet government as a whole? If there was indeed evidence of KGB involvement, do you think for a minute that any American would stop to make this distinction between "renegade KGB," "KGB," and "the Soviet government"? Certainly not. And why not? Because the Soviets are (were) the enemy. It is nothing more than our naive belief that our government cannot possibly be our enemy that allows us to rationalize in this way. Eliminate the initial premise ("Uncle Sam is a good guy") and the "renegade CIA" theory appears — correctly — as naive and preposterous as the "renegade KGB" theory.

Perhaps you do not realize just how deeply suspicious many of us have become of our government. That 81% figure that Dan Alcorn cited of people who "mistrust" the government hardly scratches the surface, in my opinion. (Furthermore, I don't think this is necessarily an unhealthy state of affairs: are we not <u>supposed</u> to mistrust government? That is what Thoreau teaches us, at least, and history too.) We, especially a group such as the one assembled in COPA, are so accustomed to the "string 'em along and jerk 'em around" strategy of the US government that we have learned to think in ways that government propagandists eagerly dismiss as "paranoid," but which we know are quite realistic.

Let me give you an example of such a scenario — "paranoid" by mass media standards but not far-fetched at all to me — where you, willy nilly, fit in quite neatly. Time Warner, the biggest propaganda machine in history, produced the Stone film (*JFK*). This is in itself a wonder, since I think *JFK* can safely be called the most <u>potentially</u> revolutionary film ever made, although Time Warner can hardly be assumed to be in the business of fomenting revolution. They also published your book (*JFK and Vietnam*, Warner Books, 1992), which is supposedly the basis of the main thesis of the film — that JFK was killed because he was threatening to withdraw from Vietnam. Then, in addition to the shallow but widespread (and no doubt orchestrated) media attack on the film, the most prestigious elements on the "radical left," led by Alexander Cockburn and Noam Chomsky, attacked both the film and your book by showing (I'm afraid correctly) that the only evidence for <u>your</u> thesis — that JFK secretly planned to withdraw regardless of the military situation — is anecdotal. Thus the end effect of your book was to provide a straw man — an extremely speculative thesis — which the most astute critics on the left (and I suppose elsewhere, but these are the ones I pay attention to) promptly demolished, and along with it the potential political impact of the film.

The point is that if this was a managed scenario, it could not have been more successful. The discussion of the (possible) connection between the assassination and the Vietnam War, which should have exploded in the American public consciousness like a nuclear bomb, was over before it began. It has now devolved to an academic historical question between those who believe you and those who believe Chomsky. Cui bono? Could it be that both you and Chomsky were cleverly (and hopefully unwittingly) seduced into playing your parts in this scenario?

The problem is that you, Chomsky, Peter Scott, and everyone else I've read have skipped over the one most important and undeniable fact in this matter: the <u>assessment of the military situation</u> in Vietnam changed radically — was reversed — <u>after</u> the assassination. Chomsky makes this point very clearly in *Rethinking Camelot* (South End, 1993, pp. 91-93), although he fails to recognize its importance. He is too busy trying to refute your thesis about JFK's secret intentions. This is the wrong debate. The documentary record is perfectly clear that JFK was planning to withdraw on the assumption (not "condition," as Chomsky insists) of success. The point of departure for reasonable debate should be: When did the optimism become pessimism (which in turn caused the reversal of the withdrawal policy)? Then the question and speculation as to whether this change was coincidental can begin. Instead, we have everyone discussing a quite different (and unanswerable) question: What were JFK's secret intentions and <u>would</u> he have withdrawn regardless of the military situation? And even this question jumps the gun. It should be: Would the intelligence consensus on the military situation have been reversed had JFK lived?

I agree with you and Peter Scott (and Schlesinger) that 273 reversed 263, and I also suspect that JFK could not have been stupid enough to think we were winning the war or that it was winnable, so my speculation about what he would have done is the same as yours. But as I said, this is not, or should not be, the issue. The issue is when the assumption of military success changed, and when the withdrawal policy changed accordingly. Chomsky is actually much clearer on these issues than you are, despite his thesis. He says the CIA and the other intelligence agencies began their radical and <u>retrospective</u> reassessment two days after the assassination. This should have raised the obvious question of why it took the CIA five months to realize they were losing the war instead of winning it, but Chomsky doesn't ask, so we must assume he takes this as coincidence.

You, on the other hand, give a more muddled picture of the intelligence consensus at the time of the assassination. Despite the almost total lack of documentation regarding what happened at the Honolulu conference on Nov. 20, you seem to argue that the change from optimism to pessimism occurred on that day:

> The upshot of the Honolulu meeting, then, was that the shocking deterioration of the war effort was presented in detail to those assembled, along with a plan to widen the war, while the 1,000-man withdrawal was turned into a meaningless paper drill (p. 435).

"Upshot" is a vague term. Do you mean immediately or within the following days or weeks? You say Lodge's assessment of the situation was "contradictory" and you gloss over his overall judgment that it was "hopeful" (p. 431), whereas FRUS is quite clear about this in a passage you do not quote:

> Ambassador Lodge described the outlook for the immediate future of Vietnam as hopeful ... Finally, as regards all US programs — military, economic, psychological —

we should continue to keep before us the goal of setting dates for phasing out US activities and turning them over to the Vietnamese; and these dates, too, should be looked at again in the light of the new political situation [after the assassination of Diem]. The date mentioned in the McNamara-Taylor statement of October 2 on US military withdrawal had — and is still having — a tonic effect ("Memorandum of Discussion at the Special Meeting on Vietnam, Honolulu," *Foreign Relations of the United States, Vietnam*, 1961-1963, Vol. 4, p. 608-610).

Thus, your conclusions about the "upshot" of the Honolulu conference seem unwarranted and in fact misleading.

If we follow your lead, we have JFK secretly engineering withdrawal under the pretense of success, then seeing this pretense dropped on Nov. 20 (was this good or bad for his secret plan?), then presumably about to sign a draft of 273 which is, however, significantly different from the version LBJ signed. The problem with this is not just that it is all speculation, as Chomsky says. More importantly, it confuses the crucial question of when the intelligence consensus changed. If it changed on Nov. 20, as you imply, then we can speculate ad infinitum as to whether and when Bundy informed JFK, what JFK's reaction was, etc. Where does that leave us? With the minute differences in language between draft 273 and final 273 as the only hint of discontinuity between JFK and LBJ's Vietnam policy — a very weak argument indeed. Of course, none of this really matters, since there is no evidence that JFK had any idea what happened in Honolulu, much less changed his policy as a result, but it fuels the false debate.

It is far more important to establish and emphasize what Chomsky presents correctly but ignores, and what you seem to misrepresent: the fact that the intelligence assessment and the withdrawal policy both changed radically after Nov. 22. Chomsky would have to agree with this — if we could get him to stop playing word games with the phrase "withdrawal policy" — because he cites the documentary evidence for it himself. Once this fact is established, we can then engage in a more speculative debate about whether the assassination and the subsequent assessment/policy change were merely coincidental or not. I would like to hear your reprise on this.

Since COPA is putting a lot of faith into what I cynically call the "paper chase" (which I will help with if I can but have no faith in at all), I want to add a word of warning. Government documents are not sacred, any more than government autopsy photographs, X-rays, etc. are. We have every right and reason to doubt the authenticity of government documents. For example, I doubt the authenticity of Bundy's draft of NSAM 273. It was declassified on January 31, 1991, by which time government agents were surely well aware of what Stone was up to. How very convenient that when the film came out in December, promulgating the explosive thesis (not new, but new to the general public) that 273 reversed 263, there was a draft of 273 to thoroughly confuse the issue: Did Bundy write it for Kennedy or for Johnson (i.e., was Bundy in on the coup)? Does draft 273 contradict 263, and if so does this mean JFK would have reversed his own withdrawal policy? Does draft 273 differ significantly from the final version? Apart from general obfuscation, the most obvious effect that the entrance of this document had on the discussion that the film engendered was to undermine Peter Scott's 1972 thesis of the discontinuity between 263 and 273 (e.g., for Chomsky, although he had never been convinced by Scott's argument anyway, despite having published it in Vol. 5 of the Gravel *Pentagon Papers*). After all, the government had had 19 years to think about how to handle Scott's disturbing theory, and what better time to release that draft than just before the film came out?

One last point. You may recall that when I talked to you briefly at the reception before the conference began, I asked you how you felt about Colby's endorsement of your book (jacket blurb).

It seemed quite strange to me that the CIA's Chief of the Far East Division from 1962-67 should feel so positively about a book that, to me at least, implicated the CIA along with the rest of the military-industrial-intelligence complex in the murder of the president. You seemed surprised at my question, as if the CIA had nothing to do with Vietnam policy and therefore could not have been part of a coup intended to reverse the withdrawal plan. But it is well known that DCI John McCone was a superhawk on Vietnam before and after the assassination, and I hardly think Colby was any different, despite whatever he might say in his memoirs, which I will certainly not waste my time reading.

On re-reading your book, I can see why Colby was pleased with your treatment of him and the Agency. They emerge virtually unscathed. The brunt of your attack falls on MACV (Military Assistance Command, Vietnam) and the military brass. But isn't it accurate to say that MACV <u>was</u> the CIA, at least until the Marines landed in April 1965? On pp. 434-5, quoting Colby himself, you even imply that Colby was opposed to escalation in November 1963, and that after Honolulu "the military started the planning and activity that would escalate finally to full-scale air attacks" against the North, although Colby "never thought this would work."

I haven't heard even the most prostrate apologist for the CIA contend that there was anything but a hawkish consensus in the Agency for the war until 1965 at the earliest (cf. John Ranelagh, *The Agency*, Touchstone, 1987, p. 417). Will you have us believing that Colby was arguing against escalation at the end of 1963?

I think most of us are aware of the CIA's Jekyll (Intelligence) and Hyde (Operations) tactics, whereby Hyde's covert maneuverings can be hidden and denied behind the relatively overt and supposedly well-intentioned face of Dr. Jekyll. This tactic is certainly used by the other intelligence "services" as well.

And of course Dr. Jekyll says many different things, sometimes contradictory, and very likely the exact opposite of what Mr. Hyde is actually doing. Thus in reconstructing history, one can always choose among conflicting intelligence estimates and advice to argue that X or Y faction in the so-called "intelligence community," which of course includes the military, were the bad guys and the others the good guys. Your choice seems to be that CIA were the good guys and MACV, or specifically the military honchos (Harkins, Taylor, perhaps McNamara) were the bad guys.

This sounds very similar to the "renegade" theory of the assassination, this time applied to the larger crime of Vietnam: it wasn't the CIA or "the intelligence community" or even "the military," but just a few "renegade" military honchos who pulled it all off. I can't buy into this, for the same reasons I've already discussed. And the CIA would be the last institution I would attempt to exonerate, not the first. The job of the Central Intelligence Agency, as I understand it, is to establish the consensus and present this to the President, who after all has to listen to somebody. So I find it ludicrous to assert that the CIA (as an institution, regardless of various stray voices within the institution) ever did anything but push as hard as it possibly could to promote the war in Vietnam (and Laos and Cambodia) –until Tet 1968, of course, when the consensus finally changed. As for Colby, it is even more ludicrous to take such a man at his word.

Furthermore, as I've said, according to Chomsky, whose scholarship I trust, even if I disagree with his conclusions, the source of the radically changed intelligence consensus after the assassination, which led to the reversal of the withdrawal policy, was specifically CIA.

So it's not all that hard, even 33 years after Gen. Smith's revealing comment, to know where the shit bucket is. Maybe Smith was being overly cautious. Maybe they figure there's no need to go to too much trouble hiding it, people are so used to the stench.

Sincerely,
Michael Morrissey

1994.11.5 TO MICHAEL PARENTI

[Newman did not reply. Of the dozen or so other COPA board members I sent copies to (e.g., John Judge, Peter Scott), only Michael Parenti replied. This is my reply to him]

Nov. 5, 1994

Open Reply to Michael Parenti (10/30/94)

Copy to COPA

Dear Michael,

Thanks for your reply to my letter to Newman. I realize that exaggerated suspicions are counterproductive, but I don't think my questions to John are exaggerated or that they constitute an ad hominem attack. I would ask the same of anyone with an intelligence background. My questions in that regard are not rhetorical. I don't think people "retire" from intelligence work the way other people retire. The oaths they take are binding for life, and not trivial. Philip Agee, for example, the first CIA renegade, still has to submit to CIA censorship. For him to admit that (as he did to me), or for me to say it here, does not cast doubt on his "integrity and motives," as you imply my questions to Newman do. On the contrary, being open and honest about it speaks <u>for</u> one's integrity. Perhaps John will welcome the opportunity to clear the air. That is the spirit in which I challenged him.

Of course you are right that I (or you) could be similarly challenged, but the analogy is not very fair. I do not have an intelligence background. I did not predict that our investigations would not point to an institutional conspiracy on the part of the CIA, but rather (perhaps) to a conspiracy of certain rogue elements within that institution. I did not write a book that minimizes the CIA's role in promoting the war in Vietnam, presents William Colby as an early "critic" of US war policy, is highly praised by Colby on the cover jacket, and in my opinion muddles the crucial question of when the intelligence assessment of the situation in Vietnam actually changed.

On that last point, you say I could be accused of "salvaging Chomsky's research," but since you haven't read Newman's book I have to wonder how much you've really thought about this. I disagree strongly with Chomsky on the importance of the assassination(s), the (false) dichotomy of "conspiracy" vs. "structural" critique, and specifically on the Vietnam withdrawal issue, but the point I made to Newman was that Chomsky makes it clear that the intelligence assessment changed radically <u>after</u> the assassination. Newman's account implies that it changed <u>before</u> the assassination. This is a crucial difference, and if I find Chomsky's account here clearer and more convincing, it doesn't mean I buy his overall argument. On the contrary, I was trying to point out the irony of Chomsky clarifying the very fact that <u>contradicts</u> his own overall thesis of continuity in JFK's and LBJ's Vietnam policy — a fact whose significance Chomsky obviously refuses to see.

It might interest you to know that I tried, in the course of a long and intensive correspondence with Chomsky (before *Rethinking Camelot* came out), to get him to state his position as follows: JFK's withdrawal plan was reversed, after the assassination, because the assessment of the military situation was reversed (also after the assassination). This is in fact his position, but you will see that in his book, as in his letters to me, he refuses to put it this way because he is so determined to make the truly specious argument that "there was no withdrawal policy." The reason is obvious to me, and I told him so: Once you admit that there was a radical policy change immediately after the assassination (exactly when doesn't matter), you must deal with the question of the possible relation between the two events. (I said this in my COPA talk too, but I guess you missed it.) That means you are automatically involved in "conspiracy theory," which is anathema to Chomsky (and others like Alexander Cockburn and the late I.F. Stone) for I suppose ideological or psychological reasons. The other alternative is to admit the withdrawal policy reversal but deny any relation to the assassination, as Arthur Schlesinger does. This is naive and irrational, as Schlesinger's hysterical condemnation of the Stone film amply demonstrates. Chomsky does not want to appear naive and irrational, so he has manufactured a tortuous and false argument that there was never a withdrawal policy ("without victory") in the first place.

Chomsky's argument is false because Newman's thesis (that JFK was secretly planning to withdraw regardless of the military situation) is 1) speculative, as Chomsky correctly says, and 2) unnecessary to establish the fact that the policy was reversed after the assassination, as Chomsky fails to realize. This is why I say it is a false debate — because it is about 1), not 2). The irony is that Chomsky's clear presentation of the facts regarding 2), as opposed to Newman's, supports a conspiracy view of the assassination. It is enough to say that two days after the assassination the CIA and other intelligence agencies began to reverse their assessment of the military situation — retrospectively, dating the deterioration from July — and hence to reverse the withdrawal policy. Chomsky says this (without using the term "withdrawal policy," which he refuses to use the way everyone else uses it) — not Newman. We do not need any secret intentions of JFK to pose the question of the relation between the assassination and Vietnam policy. All we need to do is establish what actually happened, according to the documentary record. What happened is that JFK was killed, and two days later the CIA et al. suddenly realized they had been losing the war for the past five months, and the appropriate policy change was made. This may have been pure coincidence (as Chomsky and Schlesinger both assume, Chomsky tacitly and Schlesinger explicitly), but once the facts are stated clearly, they reek of conspiracy.

A pity you could not hang around a little longer in Washington. I considered storming the podium after your fine speech and introducing myself, but you were surrounded. Next time I will. I did talk with John briefly, and I found him very pleasant and friendly. I wish we could have talked more, and I hope we will be able to another time. I'm surprised, frankly, that you take my letter as a personal attack on him, which it clearly is not. I am asking him about things that are "public domain," i.e., his acknowledged intelligence background and what he has publicly stated and written. Since these are fairly complicated issues, it is better to discuss them in writing and publicly, so that other people can participate. You are the first to reply in this mode, and I'm glad you did. I hope John also replies. I think such exchanges will lead to more solidarity, not less — unless, of course, it turns out that there is something seriously dividing us, in which case solidarity has no virtue anyway. That is what we need to find out. There is nothing to be gained by keeping mum and pretending to agree on things that in fact we've never even discussed.

Sincerely,
Michael Morrissey

1995.02.21 TO CHOMSKY

[In his letter of June 1, 19936, Chomsky repeated his claim that JFK "reluctantly authorized withdrawal on the explicit condition that victory was guaranteed," that NSAM 263 "endorses the McNamara-Taylor recommendations for withdrawal, but only if this can be done 'without impairment of the war effort' – that is, on condition of victory."

All of my efforts to challenge his interpretation of that phrase as an "explicit condition," as opposed to an "assumption" or at best "implicit condition," were in vain. This was, Chomsky said, merely my "tortured" attempt "to show that NSAM 263 doesn't mean what it says." My argument concerning conditions vs. assumptions, he said, "does not merit further discussion."

This is where things stayed for the next year or so, until after the first COPA (Coalition on Political Assassinations) meeting in October 1994, where I had been invited to give a talk on the Bay of Pigs (see *Looking for the Enemy*, Ch. 1). John Newman, about whom I had my misgivings, was on the governing board, and believing the best way to express my suspicions was openly and publicly, I sent "An Open Letter to John Newman" (see 1994.10.20) to all the members of the board. I also sent a copy to Chomsky.

Newman did not reply. Michael Parenti sent me an "Open Letter" reply, to which I responded with an "Open

Reply" (1994.11.05). I sent copies of these letters, too, to Chomsky. He replied briefly on February 9, 1995, fully exasperated, but "for the record" enclosing "a few excerpts" from *Rethinking Camelot* that I had supposedly misquoted, without further commentary:

> Meanwhile [early Nov., 1963], evidence that undermined the optimistic assessments was becoming harder to ignore. A week after the coup, State Department Intelligence, with the concurrence of the CIA, reported that by late October the military situation had sharply deteriorated, predicting "unfavorable end-1963 values" for its statistical factors. The new government confirmed that the GVN "had been losing the war against the VC in the Delta for some time because it had been losing the population." A top-level meeting was held in Honolulu on November 20 to consider the next steps. The US mission in Vietnam recommended that the withdrawal plans be maintained, the new government being "warmly disposed toward the U.S." and offering "opportunities to exploit that we never had before." Kennedy's plans to escalate the assault against the southern resistance could now be implemented, with a stable regime finally in place. McNamara, ever cautious, stressed that "South Vietnam is under tremendous pressure from the VC," noting a sharp increase in VC incidents after the coup, and urged that "We must be prepared to devote enough resources to this job of winning the war to be certain of accomplishing it..." At an 8AM White House meeting on November 22, Bundy was informed that "for the first time" military reporting was "realistic about the situation in the Delta" (pp. 81-82).
>
> ... On Nov. 13, Jack Raymond reported that Defense officials say that the 1,000-man withdrawal plans remain unchanged. Two days later, he reported that at a

news conference, while keeping the "official objectives announced on Oct. 2 to withdraw most of the troops by the end of 1965," Kennedy weakened the withdrawal plans, reducing the estimate for 1963 to "several hundred," pending the outcome of the Honolulu meeting. JFK again emphasized the need to "intensify the struggle" (p. 83).]

Feb. 21, 1995

Dear Noam,

Thanks for answering. It is more than Newman himself or Peter Scott have done — and we presumably agree on the political significance of the JFK assassination!

I did not "misquote" you in my letter to Newman. I referred to pp. 91-93, where you state clearly that the assessments of the military situation in Vietnam were radically revised after JFK's murder, beginning with McCone's report to Johnson on November 24.

You now quote to me from pp. 81-83, where you say there were negative reports in early November. I don't think anyone denies this. The question is when the consensus changed from optimistic to pessimistic. Your remarks on pp. 91-93 are the clearest statement I know of that the consensus changed after Nov. 22, and they are confirmed by Lodge's optimistic appraisal at the Honolulu conference on Nov. 20, which I quoted in the Newman letter.

Why are you hedging now? Do you want to say now that what you say on pp. 91-93 is misleading, or that only stupid readers like me would understand it the way I have? Do you want to say now that the consensus changed before Nov. 22, or that there never was a consensus either way?

The fact is that you say clearly in the book what I tried in vain to get you to say in our correspondence: that the assessment of the military situation changed radically — after Nov. 22, but only coincidentally — which caused the withdrawal policy to be reversed (or in your words, "which canceled the assumptions on which the withdrawal plans had been conditioned" [p. 91]). The facts are thus:

1. JFK was murdered (quite coincidentally, from your point of view) on Nov. 22.

2. "The first report prepared for LBJ (November 23) opened with this 'Summary Assessment': 'The outlook is hopeful. There is better assurance than under Diem that the war can be won. We are pulling out 1,000 American troops by the end of 1963'" (p. 91).

3. "The next day, however, CIA Director John McCone informed the President that the CIA now [my emphasis] regarded the situation as 'somewhat more serious' than had been thought, with 'a continuing increase in Viet Cong activity since the first of November' (the coup). Subsequent reports only deepened the gloom" (p. 91).

4. McCone's reassessment was retrospective: "McCone agreed [in December] that 'indices on progress of the war turned unfavorable for the GVN' about July 1963, moving 'very sharply against the GVN' after the coup" (p. 92).

5. In the light of the "radically revised assessments of the military situation, which cancelled the assumptions on which the withdrawal plans had been conditioned" (p. 91) — all (coincidentally) after Nov. 22 — the US position moved, as you put it in the title of this chapter, "from terror [JFK's policy of counterinsurgency] to aggression" (LBJ's policy of direct involvement).

Note that I have avoided saying that LBJ "reversed the withdrawal policy," since you made it clear in our previous correspondence that you will not accept this formulation. For you, LBJ was if anything less hawkish than JFK, and their policy of winning the war, and withdrawing only on condition of victory, was the same. As you know, I disagree with you on this, but this does not mean we have to disagree on points 1-5 above.

Can we agree, finally, on these five points? Or do you think I have "misquoted" you again?

I cannot understand why you think our discussion is a "waste of time," particularly since in one of your previous letters you said my questions had helped you clarify your own thinking on these matters (albeit with conclusions opposite to mine). I am hoping that you will be kind enough to return the favor, at least as far as my understanding of your position is concerned. Your book, especially pp. 91-93, made it clear to me that we agree on the one crucial (to me, anyway) point that I was trying to establish during our correspondence (or 5 points, as above). Now you say that I have misunderstood and misrepresented what you say in the book. Is it too much to ask you to say, as clearly as possible, whether you agree with points 1-5 above, which are stated almost entirely in your own words?

Sincerely,
Michael

1995.03.23 TO CHOMSKY

March 23, 1995

Dear Noam,

Your resort to sarcasm demonstrates not only the poverty of your arguments but a very large measure of *mauvaise foi.*[47] Perhaps I should thank you for liberating me from the obviously exaggerated esteem in which I once held you, but you do not deserve to be thanked and the transition from profound disappointment to "liberation" has been neither easy nor pleasant, so I'll skip it.

You show how willing, eager in fact, you are to slug it out with all the dirty tricks of a street thug (or our friends from Langley) when it is clear that your opponent is winning the argument. I noticed this before, when I saw how you insisted on simply repeating your own arguments rather than responding to mine, and how easily you resorted to name-calling in lieu of argumentation. I'm referring to your description of Prouty as a "raving fascist" and a "fraud." When I asked you to explain why you think so, besides the claim that he is "associated" with Liberty Lobby, you did not respond. And this from a guy who himself has been denounced as an "anti-Semite" because he defended Faurisson's right to speak!

I did not say or imply that the pessimistic reports you mention on pp. 81-83 of *Rethinking Camelot* came after Nov. 22, and you know it. I said that YOU SAY (on pp. 91-93) that the consensus changed radically immediately after Nov. 22. This is merely a ridiculous and totally transparent attempt on your part to avoid my question.

You protest far too much. If you were half as intelligent as I once thought you were, you would long ago have accepted the fact (especially since you make it clear yourself on pp. 91-93, and as the Gravel *Pentagon Papers* also make clear) that the military assessment was reversed immediately after JFK's murder. You would also have admitted that you consider this a coincidence unless it can be proved otherwise (which makes your position, as I have told you, essentially identical to Schlesinger's). I'm sure you could have trotted out a long list of similar coincidences, and any freshman composition student is aware of the *post hoc, ergo propter hoc* fallacy.

But no. Out of arrogance or just plain stupidity, you refuse to admit that the military assessment was reversed after Nov. 22 — plainly contradicting yourself as well as the documentary record. You also continue to ignore my point, which I have made abundantly clear, by treating it as if it were the same as John Newman's, which it quite obviously is not.

The only people who are arguing about JFK's "secret intentions to withdraw without victory" are you and Newman.[48] I am talking about JFK's documented and public intention to withdraw on the assumption (not condition) of continued military success. This assumption was reversed, AFTER Nov. 22, and subsequently the withdrawal policy was also reversed. I cannot believe that you are too stupid to understand the difference between this and Newman's much more speculative thesis, so I can only ascribe your stubbornness here to arrogance: How can a mere Michael Morrissey be right, and Noam Chomsky be wrong?

I don't think you are an agent. It has crossed my mind, but I don't think you would have written to me if you were. You would have been more likely to ignore me, as John Newman has done. I think you are a man who has been told far too many times how brilliant he is, an American who cannot rid himself of the illusion that the United States is still "the freest country in the world" (as you said in the film *Manufacturing Consent* — and you should have heard the German audience groan at that), and the best example of a propagandized intellectual that I can think of. I'm sure that your IQ by the Bell Curve's standard is impressively high, but you are still an American, and the idea that a coup d'état could take place in America, especially without perspicacious commentators such as your friend Alexander Cockburn and geniuses such as yourself even being aware of it, is simply beyond your capacity. The idea is too big for you. You cannot take the shock, confusion, and fear that this idea brings with it when you let it into your brain, especially the shock of recognizing that you are as subject to mind control as anyone else, and that you are a slave just like the rest of us.

And yes, I believe I am beyond you in this respect, because I KNOW that I can be wrong, can be deluded to a point that I would never have dreamed possible, especially because I always thought of myself as fairly well-informed, skeptical, independent, etc. I don't think you have ever had such an experience. You think you can see through the self-delusion and propagandization of others, and perhaps you do, but you have not seen through yourself. The idea that you can be (and are) a victim has not penetrated, and IQ doesn't help at all here.

My best defense against your snide suggestion that I am an agent is my quarrel with you. I believe the CIA killed JFK and have said so publicly, and about half of the American population have similar suspicions, according to a *Time*/CNN poll taken <u>before</u> the Stone film came out (*Time*, Jan. 13, 1992, European ed., p. 40). Your foolish insistence that there is no evidence of high-level conspiracy, and your even more foolish and (now) blatantly self-contradictory "position" on the withdrawal question, support the established lies on both issues and thus help to exonerate the CIA, the government as a whole, and the complicit media Establishment. Which of the two of us looks more like an agent? Your long association with MIT, despite the incongruity of the nation's most prominent "radical leftist dissident" being so tight with the nation's No. 1 educational institution with military and intelligence ties, is also suspicious.

But I do not stoop as easily as you do to mud-slinging, and I will not accuse you of being an agent, even though your actions aid the enemy much more than mine. Nor did I accuse Newman of being an agent. I referred to his well-known intelligence background and asked him a few perfectly legitimate and justifiable questions. If he were honest, he would have nothing to fear by answering them, and everything to gain — namely, credibility. But his silence is also an answer, and it speaks even worse for him than your sarcasm does for you.

Sincerely,
Michael

[I did not have the last word. In his curt reply (and last letter to me) on April 3, 1995, Chomsky referred me to *Rethinking Camelot* concerning his "alleged refusal" to answer my question about Prouty (though in the book he says only that Prouty's evidence is "anecdotal"). "The remainder," he said, "is at the same level of respect for fact, making it clear that there is no point proceeding."]

1995.03.23 TO PROUTY

March 23, 1995

Dear Fletch,

Enclosed is a copy of the letter I sent today to Chomsky. Thought you might be interested since I mention your name.

He still doesn't want to admit that the assessment of the military situation in Vietnam (the consensus, that is) did not change until after the JFK assassination, although he says so himself in *Rethinking Camelot*. I'll spare you the details but can send them if you wish.

This is a strong letter, but as you know I have not come to this opinion rashly.

You are still the only person who has been strongly favorable about my letter to Newman, and one of a very few that have responded at all. Newman, Peter Scott, and also Oliver Stone, whom I wrote to at 201 Santa Monica Blvd., 6th Fl., Santa Monica, CA 90401, have not responded. I would particularly like to know Stone's opinion, so if you ever get a chance to urge him to answer, please do!

I hope you won't mind that I have taken the liberty of giving your address and phone no. to Vince Salandria in Philadelphia. He's an early assassination researcher and you probably know the name. He organizes a group of a dozen or so of us that correspond on things loosely associated with the assassination (what isn't?), and all of us more or less agree that Garrison/ Stone got it right. I recommended that Vince include you in the group (it's up to him since he does the photocopying and mailing), and I hope he does. So you may hear from him.

Best regards,
Michael

2000.09 MY BEEF WITH CHOMSKY

[This was published in the Fall-Winter 2000/2001 issue (#36) of John Kelin's Fair Play online magazine[49] It is also included in *Looking for the Enemy, Addendum 5*.]

Chomsky and AIDS

In my first letter to Chomsky, in April 1989, I included my review of the Turner film, *The Men Who Killed Kennedy* [see Addendum 7], which I had seen a few months earlier and had so turned my head around. He replied (5/15/89) that the review was "interesting" and that he "didn't know about the events" I described.

In retrospect, this is a puzzling remark. Three years later (3/3/92) he told me he had "read a good bit of the critical literature" (meaning critical of the Warren Report), so I suppose he did this reading in the meantime, the Gulf War notwithstanding.

I learned in 1995, however, after reading Ray Marcus's *Appendix B* (1995, self-published), that Chomsky had been well informed about the evidence of high-level conspiracy in the assassination twenty years before I wrote to him. Marcus tells the story of trying to enlist the support of a number of progressive intellectuals in reopening the JFK case in 1969:

I first met with Noam Chomsky. Soon after our discussions began, he asked his secretary to cancel his remaining appointments for the day. The scheduled one-hour meeting stretched to 3-4 hours. Chomsky showed great interest in the material. We mutually agreed to a follow-up session later in the week. Then I met with Gar Alperovitz [a professor at Harvard]. At the end of our one-hour meeting, he said he would take an active part in the effort if Chomsky would lead it...

[The second meeting] again lasted much of an afternoon. The discussion ranged beyond evidentiary items to other aspects of the case. I told Chomsky of Alperovitz' offer to assist him if he decided to lead an effort to reopen. After the meeting, as they drove me back to my apartment, Bromberger [another MIT professor who had attended the meeting] expressed the view that, "If they are strong enough to kill the president, and strong enough to cover it up, then they are too strong to confront directly...if they feel sufficiently threatened., they may move to open totalitarian" ("they" was not further defined).

As we have seen from previous reactions by I.F. Stone, A.L. Wirin, and Carey McWilliams, this was similar to the fears expressed or implied by many leftist intellectuals among those who nevertheless professed faith in the Warren Report. From Bromberger, I was hearing it for the first time from someone who believed the report to be false.

I phoned Vince Salandria, of whom I had spoken to Chomsky, and asked him to send Chomsky his research and thinking. Salandria told me he was skeptical that Chomsky would actually get involved, based on his previous experiences with such left-oriented people.

He reasoned that had they entertained any such intentions, they would have acted on them long before this. Nevertheless, he agreed to send the material.

Upon returning to Los Angeles, I wrote a lengthy letter to Chomsky summing up my overview of the case to that time, and stating as cogently as I could the arguments for his active involvement. He responded on April 18, 1969:

> Just a quick note. I got your long letter, and some material from Salandria. I'll read both carefully. But I won't be able to decide anything until I return from England, in mid-June. Right now things are simply too rushed, and I'm too harassed to give serious thought to anything. I'll be in touch with you then. I don't know what the odds are. I'm still open-minded (and I hope will remain so).

From the context of our previous meetings it was clear that what Chomsky "...won't be able to decide" until he returned from England was not the question of whether or not there was a conspiracy – that he had given every indication of having already decided in the affirmative – but whether or not he wished to participate actively, even to assume a leading role, in the movement to reopen the case.

I never heard from him again, and Chomsky did not join such a movement. On the contrary, in recent years he has on a number of occasions gone on record attacking the critics' position and supporting the Warren Report (pp. 67-68).

What "events" had I described in my little review that Chomsky "didn't know about," after being informed by Marcus and Salandria twenty years earlier?

There is a telling parallel to this behavior in Chomsky's reaction to the AIDS origin issue.

In late summer 1989, I sent Chomsky an early (1986) paper by Segal in English and a copy of his first book, *Aids: Erreger aus dem Genlabor* ("AIDS: Virus from the Pentagon," Berlin: Simon und Leutner, 1987), which, though in German, I thought he would be able to read. (After all, I had to pass a German reading exam to qualify for my Ph.D. in linguistics, and he is the most famous linguist in the world!) He thanked me (8/26/89) for "the surprising and very interesting material," without further comment.

I had "surprised" him with the "very interesting" argument that the Pentagon had created AIDS, and this was all he had to say? It was my turn to be surprised. On Sept. 14, 1989 I sent him a copy of an article I had written summarizing Segal's theory ("Is AIDS Man-Made?"). He thanked me (9/22/89) for the "information," which he said was "most intriguing," but again had no further comment.

On Nov. 29, 1989, I sent Chomsky a photocopy of the MacArthur testimony from the Congressional Record (see "Informing the Press" in Chapter 4). He replied (12/28/89):

> Thanks also for the material from the Hearings. Sends a chill up the spine. This is very far from my field, and I have no scientific judgment. But it is hard for me to believe that one can't obtain a scientific judgment from some knowledgeable and unprejudiced source. I don't know people directly involved in AIDS research, but there are plenty of them around.

A year later, on Nov. 30, 1990, I sent him another article about Segal, focusing on the MacArthur testimony (see Ch. 4.1). Chomsky's reply (12/17/90) was: "Quite a story." These were his last words on the subject to me. A "chill up the spine," but the man who calls Washington the "terrorist capital of the world" has no more to say on the subject.

The parallel is clear. In 1969, he learns from Marcus and Salandria about the evidence for conspiracy in the assassination, but has not a word more to say about the subject until twenty years later, when I write to him, at which time he professes "surprise" to hear about it. In 1989, he also expresses surprise and horror at the idea that the "terrorist" US government may have created AIDS, but has nothing further to say on this subject either. This behavior strikes me as very much out of character – at least out of the character that I thought, from reading his books, that Chomsky possessed.

There is another significant parallel. Chomsky's trust in the integrity and objectivity of the "scientific community" (in quotes because I think it is more like the Mafia than a community) is astonishing, and again totally out of character for a man who is considered by many to be the "leading intellectual dissident" in the country. In 1989 he assures me that "knowledgeable and unprejudiced" sources can answer the question of the origin of AIDS (although he obviously does not wish to pursue the question, despite a "chill up the spine"). A couple of years later, Chomsky reveals his absolute faith in the National Academy of Sciences. In dismissing the notion of conspiracy in the JFK assassination, he gives this example of conspiracy logic (July 1, 1992):

> Thus when the National Academy of Sciences refutes by careful experiment the one reason offered by the House Committee to question the Warren Report, we can simply conclude that the scientists are in on the conspiracy. Anyone who knows them personally knows that this is laughable...

It is hard to remember, reading this, that the author is Noam Chomsky, author of many books and articles excoriating other academics and journalists, not to mention politicians and government officials, for their conformist, propagandized mentality (e.g., *Manufacturing Consent*). But in these lines we learn not only that it is "laughable" to doubt the judgment of a member of the National Academy of Scientists, but also, implicitly, that the House Select Committee on Assassinations 1979 report is trustworthy.

No one who has read "a good bit of the literature" could maintain such faith in either of these institutions – even before Gaeton Fonzi's definitive exposé of the HSCA's thoroughly compromised "investigation" (*The Last Investigation*, NY: Thunder's Mouth Press, 1993). No one, at least, who is not either incredibly naive, or the worst example of the kind of propagandized intellectual that Chomsky has so often (and effectively and correctly) warned us about.

Chomsky and CAIB/CAQ

Chomsky suggested that I send my review of the Turner film *(The Men Who Killed Kennedy)* to *CovertAction Information Bulletin* (now *Quarterly*). This was the first I had heard of it. One of CAIB's editors, Bill Vornberger, answered on 10/25/89 that they could not print my review because they were planning to run a review of Jim Garrison's *On the Trail of the Assassins*, which had just come out, in their next issue. This review never appeared, and as far as I know CAIB/CAB has never published anything about the Kennedy assassination.

Thus the first obvious question: Why has a journal devoted to exposing the misdeeds of the CIA so conspicuously avoided the subject of the JFK assassination, when a large portion of the general public believes the CIA was involved, and especially since the journal's longtime editors, Bill Schaap and Ellen Ray, were also the editors at Sheridan Square Press, which published Garrison's book, and the editors of *Lies Of Our Times*, a political monthly (now defunct) that published favorable (and reasonable) reviews of the Stone film?

Chomsky has always been a supporter of CAIB/CAQ; his photo adorns the magazine's subscription inserts. "Quite a good rag," he told me (May 15, 1989). "I write for it a lot." Here again is a statement which in retrospect I find very puzzling. If I had bothered to check, I would have found that Chomsky had published only two articles in CAIB – actually only one, since the second one (No. 32, summer 1989) was simply a shortened version of the first (No. 26, summer 1986), and they were identically titled ("Libya in US Demonology").

Why did Schaap and Ray publish virtually the same article twice within three years? They had never done such a thing before, and they haven't since. Why would Chomsky refer to this one article, published twice, as "a lot"? How could he write for it "a lot," if it was only one article?

On May 21, 1992, referring to Alexander Cockburn's review of the Stone film in *The Nation*, Chomsky wrote to me:

> But so far, his account is the only one in print that does justice to the factual record. Perhaps I should abstain from comment on this, since I did a lot of the background research for it (though what he wrote is his way of using it).

I would like to know how many professors, especially famous professors, do "background research" for journalists. Chomsky is the only one I have ever heard of. Maybe this is the way to understand his remark about having written "a lot" for CAIB, although only one article had appeared under his name. If he does "background research" for Alexander Cockburn, why shouldn't he do it for others?

Although CAIB/CAQ has strictly avoided the assassination in print, Vornberger told me in the same letter that "we are very much aware of the fact that Kennedy was killed by members of a conspiracy." "In fact," Vornberger continued, "it is our opinion that these men were current or former employees of the CIA." Vornberger also said "we highly recommend" Jim Garrison's *On the Trail of the Assassins*. The question screaming at us here is: If that's what they think, why haven't they written about it?

CAIB/CAQ and AIDS

I also sent the AIDS material, which Chomsky found to be "quite a story," to *Lies Of Our Times*. Bill Schaap replied (12/27/90) that they had "real problems" with it (see Ch. 4.1). CAQ did not come out with an AIDS article until six years later, in their Fall 1996 (No. 58) issue. This article, "Tracking the Real Genocide," by David Gilbert, a prison inmate, hardly fulfilled Schaap's call for fair coverage of "alternative theories." Gilbert offers a two-sentence summary of Segal's theory, failing to mention that Segal claims the virus escaped by accident, thus making it appear that Segal blamed the Pentagon for spreading it on purpose, which he did not. This gross misrepresentation of Segal is especially surprising considering what Schaap had written to me six years earlier (12/27/90). But in 1996 Schaap allows Gilbert to get away with this blatant misrepresentation.

What "problems," one must ask, did the CAIB editors have with the Segal material? Why did they have no problems with the Gilbert article, which they must have known was a travesty? Gilbert not only misrepresents Segal but fails completely to mention other dissident AIDS researchers, notably Robert Strecker and Alan Cantwell. He dismisses the science of the matter by asking his microbiologist friend Janet Stavnezer, who assured him that "the Segals' splice theory is scientifically impossible."

In the issue of CAQ following the Gilbert article (No. 59, Winter 1996), Nathaniel Lehrman writes in a letter to the editor that his 1987 article "Is AIDS Non-Infectious" (CAIB No. 28) "examined and demolished the Segal hypothesis of a synthetically created AIDS virus." This is truly astonishing. It will be clear to anyone who reads the earlier article that exactly the opposite is true. In that article, Lehrman suggests that HIV, although it is only "closely associated " with AIDS [following Duesberg], might be "a laboratory-created, minimally infective agent intended to be blamed for the chemical poisoning it actually accompanies."

Far from "demolishing" Segal, Lehrman affirms and goes considerably *beyond* it, suggesting that AIDS was not only man-made, but created *as a weapon*:

> The information described here, and the history of CBW research, suggest that AIDS may indeed be another example of a deliberately created disease (p. 62).

How is one to understand such self-contradictions? Schaap tells me in 1990 that his magazine wants to give decent coverage to "alternative" theories like Segal's, and six years later he publishes an article that does just the opposite. Gilbert gives us "official AIDS doctrine," as Lehrman puts it, grossly misrepresenting Segal, and Lehrman responds with an even grosser misrepresentation of what he himself had written in the same magazine nine years earlier!

One thing is clear: the message, flawed as it is, from CAIB/CAQ is that theories of the artificial origin of AIDS are not to be taken seriously.

Chomsky and Vietnam

Chomsky's argument is that

1. Vietnam policy did not change after the assassination (until 1968, of course)

2. Only tactics changed, quite coincidentally, at the same time

as the assassination, in response to the changed military situation.

3. The change in tactics was first made by JFK, not LBJ.

The first argument is justified by Chomsky's definition of the word *policy* to mean "withdrawal if and only if victory is assured." This is his interpretation, from which he refuses to budge an inch, of one sentence in the McNamara-Taylor recommendations approved by NSAM 263:

> This action [troop withdrawals] should be explained in low key as an initial step in a long-term program to replace U.S. personnel with trained Vietnamese without impairment of the war effort.

Chomsky insists that the last six words constitute an "explicit condition" of victory before any withdrawal would take place, and that this was the policy of both JFK and LBJ.

This is pure linguistics. Now, Chomsky is the greatest linguist in the world, but look at the linguistic facts he ignores in his interpretation:

First, the sentence can easily be understood to mean "This is the way we should explain it, but not necessarily the whole truth." Obviously, McNamara and Taylor (and JFK) would not have wanted it to look like they were simply abandoning the South Vietnamese.

More importantly, the phrase "without impairment of the war effort" is *not* an explicit condition, even if the most famous linguist in the world says it is. Consider:

> My plan is to wash the windows without hurting the plants.

Does this mean (Chomsky's interpretation):

> My plan is to wash the windows if and only if I can do

so without hurting the plants.

Or does it mean, as I am quite certain it does,

> My plan is to wash the windows and not hurt the plants (and I think I can do so).

This is what the sentence means, and it is what McNamara and Taylor meant:

> The plan – at least the way we should explain the plan – is to withdraw and do so without impairment of the war effort (which as we have said should be taken over completely by the Vietnamese by the end of 1965).

But Chomsky wants us to understand it as:

> The plan is to withdraw if and only if victory is assured.

Who is right? You be the judge.

The second argument is meant to back up the first. If the policy never changed, it does not matter when the tactics changed, whether under JFK or LBJ, but we would still be left with the troublesome coincidence that the change in tactics (in fact a reversal, from withdrawal to escalation, from not fighting the war to fighting the war) took place immediately after the assassination.

But lo and behold, on Jan. 31, 1991, right out of the blue, apparently, a draft of NSAM 273 appears from the black box that houses "national security" secrets, with no explanation as to why it was being released 13 years after the final document was released (NSAM 273 was declassified in 1978), or who or what was causing it to be released (an interesting question in itself, as is the question of its authenticity).

This is all Chomsky needs for his third argument: If anyone

should insist that even a reversal of tactics, if not of policy, so close on the heels of the murder of the head of state in charge of both the policy and the tactics, could be suspicious, thanks to the Bundy draft we now know that the person behind the change in tactics was not Johnson, but Kennedy.

Why? Because Bundy wrote the draft on Nov. 21, one day before the assassination! Therefore, Chomsky concludes, JFK would have signed it (although he never saw it or discussed it with Bundy or anyone else). Therefore, Chomsky further concludes, the people who say NSAM 273 shows a change in policy (Peter Dale Scott, John Newman, Arthur Schlesinger) are right, but wrong about who was responsible for it.

Chomsky's third argument actually contradicts the first. It's like saying, "I don't care what flavor it is, but make sure it's vanilla." If "tactical" changes don't matter, they don't matter. If they don't matter, there is no reason to make the further point – dubious in itself – that JFK made the change. By adding this third argument, Chomsky allows for the possibility that the "tactical" change was indeed significant, which destroys the premise expressed in the first argument.

What does all this mean? What is the message we are hearing from Chomsky and CAIB/CAQ? It is clear:

No AIDS conspiracy

No assassination conspiracy

No connection between Vietnam and the assassination

Surely it cannot escape our attention that this is precisely the same message we have been hearing from the government, from the mainstream press, and the so-called "scientific community." Nor should it escape our attention, as I think even this brief summary shows, that the argumentation presented to support these conclusions is patently false in each case.

Of course it is not necessarily wrong to agree with the government. But when "radical dissidents" agree so completely with the government, on such important questions, and the reasoning employed is so clearly wrong, the warning bells should sound.

Ding dong.

2019.01.26 HOW THEY PLAY(ED) US

[This was published in *Veterans Today*, Jan. 27, 2019.[50] N.B.: I am not a vet, nor do I share the editorial views of VT re "Zionism," which have nothing to do with this article. I was just glad that Gordon Duff agreed to publish such a long piece, which might indeed be of interest to Vietnam veterans. Unfortunately I did not get any substantive replies, because as I wrote in a comment:

> I sent copies of this to Chomsky, Scott, Newman, et al. None of these three have replied, which encourages me to think I got it right. On the other hand, it's too bad because they, if anyone — since they are all dedicated paper chasers — would be able to confirm or deny what I seem to have discovered, namely, the deceitful treatment of the (actual) Gravel Pentagon Papers by the New York Times' selective and misleading summary of same in their book, also called "The Pentagon Papers" (Bantam paperback). I couldn't even find some of the crucial texts the NYT quoted to make their points. So either I missed something or the NYT authors were deliberately deceitful, making stuff up or getting it from secret unnamed sources. At best they were extremely careless in citing their sources. If I am wrong, document sleuths like Newman, Scott and Chomsky should be able to set me straight. Instead

they have chosen to ignore me. Sometimes silence speaks louder than words.

As far as I know, Chomsky has not changed his mind on the issues I discuss here.[51]]

Oliver Stone says he heard about L. Fletcher Prouty, the real-life "Mr. X" in Stone's film *JFK*, from Jim Garrison. But I know he heard about Nigel Turner's documentary *The Men Who Killed Kennedy*, in which Prouty also features prominently, from me. How do I know this? After I sent him (Stone) my review of the Turner film,[52] he replied on July 14, 1989: "I will look for the film you mention, but I am fully occupied now with three films and cannot pursue at this point." One year later he was meeting with Prouty in Washington. I surmise from that that Stone watched the Turner film, was as impressed with Prouty's performance as I was, and created a role for him in *JFK*.

The Turner film aired in the US in September 1991, three years after it had come out in the UK and internationally. I saw the German version, *Präsidentenmord*, in November 1988. *JFK* came out in December 1991. Why did it take so long for the Turner film to appear in the US? It's a better film, in my opinion, if only because it is not fiction, and has a much greater emotional impact (at least it did on me), but it was immediately overshadowed by the Stone blockbuster and the ensuing firestorm of controversy. I was and remain skeptical of Time Warner's motives in producing the film, as I wrote in my review of the Stone film[53] and later in the introduction to *Looking for the Enemy*:

> When information and ideas gain enough momentum on their own to become dangerous, that is, when they spread among the population despite monumental efforts of the mainstream media to confine them to marginalized political groups ("extremists," left and right) and wackos ("conspiracy buffs"), the strategy of

suppression–since it cannot become overt–is replaced by a direct offensive. Fire can be fought with fire, as long as the firefighters are under control. Hence *JFK*.

JFK was released in December 1991, three months after the Turner film was finally given limited exposure–on A&E cable in September 1991. This was no accident. The Stone film tells the whole story, but as a work of "fiction," it is much easier to discredit than a documentary. Whatever impact the Turner film might have had was lost in the furor over JFK. I don't doubt Oliver Stone's intentions. He is a vet, i.e., a victim; I was a draft-dodger and protester. But we feel the same rage. The question is, what was Time Warner's interest in producing the film? Money is one answer, of course, but it is not enough. The largest propaganda machine on earth is not in the business of fomenting revolution, even for big bucks. And there is no doubt that *JFK* is a – potentially – revolutionary film. Why should Big Brother's favorite mouthpiece make a revolutionary film?

The answer is clear. *JFK* was intended to be exactly what it has become: the assassination film to end all assassination films. Stone wrote the message loud and clear across the silver screen, but the media campaign against it was louder. The result was a general consensus among the skeptical that the truth was unknowable, and even deeper resignation among those of us who believed the film was the truth. I'm not the only person who has asked himself: "If that doesn't do it, what will?" Thanks to *JFK*, despite Stone's good intentions, the assassination is a burnt-out case. It will not flare up again soon. It is Old News.

I think the past 27 years have proved my point. The big guns were ready and waiting as soon as the film hit the theaters. Officialdom was certainly well aware of everything Time Warner was doing, Garrison had published *On the Trail of the Assassins* in 1988, fingering the CIA and Kennedy's decision to withdraw from Vietnam as the perpetrators and the primary motive, respectively, just as he had in his earlier (1970) book *A Heritage of Stone*. The difference was that this time Oliver Stone read the book. He was given a copy in December 1988 and, according to Patricia Lambert, was

> "deeply moved and appalled" by Garrison's story. Until then, he had thought little about the assassination and had accepted the conclusion of the Warren Report... Garrison, Stone said, opened his eyes... In Garrison's story, Stone had found his own personal Rosetta stone, an explanation for why he had ended up in the jungles of southeast Asia.[54]

Garrison and Prouty had both published in Freedom magazine[55] (Prouty's articles therein were the basis of his 1992 book *JFK and Vietnam: The CIA, Vietnam and the Plot to Assassinate John F. Kennedy*) and Prouty read the manuscript of Garrison's book, so all three were well acquainted by the time Stone contacted Prouty in July 1990 and asked him to consult on the film. But Prouty was not the only "military expert" consultant on the film. After the film came out, and after Prouty's book was published, he wrote to me (Oct. 14, 1992):

> [John] Newman is an active duty U.S. Army Major in Intelligence. He lives in Odenton, MD on the border of Ft. Meade which is the headquarters of the National Security Agency. I believe he is on duty with them and that he was told to infiltrate the Stone organization with his phony book [*JFK and Vietnam*, Warner Books, 1992]. He tried hard to get me to work with him; but I recognized his game and then he got mad at me. He is the guy who gave all the lies to Robert Sam Anson for that libelous job that appeared in *Esquire* ["The Shoot-

ing of JFK," *Esquire*, Nov. 1, 1991[56]] Newman is bad news...but I know the type all too well. Stone had no protection. I had warned him; but the NSA/Newman approach was too smooth. Newman screwed up the film's accuracy.

One of the things Prouty emphasized strongly was that everything in Vietnam up until March 1965 was under the control of the CIA, not the military. "Researchers and students fail to see in JFK's hard-hitting words, 'the bulk of U.S. personnel out before the end of 1965' that he was not predicting the end of a war we were not ourselves fighting; but that he was getting the 'make-war' gang of the CIA out of Southeast Asia" (his letter to me, Jan. 19, 1993).

As for the putative "secrecy" of JFK's withdrawal plan (as elaborated by Newman in *JFK and Vietnam*, 1992), and the putative "conditionality" of withdrawal on "victory" (as elaborated by Chomsky in *Rethinking Camelot, 1993*), Prouty said:

> His [JFK's] policy was not predicated on some "military campaign progressing well," And of course no one in 1963 was so stupid as to say, "If we win the war, we will withdraw." If we had had a war to win, then winning would be victory and that is an unconditional term by itself. We could win and stay there as we have done in Germany and Japan, since the end of WWII. Instead we lost [in Vietnam] and then left. That's a hell of a difference. [His letter to me, Jan. 19, 1993]

So for Prouty, Kennedy's withdrawal plan was aimed at the CIA, not the military:

> We had military personnel there aiding the Vietnamese and supporting the CIA. It was like the Indonesia rebellion and the Bay of Pigs. We had military there but only in a support role. After all that was the limit of the NSC [National Security Council] authority that estab-

lished the parameters of my own office, i.e. support.

No one had ever visualized that such a minimum cadre was there on any "assumption [my word; Chomsky insisted on "condition" — see below] of military success." The military did not arrive until 1965.The removal of "U.S. personnel by the end of 1965" was simply that. JFK was not going to add to what was there, in fact he was taking 1,000 men home in 1963. He was just leaving and letting the South Vietnamese do the best they could with our aid and money. [His letter to me, Jan. 19, 1993]

Prouty describes his first meeting with Newman, which must have been sometime in 1990:

After several calls Newman pleaded with me to meet with him. I did not know him and did not know that he had somehow gotten into the Stone group. I had turned him down many times because I saw no reason for it. One day I was going to be at the National Press Club; so I told him I would be there. I went after I had had lunch with someone else and expected it to be brief.

He introduced himself as a student working on a Ph.D. He did not call himself Major, nor did he mention the Army, Intelligence or NSA. Nor did he mention Stone. He said he needed some help with his thesis on the subject of NSAM #263. He wanted to know if it existed and if so was it formal, etc. I could not believe that someone who claimed to have studied Vietnam for 15 years did not know about NSAM #263 and its great significance. I told him to go to the library, get the Gravel edition of the Pentagon Papers, open Vol. II and find NSAM #263. That would be the Bundy "Cover Letter" only. He would have to turn back many pages and find the content, i.e. McNamara/Taylor "Trip Report." Put that together and he'd have NSAM #263. I got up to leave as he still pleaded with me to stay and discuss other things. Then he said something about wanting to work with Stone. I just turned and said something like, "You had better do your own homework first."

I was completely perplexed by that meeting. How could he be an expert, and be writing a book? How could Stone need him? To get that question off my back I called Stone's office and asked if some fellow named Newman had been there. The answer was "Yes" but they could not explain in what capacity. (I know all too well that the CIA and the NSA use ranking go-betweens to open the door for special agents such as Newman. That could be his role, i.e. the role of a mole.) From that time on I just avoided him.

Later as with the Anson case I kept discovering that Newman was constantly setting me up, even with Stone, from behind the scenes. [His letter to me, Jan. 19, 1993]

Prouty's book appeared in the same year as Newman's book, but Newman beat him to it (February 1992). According to Anthony and Robbyn Summers ("The Ghosts of November," *Vanity Fair*, Dec. 1994), Newman did not retire from US Army Intelligence until August 1994 (his last assignment was as Executive Military Assistant to the Director of the National Security Agency at Ft. Meade, 1988-90[57]), so he was still on active duty with the NSA while he was writing his book and consulting on the Stone film. This in itself raises questions about the motives and intentions of someone coming directly from the heart of the military and intelligence establishment and supposedly supporting the thesis that the president was assassinated by the same military and intelligence establishment. I still fail to understand why I seem to be the only person, even within the so-called assassination "research community," to have even brought this up. I wrote an "open letter" to Newman in November 1994[58] to which, strangely, only Michael Parenti replied, defending Newman from my "attack," but as I replied to him,[59] my letter had been courteous and fully appropriate. The only other person to react to my letter was Fletcher Prouty, who wholeheartedly approved and wrote a long letter in response on Nov. 5, 1994.

In January 1992, before Newman's book appeared, Alexander Cockburn wrote in *The Nation*, Jan. 6/13 ("J.F.K. and JFK"):

> Newman's *JFK and Vietnam* first came into the offices of Sheridan Square Press, Ray and Schaap's publishing house, whence it was passed on to Stone, who assisted in its dispatch to Warner Books (part of the conglomerate backing *JFK*), which is publishing the book in February.

So Cockburn had an advance copy of the book, which he proceeded to savage mercilessly. This would not be noteworthy except for the underlying relationships of the people involved. Cockburn tells us that Bill Schaap and Ellen Ray also published Garrison's *On the Trail of the Assassins* (1988) and, as already mentioned, gave a copy to Stone, and were also the publishers of *Covert Action Quarterly*[60] (formerly *Covert Action Information Bulletin*) and *Lies of Our Times*[61] (both now defunct). Noam Chomsky was a frequent contributor to LOOT, and he told me in his letter of May 15, 1989 that CAIB was "Quite a good rag. I write for it a lot." This was puzzling since I could find only two articles of his in all the back issues, one of which (No. 32, summer 1989) was simply an abbreviated version of the other (No. 26, summer 1986) both identically titled "Libya in US Demonology."

Obviously Schaap and Ray differed sharply with their former close colleague Chomsky over the Kennedy issue, and Cockburn puts his acerbic touch on it:

> Ray...has long felt that history did a U-turn for the worse when conspiracy laid J.F.K. low. Why the publishers of *Covert Action Information Bulletin* and *Lies of Our Times* should take this position I'm not sure, unless we take a biographical approach and argue that maybe it all goes back to Ellen's Catholic girlhood in Massachusetts, with an icon of J.F.K. on the wall.

I was corresponding intensively with Chomsky at the time (1992-93), and I asked him if he knew Cockburn and Christopher Hitchens (another *Nation* columnist): "Yes," he said. "Very well, in fact. In the case of Alex Cockburn, we are in very regular contact, and have a good deal of exchange as well" (March 3, 1992). In May I published my own review of the Stone film,[62] and I sent Chomsky a copy. He replied (May 21, 1992), in the first of several long letters, that Cockburn's review was, "so far,"

> the only one in print that does justice to the factual record. Perhaps I should abstain from comment on this, since I did a lot of the background research for it (though what he wrote is his way of using it).

The reader of Cockburn's review, then, should not be surprised to recognize the same arguments reappearing, first in Chomsky's article in *Z* magazine in September 1992, "Vain Hopes, False Dreams,"[63] and later in his 1993 book *Rethinking Camelot*.

In his July 1, 1992 letter (11 single-spaced pages!), Chomsky said the only positive thing he ever said about any of my arguments: "Your letters, incidentally, have helped me clarify the issues to myself, as I hope will show up in what I'm writing about this." He said he had "about 100 pages in draft" (July 1, 1992). The book, *Rethinking Camelot*, turned out to be 148 pages, plus index and footnotes — in which by the way I found no acknowledgement of my "helpful" arguments!

Chomsky's "Vain Hopes, False Dreams," a prequel to the book, appeared in the September issue of *Z*, and I wrote a letter to the editor[64] about that, with a copy to Chomsky. *Z* did not print my letter, but Chomsky replied in what I suppose he hoped would be our last exchange on the subject:

> I'm afraid that I'll have no more to say about this matter unless you can come up with some particle of evidence, however fragile, to suggest that your beliefs about JFK and the assassination have some merit, and some reason why the huge mass of evidence to the contrary must be entirely disregarded and ignored, as you demand. [January 7, 1993]

Just to recap briefly, Chomsky said (and still does) there was no withdrawal plan, ergo there could have been no reversal of it. This despite Ch. 3, Vol. 2 of the Gravel *Pentagon Papers* (of which he himself edited Volume 5) titled "Phased Withdrawal of U.S. Forces, 1962-1964"[65] because, Chomsky said, Recommendations B 2-3 of the McNamara-Taylor report[66] of Oct. 2, 1963 constitute an "explicit condition of victory" on the proposed withdrawal, so that it was not a "withdrawal policy" but a "withdrawal *after victory*" policy. I kept insisting that this is not what the document says, that it could only be interpreted as based on an *assumption* of "military progress" ("progress" not being the same as "victory"), not a *condition*.

Painfully aware that I, one of the least famous linguists in the world, was arguing with the most famous linguist in the world about the difference between an assumption and a condition, I repeatedly pointed out that the wording of the McNamara-Taylor report, i.e.:

> I.A.1 The military campaign has made great progress and continues to progress.
>
> I.B.2 ...It should be possible to withdraw the bulk of U.S. personnel by that time [the end of 1965].

was exactly analogous to sentences like:

Barbara is doing well with her studies.

She should graduate by the end of next year.

But I got nowhere. Withdrawal was absolutely conditioned, if and only if there was "victory." And never mind that "victory" was defined in the same document (B 6) as "reducing it [the Viet Cong insurgency] to proportions manageable by the national security forces of the GVN [South Vietnamese], unassisted by the presence of U.S. military forces," or that if "victory" had been understood in the usual sense of, say, the Allied victory in World War II, there hardly would have been a need for a "withdrawal plan."

The closest I came to any kind of agreement with the famous professor was when I finally managed to get him to use the word "assumption" rather than "condition." He wrote on Jan. 7, 1993:

> Let's distinguish two different theses: (1) the M-thesis (yours), and (2) the C-thesis (mine). The M-thesis holds that there were plans to withdraw from Vietnam, "predicated on the assumption of military success" (your words). The C-thesis holds that JFK planned to withdraw without victory, that is, whether the assumption of military success were to hold or not.

What he called the "C-thesis" he should have called the "N-thesis," since it was John Newman's thesis that he was really attacking, as he did in the book that appeared later that year (*Rethinking Camelot*). His own "C-thesis" was precisely the opposite — that JFK did *not* plan to withdraw without victory. Hurray, I thought, he got my point. However:

> The M-thesis is uncontroversially true, and completely — totally — without interest. Furthermore, it has been known to be true, and uninteresting, for almost 30 years. The basic content of the withdrawal plans was made public at once, in October 1963.

The C-thesis (the Newman thesis), however, said Chomsky, is refuted "across the board, without exception, from whatever angle we approach it." He says of Newman's book:

> Newman's work is perhaps the most incompetent and comical piece of work ever called "history." ... I wouldn't say that Newman totally destroys his [own] withdrawal-without-victory thesis, but he certainly weakens an already hopelessly implausible case. [His letter to me, July 1, 1992]

Strangely, although Chomsky devoted virtually the whole of *Rethinking Camelot* to demolishing Newman's book, Newman, who has gone on to produce the first three of a multi-volume study of the JFK assassination and has a website devoted to the subject,[67] has never seen fit to respond directly to any of Chomsky's arguments or even mention his name, except to say in the Appendix to the revised edition of *JFK and Vietnam* (2017) that "Noam Chomsky claimed that I had made a saint out of JFK."[68]

Howard Jones entered the fray in 2003 with *Death of a Generation*, which according to the summary on Amazon "argues that Kennedy intended to withdraw the great bulk of American soldiers and pursue a diplomatic solution to the crisis in Vietnam....Jones argues forcefully that if Kennedy had not been assassinated, his withdrawal plan would have spared the lives of 58,000 Americans and countless Vietnamese."[69] Here again, Newman is cited copiously (35 times), but Chomsky not at all. James Douglass, whose *JFK and the Unspeakable* (2008) is considered by many to be the "definitive" work on the assassination, also accepts Newman's version of the Vietnam issue and cites him 24 times, but doesn't mention Chomsky at all.

I seem to be the only person who has gone toe-to-toe with Chomsky on this issue, in our correspondence, which I documented as thoroughly as I could and posted on the internet in 1993 and published later as an addendum to *Looking for the Enemy* (2007), and also in my articles "Chomsky on JFK and Vietnam " (1993), "Rethinking Chomsky" (1994), "My Beef with Chomsky" (2000), and "Chomsky and Newman – The False Debate" (Nov. 2009).[70]

In 2003 there was an exchange between Chomsky and James Galbraith, a respected historian and son of the famous economist, who wrote in the *Boston Review* ("Exit Strategy," Oct./ Nov. 2003[71]) that "most Vietnam historians...have asserted continuity between Kennedy's policy and Lyndon Johnson's." That is precisely the point I made to Chomsky in my letter of June 18, 1992[72] and became Ch. 2.3 of *Looking for Enemy*. Chomsky's reply at the time (July 1, 1992) was:

> The quotes you give to illustrate that histories have falsified the record are, in this case, pretty much accurate. As far as any evidence goes, LBJ "took the same view of the importance of Vietnam" as JFK. He did "follow Kennedy's lead" in all important respects, and JFK's advisers agreed until the thing began to go sour and they sought ways to distance themselves from the disaster. LBJ did indeed "inherit and expand the VN policy of his predecessor." I don't know why you find these statements questionable. They are completely supported by the huge internal record. JFK's policy was withdrawal <u>after victory</u>; LBJ's was the same. As assessments of the precondition changed, so did policy. That's about it.

In other words, most historians have asserted continuity because there *was* continuity.

Galbraith, though corroborating my point on the false impression of continuity given by Vietnam historians, makes a puzzling remark about the *Pentagon Papers* (henceforth PP Gravel unless otherwise noted):

> You will not find it [Kennedy's *decision* to withdraw]

in Leslie Gelb's editorial summary in the Gravel edition of *The Pentagon Papers*, even though several documents that are important to establishing the case for a Kennedy decision to withdraw were published in that edition. Nor, with just three exceptions prior to last spring's publication of Howard Jones's *Death of a Generation*—a milestone in the search for difficult, ferociously hidden truth—will you find it elsewhere in 30 years of historical writing on Vietnam.

But Gelb's summary of Ch. 3, Vol.2, "Phased Withdrawal of U.S. Forces, 1962-1964,"[73] begins with the sentence: "A formal planning and budgetary process for the phased withdrawal of U.S. forces from Vietnam was begun amid the euphoria and optimism of July 1962, and was ended in the pessimism of March 1964." Perhaps Galbraith's emphasis on the word *decision*, as if it had an exceptional meaning, is the point, but why should that word be more important than the word *policy*, which is used more than three times more often in the document and almost always collocated with *withdrawal*? Where there is a policy, there must have been decisions, and policy was set, as I think everyone agrees, with the issuance of National Security Action Memorandum (NSAM) 263, which was signed by McGeorge Bundy for the president on Oct. 11. What difference does it make whether the *decision* to sign it was made on Oct. 2, 3, 5 or 11?

Galbraith, following Newman, favors Oct. 5 as decision-day, and quotes Newman quoting Michael Forrestal's memo of a meeting with the president on that day:

> The President also said that *our decision* to remove 1,000 U.S. advisors by December of this year should not be raised formally with Diem. Instead the action should be carried out routinely as part of our general posture of withdrawing people when they are no longer needed.[74] [Emphasis added.]

Galbraith treats this, as Newman does, as if it were a discovery:

> The passage illustrates two points: (a) that a decision
> was in fact made on that day, and (b) that despite the
> earlier announcement of McNamara's *recommendation*,
> the October 5 decision was not a ruse or pressure tactic
> to win reforms from Diem (as Richard Reeves, among
> others, has contended but a *decision* to begin with-
> drawal irrespective of Diem or his reactions.

But this has been part of the record since PP Gravel: "Three
days later, on 5 October, in another meeting with the President, followed by another NSC meeting, the McNamara-Taylor
recommendations themselves were addressed. The President
'approved the military recommendations contained in the report.'" PP Gravel also says "The President approved the military
recommendations" at a meeting with McNamara and Taylor
and the NSC on Oct. 3. Furthermore, the president would
never have ordered the public White House statement of Oct. 2
unless he had already decided to accept the recommendations.
PP Gravel says this "statement of United States policy was approved by the President," so the approval must have occurred
on or before Oct. 2. It is true that the text of NSAM 263[75] mentions the Oct. 5 meeting at which the recommendations were
"considered" and "approved," but the important date is still
Oct. 11, when the NSAM was issued.

So I do not understand why Galbraith accuses Gelb of ignoring
JFK's decision to withdraw since it is obviously the subject of
both the summary and the body of Ch. 3, Vol. 2[76] of PP Gravel.
But more importantly, I think, and what Galbraith, Newman
and as far as I can tell everyone else seem to have overlooked
is how the popular version of the PP, which is quite different
from PP Gravel, also ignores Kennedy's withdrawal plan and
creates the same illusion of continuity, so that we can add this
to Galbraith's list of "30 years of historical writing on Viet-

nam" guilty of this distortion. This "popular version" of the leaked PP was published by more than a dozen newspapers, and it would be interesting to find out if and how the other newspapers treated the material differently than the New York Times.[77] But I will use the New York Times version (henceforth PP NYT), which they also published as a paperback in 1971, to make my point.

PP NYT became available in July 1971 and was not really a "version" or "edition" of the PP at all; it was a summary by NYT reporters with some excerpts from the actual documents, the complete (and only) edition of which is the four-volume so-called "Gravel edition" (PP Gravel) published by Beacon Press in October 1971 (plus a fifth volume of essays edited by Noam Chomsky and Howard Zinn, 1972). As I also pointed out in *Looking for the Enemy* (and to Chomsky in my letter of Aug. 3, 1992), PP NYT glosses over the entire chapter of PP Gravel covering the "Phased Withdrawal of U.S. Forces, 1962-1964"[78] thus:

> The Pentagon account [i.e., the actual Pentagon Papers, of which this is only a summary], moreover, presents the picture of an unbroken chain of decision-making from the final months of the Kennedy Administration into the early months of the Johnson Administration, whether in terms of the political view of the American stakes in Vietnam, the advisory build-up or the hidden growth of covert warfare against North Vietnam. [Bantam, 1971, p. 114]

This is simply not true. PP NYT does not mention NSAM 263 at all, the "advisory build-up" is mentioned as if there were no "advisory build-down," i.e., "phased withdrawal," at all, and the "hidden growth of covert warfare" is presented quite slyly as having begun under Kennedy, whereas it actually began under Johnson:

> Particularly in the sphere of covert operations against

North Vietnam, which became a prelude to the Tonkin Gulf clashes in 1964, the Pentagon narrative describes a smooth transition in the decision-making process. The Honolulu conference, set up under President Kennedy, ordered planning for a stepped-up program of what the account calls "non-attributable hit-and-run" raids against North Vietnam. In his first Vietnam policy document, on Nov. 26, President Johnson gave his personal sanction to the planning for these operations. [PP NYT, p. 189]

The Nov. 26 policy document, of course, was NSAM 273. At the end of this chapter PP NYT offers in addition to their summary a few "key documents" from PP Gravel, each adorned with a boldface heading. This one, NSAM 273, is titled "Order by Johnson Reaffirming Kennedy's Position on Vietnam" (pp. 232-233) and includes some "excerpts" from NSAM 273 and, in italics, "the study's paraphrase" of this document. The excerpted paragraphs are Paragraphs 2, 4, 5 and 3, in that (jumbled) order. NSAM 273,[79] however, was not declassified until May 1978, so how did these paragraphs, even in jumbled order, get into PP NYT in 1971? They are not in PP Gravel. It would seem the NYT had access to documents that were not in the PP at all, and published them as if they were. I find it hard to believe this, even as I write, but I see no other explanation.

PP NYT concludes the section on NSAM 273 in italics, which means this is "the study's paraphrase," that is, the words of Leslie Gelb and his team of writers, as follows:

> And in conclusion, plans were requested for clandestine operations by the GVN against the North and also for operations up to 50 kilometers into Laos; and, as a justification for such measures, State was directed to develop a strong, documented case "to demonstrate to the world the degree to which the Viet Cong is controlled, sustained and supplied from Hanoi, through

Laos and other channels..." (p. 233).

Now, where did this text come from? I could not find anything like it in PP Gravel, and I searched through all the chapters of Volumes 2 and 3. The portion enclosed in quotation marks is from Para. 10 of NSAM 273, but again, this text was still classified in 1971 and does not occur in PP Gravel. So where did it come from? Wherever it came from, it is inaccurate, because the actual text of Para. 8 of NSAM 273, which we now have, is:

> With respect to Laos, a plan should be developed and submitted for approval by higher authority for military operations up to a line up to 50 kilometers inside Laos, together with political plans for minimizing the international hazards of such an enterprise. Since it is agreed that operational responsibility for such undertakings should pass from CAS to MACV, this plan should include a redefined method of political guidance for such operations, since their timing and character can have an intimate relation to the fluctuating situation in Laos.

As a side note, we might note that "CAS" is a "code name for CIA" according to the glossary at the back of the NYT book, and the transfer of responsibility from the CIA to MACV (the military) accords with what Prouty told me had been JFK's plan since the Bay of Pigs: to get the CIA out of the "make war business."

But yet again, where did this text come from? I can find no mention of "clandestine operations by the GVN against the North," either in PP Gravel (which is all the NYT supposedly had access to) or in the actual document (NSAM 273).

Galbraith seems to follow Newman and Peter Dale Scott in asserting that LBJ's NSAM 273 shows a significant departure from JFK's policy. In his 1972 essay in Vol. 5[80] of PP Gravel, Scott reconstructs the then still classified NSAM 273 and tries to show that it differs significantly from the McNamara-Taylor recommendations of Oct. 2 (that are in PP Gravel). According to Newman (in *JFK and Vietnam*, 1992), the *draft* of NSAM 273, written on Nov. 21 for JFK but not seen or approved by him, differs significantly from the version written for and approved by LBJ on Nov. 26, namely, in the revision of Para. 7.[81] Both Newman and Chomsky spend a lot of time making and rebutting this argument, respectively, in *JFK and Vietnam* and *Rethinking Camelot*), but I don't think it matters at all. Like the question of exactly when JFK made the decision that resulted in NSAM 263, the question of exactly when LBJ reversed that decision is not important since we know that it came almost immediately after the assassination, as described in Ch. 3, Vol. 2 of PP Gravel.[82]

What strikes me as noteworthy about this draft of NSAM 273 is the date of its declassification: Jan. 31, 1991. I would like to know who requested this declassification. The final version was declassified in May 1978. When and why did the draft become important enough to require declassification in 1991?

I will speculate: it provided a straw man for people to argue about. *JFK* (the film) would appear in December of that year (1991) followed by a host of articles pro and contra, conveniently collected in *JFK: The Book of the Film* (Applause Books, 1992), Newman's book a couple of months later, and Chomsky's book the next year. Here is the relevant chronology:

Nov. 26, 1963 (at the earliest) - March 1964 (at the very latest) Reversal of JFK's Vietnam withdrawal policy

... Many years of silence, that is, depiction of continuity.

1988 Publication of Garrison's *On the Trail of the Assassins*; release of Turner's *The Men Who Killed Kennedy*.

1991 Release of Stone's *JFK*; declassification of draft of NSAM 273

1992 Publication of Newman's *JFK and Vietnam*

1993 Publication of Chomsky's *Rethinking Camelot*

I agree, then, in principle with Galbraith that the policy reversal after the assassination (depending on which date between Nov. 22 and March 24, when "the policy of phase out and withdrawal and all the plans and programs oriented to it" ended "de jure") was a "difficult, ferociously hidden truth...in 30 years of historical writing on Vietnam," although I disagree on the dates. He seems to be taking the 30 years (actually 32) between the publication of the PP (1971) and the publication of Howard Jones' "milestone" *Death of a Generation* (2003), but I see the "milestones" differently. I see the first one as the thing itself, the thing people have been ignoring for decades and then, much more recently, arguing about, which is the policy reversal. The second milestone is the Stone film in 1991, which finally publicized that event and its possible significance — the event that Chomsky says is "uncontroversially true, and completely — totally — without interest" and "has been known to be true, and uninteresting, for almost 30 years."

Galbraith begins his article asking: "What, at the moment of his death, was John F. Kennedy's policy toward Vietnam?" We must note, first of all, that this has only become a public question since Stone's film. It is true that the withdrawal plan was announced publicly on Oct. 2, 1963, and subsequently reported in the newspapers. For example, I have a copy of the front page of the Pacific *Stars and Stripes* of Oct. 4, 1963 with the banner headline "U.S. Troops Seen Out of Viet by '65." The front page UPI story says:

> The White House said Wednesday night after hearing a report from a two-man inspection team that the U.S. military effort in the Republic of Vietnam should be completed by the end of 1965.

The question is, however, how deeply this news penetrated the public consciousness, and the answer can be amply provided by a search of the newspapers after the assassination. Was there any outcry, any questioning whatsoever, about the change in policy that occurred in the days or weeks following Nov. 22? I would be very surprised to find such protest, because as PP Gravel[83] says:

> On 22 November 1963, President Kennedy was assassinated. The consequences were to set an institutional freeze on the direction and momentum of U.S. Vietnam policy. Universally operative was a desire to avoid change of any kind during the critical interregnum period of the new Johnson Administration. Both the President and the governmental establishment consciously strove for continuity, with respect to Vietnam no less than in other areas. In Vietnam this continuity meant that the phase-out concept, the CPSVN [Comprehensive Plan for South Vietnam] withdrawal plan, and the MAP [Military Assistance Program] programs probably survived beyond the point they might have otherwise.

Chomsky, and as Galbraith says, "most Vietnam historians" are merely reinforcing the idea that there was no policy change (what I call "The Second Biggest Lie,"[84] the first being the Warren Report). In accordance with this principal requirement of maintaining the *appearance* of continuity, the popular (i.e., widely read) "version" of the PP, PP NYT, as I have shown, simply ignores the chapter in PP Gravel which nevertheless presents the facts clearly enough that if they had been widely *publicized*, as opposed to being merely *published* in a four-volume hardcover book that few people would buy or read, the consequences might have been different.

The only work I know of that reacted astutely to the policy

change is a book written in 1966 called *The Politics of Escalation in Vietnam*, by Franz Schurmann, Peter Dale Scott, and Reginald Zelnik (Greenwich: Fawcett Publications). The book is now out of print so I will quote the relevant passages entirely (pp. 32-34):

> ...precisely at a moment when neutralist sentiment was increasing in Saigon and elsewhere, the shift from a moderate to a militant government in Saigon was accompanied by a shift in Washington's declared policy from limited to unlimited support for the Vietnam war. It is important to recall, in this regard, the stated intention of the Kennedy administration, as announced by McNamara and Taylor from the White House on October 2, 1963, which was to withdraw most U.S. forces from South Vietnam by the end of 1965.*
>
>> *Footnote: Three weeks after the assassination, on December 19 and 20, 1963 [sic: actually 27 days], McNamara and CIA chief John A. McCone visited Saigon to evaluate the war efforts of the new Saigon government. "McNamara told the junta leaders that the United States was prepared to help...as long as aid was needed" (NYT, January 2, 1964, p. 7).
>
> The first public indication of a change in the U.S. intentions came in a letter from President Johnson to Duong Van Minh at New Year's, 1964, which promised "the fullest measure of support...in achieving victory." *The New York Times* commented, "By implication, the message erased the previous date for withdrawing the bulk of United States forces from Vietnam by the end of 1965" (NYT, January 2, 1964, p. 7).*
>
>> *Footnote: The letter reportedly renounced unequivocally "any prospect for a neutralist solu-

tion for South Vietnam...at a time when neutralist sentiment has been gaining currency in some political and intellectual circles here" (in South Vietnam). (NYT, January 2, 1964.)

A more explicit official indication of *reversal of policy* came in the testimony of Secretary McNamara before the Armed Services Committee, on January 27, three days before the coup [of Jan 30, 1964;[85] my emphasis]:

> The survival of an independent government in South Vietnam is so important to the security of Southeast Asia and to the free world that I can conceive of no alternative other than to take all necessary measures within our capability to prevent a Communist victory. (M. Raskin and B. Fall, *The Vietnam Reader*, New York, 1965, p. 394)

Immediately after the coup, James Reston reported from Washington:

> We are probably coming to the end of the period when the United States would neither fight nor negotiate. And we are probably approaching a new phase when both fighting and negotiating will be stepped up (NYT, January 31, 1964, p. 26).

Military developments in 1964 were to confirm Reston's prediction with respect to the fighting, if not to negotiations. In retrospect, *it is hard to deny that, shortly before the coup, the United States had made the crucial decision to reverse the policy, announced during the last days of President Kennedy's administration, of gradually withdrawing U.S. troops from South Vietnam. Was it all a coincidence that a change in leadership in Washington was followed by a change in policy, and a change in policy by a corresponding change in Saigon's* *government?** [My emphasis]

> *Footnote: Hanoi Radio on February 4 also saw in the coup evidence that "the United States had blotted out its decision to withdraw part of the United States troops from South Vietnam" (FBIS Daily Report, February 5, 1964, JJJ6)

Administration officials have never yet seen fit to defend publicly this important reversal of policy; thus they have not identified the threat that brought it about. Was it a radical increase in the strength of the opposing forces? As far as we know, none has ever been alleged. Or was it a radical decline in Saigon's will to resist, with a corresponding disposition toward the political proposals of de Gaulle and the NLF? [My emphasis]

One conclusion can be asserted unequivocally: The United States increased its commitment to a prolongation of the Vietnam war at a time when the drift of the Saigon junta and of public opinion was in the direction of negotiations for a neutralized Vietnam. The threat of a serious divergence between Washington's interest in the war and Saigon's was temporarily postponed by the success of the January coup.

It is interesting to note that this book was cited by Noam Chomsky in his 1967 essay "The Responsibility of Intellectuals"[86] in a footnote to illustrate his point that "the power of the government's propaganda apparatus is such that the citizen who does not undertake a research project on the subject can hardly hope to confront government pronouncements with fact." The book, he says, resulted from a "Citizens' White Paper" and "presented evidence of American rejection of UN initiatives for diplomatic settlement, just prior to the major escalation of February, 1965…"

He could just as well have said that the peace overtures ignored by the US were "uncontroversially true" and "known to be true" by people like himself and Schurmann et al. who read the newspapers assiduously, but precisely the point he is making is that "known to be true" is a very relative thing. *To whom* is it known, and by how many? The "government's propaganda apparatus" controls the mass media and therefore what the mass of people know, or think they know, and therefore what they think.

So why does this same Noam Chomsky tell me that just because something is "on the record" or "known to be true" by *some people*, it is therefore of no interest? He knows better than this, as he says in this 1967 essay. What *some people* know is not the same as what *many* or *most* people know. Again, thinking back on this exchange, I am just astounded at having to make a point that is not only screamingly obvious, but one which Chomsky himself has made many times, including in this 1967 essay. He even has his own term for it: "Orwell's problem," as opposed to "Plato's problem"; cf. Preface, *Knowledge of Language: It's Nature, Origin, and Use*, 1986.

But unlike Schurmann et al., Chomsky pays no attention to the question whether it was "a coincidence that a change in leadership in Washington was followed by a change in policy." It is clear that he agrees that the 1964 peace overtures were ignored by the US in favor of escalation, but at the same time as he is demonstrating his resistance to the "propaganda apparatus" by acknowledging these facts, he seems quite oblivious to the other glaring fact that Schurmann et al. point to, namely, the "coincidental" reversal of policy following the "coincidental" murder of the policy-maker (the president). He completely ignores this. Why? Even if he hated JFK with a purple passion, as a cognitive scientist, or as a natural scientist, or as a person of common sense, he could not have helped being struck by this "coincidence," especially after reading and citing with approval a paper by others who made the point explicitly.

The question Schurmann et al. asked, apparently alone in 1966, but was not asked again until 1991, still stands: Was the policy reversal a "coincidence" or not? Galbraith says "After Newman's book, no one seriously disputed that Kennedy was contemplating withdrawal from Vietnam," and that the question now is "Did the withdrawal plans depend on the perception of victory?"[87] But this falls right back into the trap of "the false debate."[88]

The real debate should be about what Kennedy did, and what others did after he was gone. Was there a withdrawal policy or not, was it reversed or not, and if so, why? The first two questions did not even have to be asked by Schurmann et al. in 1966 because the answer was clearly Yes to both — and this was five years *before* the *Pentagon Papers*. The question why still stands, and the question whether the assassination was merely a coincidence follows inevitably from that.

The false debate, as framed and prosecuted by the main antagonists, Newman and Chomsky, is about what Kennedy may or may not have been thinking, what he may have been secretly planning to do, and what he might have done had he lived. All of these questions are inherently unanswerable and susceptible to infinite prolongation. Who started it? Newman, I think. As one enthused reader wrote on Amazon, and which Newman liked enough to repost on his website:

> This essential work examines in detail the Shakespearean machinations of deception and counter-deception that took shape in the hidden maneuverings of a president who was determined to avoid being trapped and determined to never again repeat the mistakes of the Bay of Pigs.[89]

Chomsky, replying to Galbraith in the *Boston Globe* in December 2003, dismisses Newman's deeply flawed account, which establishes its conclusions by elaborate tales of "deception" of JFK by those around him, though "in his heart [JFK] must have known" the truth so we can ignore the documentary record which leaves no trace of what JFK, alone, "had to notice." This strange performance too is reviewed elsewhere in detail, and need not be discussed here.[90]

By "elsewhere" of course he means *Rethinking Camelot*, to which as I have mentioned neither Newman nor anyone else except Galbraith, 16 years ago[91] — and me, repeatedly for the past 26 years ago — have deigned to respond. Chomsky, in his reply to Galbraith a full ten years after the publication of *Rethinking Camelot*, may feel entitled to a bit of vitriol, but his argument has not changed a bit, asserting for the umpteenth time that there is "no hint in the record that he [JFK] contemplated withdrawal without victory." (The word *victory* occurs in his 1104-word article 10 times, that is, ca. once every 100 words.)

Chomsky — and the multitude of his admirers — certainly *does* seriously dispute that Kennedy was contemplating withdrawal *without victory* from Vietnam," an argument which I have tried to show is completely specious, but Galbraith reopens the debate by saying the questions "focused" (after Newman) on four questions, the first of which is: "Did the withdrawal plans depend on the perception of victory?" This moves the ball right back into Chomsky's court. "Depend on" means "conditional," and "victory" means "victory." These are Chomsky's words, and they are his terms for the debate. If you accept them, he wins. But they are inaccurate. So we are back to Step 1, where I was with him in 1992-93.

I'll give it one more try. The withdrawal plan was not *conditional*. It did not "*depend* on the perception of *victory*." It was based on an *assumption* of *military success*. These are the words that Chomsky would not allow into the discussion, as I have described, except ever so briefly, only to dismiss them as "uncontroversial" and "uninteresting." They are, however, much closer to the wording and intended meaning of the documents being discussed (mainly the McNamara-Taylor report of Oct. 2, 1963).[92] The reason he would not allow this vocabulary, as I also told him, is obvious: Once you accept the fact of the policy reversal, you have to ask if it was related to the assassination. This is exactly what Schurmann et al. did. But if you insist that there *was* no policy reversal because there was only a *withdrawal after victory* policy, which never changed, at least until the Tet offensive in 1968, as Chomsky does, then you can say that there was no reversal of the policy because there was no *victory*.

If I were a government propagandist concerned with the potentially dangerous idea that JFK was assassinated because he was threatening to deprive the warmongers of their lucrative Vietnam war ($1 trillion in 2017 dollars;[93] "cost" being income to the war industry and others who profit) I would have seen trouble brewing with the Garrison investigation that started in late 1966. As Garrison recalled in *On the Trail of the Assassins* (1988):

> Certainly, it never crossed my mind that the murder of President Kennedy and the subsequent arrival of half a million members of the American military in Vietnam might be related (pp.12-13).

It was a chance remark by Senator Russell Long expressing doubt about the Warren Commission's findings that piqued his curiosity and started him on his search for the truth about the assassination. The actual trial (against Clay Shaw) was unsuccessful in that the defendant was immediately acquitted, but it got a lot of publicity and brought much hidden information (such as the Zapruder film) to light, with the help of a number of volunteer investigators. The most important of these was a Philadelphia lawyer named Vincent Salandria, who helped

Garrison write his first book, *A Heritage of Stone* (1970). Garrison's conclusions were certainly enough to make the government take notice. As the book is now out of print, I will quote the passages that Salandria quoted to me in his letter of April 6, 2000:[94]

> The question of who killed John Kennedy evolved into the more meaningful query of why he was killed (p. 22).

> The President recognized his inherited obligation and increased the American advisory contingent in South Vietnam. However, he never budged from his refusal to send over American soldiers for combat in its swamps and jungles...The problem grew, however, in the form of Pentagon opposition to his restraint:... (p. 225).

> John Kennedy's desire to prevent an American war in Vietnam was remembered well by men who were close to him (p. 227).

> In the fall of 1963 he issued an order, over the objections of many around him, to reduce American military advisers in South Vietnam immediately by bringing home one thousand U.S. soldiers before the end of 1963. In the spring of 1963, reports his key White House aide, Kenneth P. O'Donnell, he had made up his mind that after his reelection he would take the risk of unpopularity, make a complete withdrawal of American forces from Vietnam. "In 1965, I'll be damned everywhere as a Communist appeaser. But I don't care."

> Shortly before his murder, the public announcement was made by Secretary of Defense McNamara that by 1965 all American personnel would be brought back home. McNamara's announcement was made not from the Pentagon but from the steps of the White House (p. 228).

Salandria had a lot to do with Garrison coming to these con-
clusions. A year and a half before *A Heritage of Stone* was pub-
lished, Salandria, who had published the first critique of the
Warren Report in 1964[95] and worked closely with Garrison
from 1967 to 1969, spoke at an antiwar rally in Central Park in
New York City on June 9, 1968 ("Confronting the Madness of
Our Military")[96] three days after the murder of JFK's brother
Robert and 66 days after the murder of Martin Luther King:

> ... almost all the people who have investigated the
> assassination of President John F. Kennedy recognized
> that the killing was motivated by the desire to per-
> petuate the Cold war which President Kennedy sought
> to end. We feel that the shooting of President Kennedy
> was a foreign policy killing done at the behest of mili-
> tary circles in the United States and executed by opera-
> tives under the control and in the employ of the Central
> Intelligence Agency.

> What changed following the assassination of Presi-
> dent Kennedy was our foreign policy and our form of
> government. Three weeks after the assassination the
> junta leaders in Saigon were told that the United States
> was prepared to help as long as aid was needed. We
> had made the critical decision to reverse the policy
> announced at the end of the Kennedy administration
> to withdraw U.S. troops from Vietnam. In Latin Amer-
> ica, the Johnson government immediately signaled the
> end of Kennedyism by supporting the military regimes
> in the Dominican Republic and Brazil. The Gulf of
> Tonkin incident was generated by the military as a
> monumental fraud — perpetrated on an all-too-un-
> skeptical Congress — to provide an excuse for further
> escalation in Vietnam. So President Kennedy's cour-
> ageous efforts to end the Cold War were shot down
> with him, and the Cold War then grew in intensity and

the democratic processes in the United States eroded in favor of more power to the military.

...There was a Bay of Pigs in which the CIA betrayed President Kennedy. There was a detente with Russia, followed by a test ban treaty which encountered heavy military resistance. And when Kennedy sought to change the Vietnam policy, he was himself fired by the military — killed on his watch. Upon his death, the military became the dominant force in our government.

Salandria said "almost all" the JFK assassination researchers felt the same way he did. But who was listening to them, and who was listening that day in Central Park? Salandria had read Schurmann et al., and quotes from that book in an essay he published in 1971 in a magazine with a tiny readership called, improbably enough, *Computers and Automation*.[97] He adds:

That there should have been a change in Vietnamese policy so immediately after the murder of Kennedy when the external situation in Vietnam did not evoke it, raises serious questions about what caused it in our internal situation. What is at stake here is the issue not of how the assassination was accomplished, but the fundamental question concerning why it was done and which elements were and are behind it. At issue are questions of war and peace that involve the whole of humanity. For the movement for peace in Vietnam not to raise these questions is and has been irresponsible.

This hits the nail precisely on the head, and for the first time, as far as I know. Likewise the rest of the article which is titled "The Assassination of President John F. Kennedy:

A Model of Explanation." The article defies summation and must be read in its entirety — not because it is difficult to understand but because it makes such devastating common sense.

17 years later, In 1988, Garrison wrote his second book, this time with the additional input of Fletcher Prouty, who had written *The Secret Team: The CIA and Its Allies in Control of the United States and the World* (1973) and a series of articles in *Freedom* magazine[98] (where Garrison also published) in the 1980s which became the basis of Prouty's second book *JFK: The CIA, Vietnam and the Plot to Assassinate John F. Kennedy* (1992). Garrison and Prouty had the same message as Salandria: JFK was killed by the CIA, primarily because he was withdrawing from Vietnam. Garrison wrote in *On the Trail*:

> By June of 1963 President Kennedy had directly and eloquently renounced the Cold War in a landmark speech at American University in Washington, D.C., underscoring that the United States and the Soviet Union had to live together peacefully on one small planet.
>
> *But none of these policy changes was as significant, in retrospect, as Kennedy's intention to withdraw all American military personnel from Vietnam* (p. 177; my emphasis).
>
> What remains as the only likely sponsor with both the motive and the capability of murdering the President is the covert action arm of the Central Intelligence Agency (p. 289).
>
> In retrospect, the reason for the assassination is hardly a mystery. It is now abundantly clear from the course that U.S. foreign policy took immediately following November 22, 1963, why the C.I.A.'s covert operations element wanted John Kennedy out of the Oval Office and Lyndon Johnson in it (p. 293).

Is all this plausible? It might not have seemed so 25

years ago. However, now that we know some of the true history of the C.I.A. and its covert operations, the answer is a distinct yes. Assassination is precisely what the Agency knows how to do and what it has done all over the world for policy ends (p. 295).

Books are bad enough from the point of view of the propagandists, but as Allen Dulles reportedly said about possible reactions to the Warren Report, "The American people don't read." The audio-visual mass media, movies and TV, are much more dangerous because they reach greater masses of people more or less simultaneously. The Turner film came out in the UK and Europe in October 1988, the Stone film three years later. What to do? If I were chief propagandist, here is what I would have done in order to keep the damage at a minimum — which turns out to be exactly what happened.

1. I would delay the US release of the Turner film long enough for it to be overshadowed by the Stone film. This was done (Sept. 1988 UK, not shown in US until Sept. 1991; Stone's *JFK* Dec. 1991).

2. I would make sure I had a preview and some control over the Stone film. This was done, via Time Warner.

3. I would insert a "military expert" into the Stone organization via my contacts in Time Warner in order to control the "historical narrative." This (says Prouty) was done in the person of John Newman.

4. I would make sure the film contained enough "dancing with facts," as some reviewers quipped, as well as facts, in order to clearly qualify as fictional. This happened. Stone himself describes the film as a "counter-myth" to the Warren Report.[99]

5. I would mention the Vietnam issue in the film

403

but make sure the blame for the assassination is widely dispersed among "members of the CIA, the Mafia, the military-industrial complex, Secret Service, FBI, and Kennedy's vice-president and then president Lyndon Baines Johnson." This was done, as the citation from Wikipedia shows.

6. I would mention and even flash on the screen (at the end of the film) some of the documents (e.g., NSAM 263, 273) that would be discussed in the anticipated controversy later. This was done.

7. I would declassify the draft of NSAM 273 to provide fodder for the anticipated debate over the significance of NSAM 263, 273, and the 273 draft. This was done on Jan. 31, 1991.

8. I would publish a documented screenplay of the film including a range of pro and contra critiques and various documents useful for discussion. This was done with *JFK: The Book of the Film* (Applause Books [Warner Bros.], 1992). Unfortunately this was published too soon to include Chomsky's rebuttal to Newman, but it didn't matter because for those (few, according to Dulles) Americans who did read, the debate continued in book form (see next).

9. I would have a "credible" book published with a controversial, speculative and vulnerable thesis, i.e., that *JFK had a secret plan to deceive the deceivers and withdraw from Vietnam regardless of the military situation*, which would keep researchers busy and discourage them from asking more dangerous questions, like those that Schurmann et al. asked in 1966. This was done with Newman's *JFK and Vietnam*.

10. I would immediately attack this book with an equally (and for many, much more) "credible" counterargument. This was done by Cockburn, Chomsky, et al.

At the same time, I would encourage the publication of as many books as possible identifying possible conspirators and motives for the assassination in order to make sure focus is not focused *only* on the Vietnam issue, and not *only* on the CIA (as per Garrison, Salandria, and Prouty). For example, I would have been pleased to see the publication of David Scheim's *The Mafia Killed President Kennedy* (the US title is *Contract on America*) in the same year as Garrison's book, 1988. This is a lengthy (480 pp.) and well-resourced book, with 53 pages of footnotes, and describes Kennedy's withdrawal policy quite accurately:

> On October 2, 1963, Defense Secretary McNamara and General Maxwell Taylor reported that it was their objective to terminate the "major part" of U.S. military involvement in Vietnam by 1965. [WH Allen, 1988, p. 187]

Quite surprisingly, in retrospect, Scheim even accepts the idea first proposed by Scott in 1972 ("Vietnamization and the Drama of the Pentagon Papers," PP Gravel, Ch. 13, Vol. 5, Beacon Press, 1972) and not taken up again, as far as I know, until John Newman revived it in 1992 after the Stone film: that NSAM 273 in itself expressed a policy reversal:

> Also aborted by Johnson was President Kennedy's attempt in his last months, as outlined earlier, to pull America out of its Vietnam quagmire. Two days after his murder — the day Ruby shot Oswald — Lyndon Johnson called a meeting of his top advisers to discuss this issue. The results of the meeting were embodied in National Security Action Memorandum 273 of November 26, 1963, parts of which were released in the Pentagon Papers. [*] This memorandum pledged total

commitment to "denying" Vietnam to communism, authorized "specific covert operations, graduated in intensity, against the DRV" (North Vietnam), and reversed President Kennedy's movement toward a military disengagement. [**] The remaining 780 of the 1,000 troops that Kennedy had ordered out of Vietnam were never withdrawn under Johnson. And after Johnson won the 1964 presidential election by styling himself a peace candidate, his administration began to escalate American involvement (p.273-274).

The casual reader might well think that Scheim is quoting from NSMA 273 here, but his footnotes (indicated here by asterisks) are to an essay by Scott called "The Death of Kennedy and the Vietnam War" in Sid Blumenthal and Harvey Yazijian, *Government by Gunplay* (1976), which includes Scott's reconstruction of NSAM 273 (not declassified until May 1978). Scott's reconstruction includes this sentence from Ch. 4, Vol. 4 of PP Gravel, in the Chronology: [100]

26 Nov 63 NSAM 273

Authorized planning for specific covert operations, graduated in intensity, against the DRV.

There is no such sentence, however, or anything similar, in the text of NSAM 273, which we can now read.[101] I have already shown how PP NYT misrepresents PP Gravel on the question of "continuity" in Kennedy and Johnson's Vietnam policy, and here is an example of PP Gravel misrepresenting *itself* with regard to the content of NSAM 273. Perhaps this supports Scott and Newman's argument that the policy reversal is manifest in this document, perhaps (according to Chomsky) not.

Far too much attention has been given to this paper chase, which started when Newman, in 1992, following Scott's lead in 1972 (and in subsequent articles, such as the one Scheim cites), made it an issue, and Chomsky then inflamed it by vehemently contesting the Scott-Newman argument. In short, it has been much ado about nothing.

Ch. 3, Vol. 2[102] of PP Gravel tells us all we need to know about the origin, implementation, phase-down, and end of JFK's withdrawal plan. It ended *de jure* on March 27, 1964, and as Chomsky himself writes:

> The first report prepared for LBJ (November 23) opened with this "Summary Assessment": "The out-look is hopeful. There is better assurance than under Diem that the war can be won. We are pulling out 1,000 American troops by the end of 1963." ...The next day, however, CIA Director John McCone informed the President that the CIA now regarded the situation as "somewhat more serious" than had been thought, with "a continuing increase in Viet Cong activity since the first of November" (the coup). Subsequent reports only deepened the gloom (*Rethinking Camelot*, p. 91).

It doesn't matter a whit whether the reversal started on Nov. 23, 24, 26 or sometime in December or January. It happened.

My point in mentioning Scheim's book is that it was not only the first book I had read about the assassination; it was also the first time I had heard about the withdrawal policy. The Turner film hadn't mentioned Vietnam, but it made immediate sense when I read about it in Scheim's book a few weeks later. I wrote in my review:[103]

> General recollection also has it that Kennedy got us in-volved in Vietnam, but in fact he had already ordered the first withdrawal of troops when he was killed, and had planned major withdrawals by 1965.

I suspect this is exactly what millions of Americans thought and felt when they saw the Stone film in 1991-92. Yes, it had been reported in the press in 1963, but it did not become common knowledge, and in fact was "ferociously hidden," as Galbraith says, by Vietnam historians (whom Chomsky defends in this respect), for decades thereafter.

In my case it was the combination of the Turner film and Scheim's book that made what Chomsky called "uncontroversially true, and completely — totally — without interest" probably the most important event in my adult life. It turned me, almost instantaneously (because the primary shock was watching the Turner film) from a "disaffected" American into a raging dissident. What Chomsky told me in his letter of Jan. 7, 1993 had been "known to be true, and uninteresting, for almost 30 years" (he must have been counting from the McNamara-Taylor announcement on Oct. 2, 1963) was complete news to me, and was as "uninteresting" to me as if the roof of my house had fallen on my head or I had fallen through the floor. I don't want to over dramatize my personal reaction, but it is important because nobody — not even the renowned Noam Chomsky whom I had always admired (and still do in many respects) — can tell me that it is "uninteresting" to put these two facts together, the assassination and the Vietnam policy reversal, or that doing so cannot have exactly the profound emotional effect that it had on me. I am my own Exhibit A for that fact, which I later expressed in a poem:

> I felt like a volcano, watching itself erupt.[104]

Scheim, of course, as the title of his book makes clear, while revealing — rather, *publicizing* — this important truth about the assassination, at the same time buries it, submerges it, subordinates it to his main thesis, which is that "The Mafia Killed President Kennedy." It is interesting, especially after 30 years have passed since my first reading — to see how Scheim subordinates the Vietnam connection to the main theme, e.g., in the first mention of it on p. 58:

> The Florida Mafia boss [Santos Trafficante] could thus
> hardly have favored two foreign policy initiatives of

President Kennedy in the fall of 1963: moves toward accommodation with Castro and the ordered withdrawal of one thousand American troops from South Vietnam, an underworld narcotics stronghold.

Vietnam does not come up again until more than a hundred pages later, when "the ordered withdrawal of one thousand American troops from Vietnam" is mentioned as one of several policies that

> aroused the wrath of a loose coalition including the Mob, extreme right wingers and elements of the CIA that had been drawn together in the early 1960s in a common campaign to eliminate Cuban Premier Fidel Castro (p. 183).

These other policies were "the test ban treaty and announced armaments reductions, civil rights initiatives...and the escalated war against organized crime."

In the next chapter, "The Anti-Castro Coalition," Scheim presents in one and a half pages an accurate enough summary of the antagonism between Kennedy and the CIA after the Bay of Pigs and his peace initiatives toward the Soviets after the Missile Crisis, which does not differ significantly from the more detailed account, for example, in James Douglass's *JFK and the Unspeakable* (Orbis, 2008), concluding with a long paragraph about Vietnam:

> In the spring of 1963, President Kennedy told aide Kenneth O'Donnell of his determination to withdraw American forces from Vietnam after the November election, commenting, "I'll be damned everywhere as a communist appeaser. But I don't care." On October 2, 1963, Defense Secretary McNamara and General Maxwell Taylor reported that it was their objective to terminate the "major part" of U.S. military involvement in Vietnam by 1965. Specifically, they predicted that

1,000 U.S. troops would be withdrawn from there by
the end of 1963. On October 31, in a news conference,
President Kennedy reaffirmed his administration's intention to pull out these 1,000 troops. The first 220
of them were withdrawn on December 3, 1963, as directed by Kennedy's prior order (p. 187).

In the next paragraph, with no logical transition, Scheim re-
turns to his main theme of the loathing of the extreme right,
anti-Castro Cubans, and Mob-connected elements of the CIA
for Kennedy, whose "aspirations," he concludes, "were dashed
by President Kennedy's steps toward détente, his civil rights
initiatives, and the Vietnam troop withdrawals he ordered" (p.
194).

There follow 79 more pages about Jack Ruby's Cuban and Mob
connections, "Nationwide Mob Contacts," etc. Scheim concludes that the "assassination of President Kennedy succeeded
in stopping the administration's crushing assault on the Mob"
but "also aborted other initiatives of President Kennedy that
the Mob's allies in the anti-Castro coalition found objection-
able." These included a "major cut in defense spending,"
"moves toward accommodation with Cuba," support of Juan
Bosch in the Dominican Republic (who opposed the Mob and
might have returned to power), and then, finally, the long paragraph quoted above about JFK's attempt "to pull America out of
its Vietnam quagmire."

Scheim embeds the Vietnam policy reversal within his larger
thesis, reducing it to merely

> the first of several hints that the sinister alliance be-
> tween the underworld and elements of the CIA that
> surfaced in assassination plots against Castro was res-
> urrected after President Kennedy's death. The point of
> collaboration this time was narcotics... For all but the
> Mob heroin traffickers, the Vietnam War was thus one

of the most unfortunate consequences of the murder of President Kennedy (pp. 274-275).

If I were a state propagandist, I would welcome a book like this. First, I would be glad to see the facts about JFK and Vietnam (the withdrawal policy reversal) getting out into the broad public where they can be seen, heard, smelled, and tossed around. This, as one may learn from "inoculation theory,"[105] is a way to expose people to potentially dangerous knowledge in an attenuated form so that they will build up a resistance to it when a stronger variety comes along. Here virtually the whole truth about the assassination is inserted into the body politic but in attenuated form, as only part of the much larger context of a conspiracy involving a sinister alliance of Mobsters, rogue "elements" of the CIA, anti-Castro Cubans and extreme right-wing fanatics.

The process of subordinating one truth to another one, perhaps both equally true from an evidentiary point of view, but where one is presented as the main, "larger" truth, and the other as the subordinate, "smaller" truth can be called *co-option*. Here, the "smaller" truth of the policy reversal is embedded in, overshadowed by, *co-opted* by the "larger" one of the sinister Mafia alliance controlling almost everything, including foreign policy.

These two processes, inoculation and co-option, pursued energetically, lead to a place which I call Ronaldland, after Stephen Leacock's hero who "flung himself upon his horse and rode madly off in all directions."[106] There we will find John Newman working on the fourth or fifth volume of his JFK assassination research[107] and his colleague Peter Dale Scott engrossed in "parapolitics" and "deep politics" (both terms he invented). To see how this relates to "Who Killed JFK?" Scott says we must look beyond (or under) "Texas oilmen, organized crime, the Dallas police, and army intelligence" to find "the key to a credible model for what happened" and to understand "the deep political system" comprised of "connections and relationships of long standing, immune to disclosure, and capable of great crimes." Echoing David Scheim, Scott says:

> The postwar international alliance between intelligence and drug traffickers is perhaps the best-documented instance of such a connection, one where denial persists despite limited revelations about the 1960-63 plots to murder Fidel Castro. It is not the only such connection, and indeed merges with others, notably unassailable networks responsible for gambling and prostitution in the United States.
>
> There are two other special reasons for suspecting the intelligence-sanctioned drug networks in particular. One is their role in connecting so many disparately centered different networks, from FBN [Federal Bureau of Narcotics] and FBI to foreign casinos to local corruption in Dallas and elsewhere. The other is their key role in transnational connections to the deep politics of Mexico and Nicaragua, two countries clearly involved in the assassination story.[108]

This exhaustively (and exhaustingly) complex "model" must be compared with the brilliant but simple common sense of Vincent Salandria's 1971 "Model of Explanation,"[109] which inspired not only Jim Garrison but also James Douglass's highly acclaimed bestseller *JFK and the Unspeakable* (2008). Like Salandria and Garrison, Douglass says:

> We have no evidence as to who in the military-industrial complex may have given the order to assassinate President Kennedy. That the order was carried out by the Central Intelligence Agency is obvious. The CIA's fingerprints are all over the crime and the events leading up to it.[110]

In the course of experimenting in the dark truth

of JFK's death, the ongoing, deepening historical hypothesis of this book has been that the CIA coordinated and carried out the president's murder.[111]

He waffles only slightly when he goes on to say:

> To tell the truth at the heart of darkness in this story, one must see and accept a responsibility that goes deeper and far beyond the Central Intelligence Agency.
>
> The CIA was the coordinating instrument that killed the president, but the question of responsibility is more systemic, more personal, and more chilling.[112]

The "unspeakable" truth involves not only the silence of various witnesses but "a larger conspiracy of silence that would envelop our government, our media, our academic institutions, and virtually our entire society from November 22, 1963, to the present."[113]

This reminds me of how I ended my 1993 book *Looking for the Enemy*: "In the end, it is we who are the enemy," which I meant much as Walt Kelly meant it when he wrote "We have met the enemy and he is us"[114] and which Douglass puts this way, quoting JFK speaking to a group of Quakers:

> "The military-industrial complex is very strong. If you folks are serious about trying to get our government to take these kinds of steps [towards disarmament], you've got to get much more organized, to put pressure on the government to move in this direction."[115]

I don't expect to see any serious challenge to Douglass's book. Noam Chomsky, I'm sure, would be no more inclined to embrace the Vietnam "withdrawal without victory" thesis as embraced by Douglass than he was in 1993 when it was put forward by Newman or in 2003 when embraced by Jones and Galbraith — and much less would Chomsky be likely to agree that "Because JFK chose peace on earth at the height of the Cold

War, he was executed" (Kindle edition, Afterword, p. 1195]. But I think the discussion is over. We can think of JFK as a hawk or a dove, as we wish. Barring another Turner or Stone film, nobody is going to get too excited about it. Time works in favor of the propagandists, and this is what they have wanted all along.

2021 EPILOGUE: STUPIDITY THEORY REVISITED

[The first part of this was published on Oct. 23, 2018 at OpEd-News.com[116] and is the best I can do as far as understanding Prof. Noam Chomsky is concerned.]

In a recent article[117] David Griffin asks how Chris Hayes and Rachel Maddow, the latter "a Rhodes scholar who earned a Ph.D. at Oxford," could have both written "such poor essays about 9/11." Then he says:

> In addition, there may be another fact: I was recently told by a man (whose name I cannot reveal) that we Truthers should not waste time trying to convince journalists: They know that 9/11 was an inside job and would have liked to report this fact, but the owners of the media forbid them from doing so.

In one of her comments on the article, Griffin's colleague Elizabeth Woodworth wrote:

> Having watched the almost entirely consistent MSM news about 9/11 for more than 10 years, I have come to a logical conclusion.

> The news people are not stupid. Many of them spontaneously observed the morning of 9/11 that the [collapse of the] buildings looked like controlled demoli-

tion.

But then all that changed. And this has been no accident.

I have come to suspect that the news networks, and also influential people like Noam Chomsky, were visited by senior members of the intelligence agencies saying that to cast doubt on the official story of 9/11 would be a massive threat to national security. The networks and people such as Chomsky may even have been threatened with treason or something akin to it.

Whatever they did has worked very well.

Woodworth hits the nail on the head. I have been struggling with Noam Chomsky's views, first on JFK, then on 9/11, since 1989. I corresponded with him over the course of almost six years (1989-95) about whether or not JFK had decided to pull out of Vietnam. I think I clearly won the argument, but you can judge for yourself as I have documented the correspondence in detail here. Subsequent evidence, such as Robert McNamara's memoir,[118] has confirmed my opinion, though Chomsky still disagrees.[119] Although Chomsky thanked me at the time for (indirectly) helping him get his thoughts together for the book he later published as *Rethinking Camelot* (1993), my arguments obviously made no dent in his thinking since they did not even merit a footnote.

This experience left me, it seemed, with two possible conclusions: either I was smarter than I thought, or Chomsky was dumber than I thought. Neither has held up over time, although the second possibility, after hearing his remarks on 9/11[120] (just google "Chomsky 9/11"), seemed even more likely. Why would a man as smart as Chomsky say such stupid things? Denial, ignorance and/or stupidity just do not satisfy in Chomsky's case. Is his career at stake, as one might suspect of a working journalist like Maddow or Hayes? Hardly. He will be 90 in December. Is he concerned about his reputation, his "legacy"? Afraid that he will lose credibility and honor by aligning himself with "conspiracy theorists"? Possibly, but this is a man who has argued many an unpopular position, a man who is not afraid to call the US "the world's leading terrorist state"[121] and to argue cogently and consistently over many decades to support this view. This makes him very different from someone like Maddow or Hayes.

Why, then, does he appear to be as stupid as they are about 9/11? We should bear in mind that although Chomsky makes a lot of the distinction between "conspiracy theory" and "institutional analysis,"[122] this is a false dichotomy. One could easily say that these events were "merely" ineluctable consequences of "the system." "Institutional" analysis does not preclude conspiracies. A conspiracy is by definition anything bad planned secretly by more than one person, which can include wars, "state terror," and all forms of oppression. Since all governments at least sometimes do these things, to that extent they could all be considered "conspiratorial."

What this false dichotomy really does is move the analysis to a level of abstraction where all the actors are seen as caught up in systemic or institutional processes in which their individual actions are relatively unimportant. This defangs the entire analysis on an emotional level, making it less volatile and less politically dangerous.

Why these two subjects, and as it would seem, only these? Because precisely the contrary of what Chomsky says about them is true: they are important, and what he says about them is also important. Just imagine the consequences of Noam Chomsky saying that 9/11 was an inside job. It wouldn't matter if this were part of an "institutional analysis" (which it easily could be) or not. The political effect of saying it either way would be the same.

I do not believe in what I have called Stupidity Theory.[123] This is the theory according to which not only is Noam Chomsky too stupid to come to grips with the assassination of JFK and 9/11, but a succession of US governments were also too stupid to do so, just as they were too stupid to realize that the Vietnam war was a bad idea, too stupid to know that the Gulf of Tonkin "attack" never happened, too stupid to defend the country against 19 box-cutter-wielding Arabs, too stupid to find out if Saddam Hussein had "weapons of mass destruction," etc. — and now, bringing us up to the present, too stupid to prevent the Russians from controlling US elections.

In opposition to Stupidity Theory I propose Anti-Stupidity, or Transparency Theory. This is a very simple theory, in fact only common sense: Some things are just too stupid to believe. This means that something else, something that would be obvious if it were not for the stupid explanations to the contrary, is true. In Chomsky's case it is his seemingly brainless accept-ance of the official account of the assassination and 9/11.

Vincent Salandria applied this notion, brilliantly and preco-ciously, in 1971 to the JFK assassination.[124] It is from him that I have the term "transparency" to refer to 9/11 because what Salandria said about the JFK assassination can be said in spades about 9/11: "If you are tempted to want to believe that our leaders are just ignorant and capable of unremitting blun-dering, I urge that you abandon any such illusion."

I don't think Chomsky is the smartest man in the world, and I also know that I am not smarter than he is. But I cannot bring myself to believe that he is on the government payroll or a deep-cover agent of some kind, either. I think he really is bril-liant, well informed, and well intentioned, so there is another possibility. Maybe he is trying to tell us something, in code. Maybe he hopes that by saying what is too stupid to believe, we will be smart enough not to believe it.

This is the end of my long odyssey in the "cloud of unknowing" that emerged from the Vietnam war and the assassination of President Kennedy, which merged almost seamlessly into 9/11 (as well as other topics such as the origin of the AIDS virus), and my attempt to understand not only these events but also the diametrically opposed attitudes of Noam Chomsky and Fletcher Prouty towards them. Fletcher died on June 5, 2001 and I was not able to learn what his thoughts may have been about 9/11, but I am fairly certain that he would agree with me — and David Ray Griffin — on that subject.

It has been a long and hard road, costing me a lot of time and energy, and many will say it has been wasted. Those who agree with Chomsky on the matters discussed here will dismiss Prouty as unworthy of attention, and those who agree with Prouty on Vietnam and the assassination and with David Ray Griffin on 9/11 will dismiss Chomsky as unworthy of attention (or worse). I have done my best to give both Chomsky and Prouty (and of course Griffin, whom I have not discussed because I agree with him on virtually everything) my full attention, and this book is my testimony to this effort.

FOOTNOTES

In some of the long links below, a hyphen (-) may be inserted at the end of the line that may or may not be part of the link itself. Otherwise the link is continuous, that is, has no empty spaces, even if it continues on the next line. The necessity to keep the link continuous, except for the occasional hyphenated word, also accounts for the irregular indentations in some of the footnotes.

---

[1] Now *CovertAction Magazine*, see https://en.wikipedia.org/wiki/CovertAction_Quarterly.

[2] I had sent Chomsky a 26-page paper written in English in 1986 by Jakob Segal called "AIDS: Its Nature and Origin" and a copy of a book in German containing the German version of that paper and discussion by various scientists: *Aids - Erreger aus dem Genlabor?* (Simon und Leutner, Berlin, 1987). I did not yet have a copy of Segals' book in English published in India in 1989: *The Origin of AIDS*, (Jacob and Lilli Segal, Kerala Sastra Parishad).]

[3] See 1989.09.

[4] See 1989.11.

[5] The MacArthur testimony. See 1990.09.

[6] "Saigon Solution" was the original title of Prouty's book JFK: The Cia, Vietnam, and the Plot to Assassinate John F. Kennedy (Carol Publishing Group, 1992).

[7] https://en.wikipedia.org/wiki/Harold_Weisberg

[8] I don't have a copy of this letter, so I don't know why the numbering is wrong or why the letter ends at this paragraph. I have this from the copy preserved in the Harold Weisberg collection at internetarchive.org. I do have copies of the other letters I sent to Weisberg.

[9] See above, 1990.11.24.

[10] *Lies of Our Times* (1.7, 4-5, 1990, now defunct) and included in *Looking for the Enemy*, Ch. 3.3. Chomsky made no comment about it

[11] See 1989.9, sent to Chomsky a year earlier (see 1989.09.14).

[12] A pseudonym.

[13] It must have been either (see) 1989.9 or 1990.09.

[14] See *Looking for the Enemy*, Ch. 4.2.

[15] "The Turkish Army 'Cleans Up' the Kurds, *Lies of Our Times* now defunct) 1991, 2.10, 18-19.

[16] Archived at https://www.maryferrell.org/showDoc.html?docId-=48765#relPageId=16&tab=page.

[17] There is a newer edition, which I have not scrutinized carefully, but I don't think there are any significant differences in his argument that I am summarizing here.

[18] The "propaganda model" proposed in *Manufacturing Consent* attributes the media's subservience to government and big business to the interlocking and pyramid-like connections of ownership. Orwell's problem, as Chomsky has expressed it, is "How is it that we know so little?" – as opposed to Plato's problem, which is "How is it that we know so much?"

[19] According to a *Time*/CNN poll taken just before the film was released, 73% of Americans thought the assassination was a conspiracy, and 68% of these (i.e. 49.6% of all Americans) said the CIA or the US military may have been involved (*Time*, Jan. 13, 1992, European ed., p. 40).

[20] Chomsky has said and written this on many occasions.

[21] "The Bay of Pigs Revisited," originally published on the internet on May 2, 1993, later in *The Fourth Decade*, Vol. 1, No. 2 (Jan. 1994, archived here: https://www.maryferrell.org/showDoc.html?docId=48679#relPageId=19&tab=page) and expanded in *Looking for the Enemy*, Ch. 1.

[22] "Taylor, for one," Chomsky had told me, "was dragging his feet on this well into 1965. The chiefs remained ambiguous. Shoup called publicly for withdrawal, in the strongest terms, in 1965, at a time when all the Kennedy folk were still extreme hawks" (May 21, 1992).

[23] Chomsky had referred to "the CIA, or whoever," who would have had far more reason to knock off LBJ in favor of a real alternative:

Goldwater. LBJ "was more dovish than JFK had been a year earlier," and Goldwater was an extreme hawk, so the putative warmongers would have profited from getting rid of LBJ more than from JFK (May 21, 1992).

[24] Chomsky had referred to Philip Green in a recent issue of *The Nation*, who had suggested that "maybe right-wing nuts thought" JFK was going to abort their war. "Sure, maybe," Chomsky wrote. "On that 'theory' anything that happens gets an explanation: it was done by right-wing nuts, who may have thought... That's desperation, not political analysis" (May 21, 1992).

[25] Chomsky had said that he thought it would be "a good idea" for people who thought the assassination was an important issue "to keep away from policy questions where there is a record that can be investigated."

[26] Chomsky had offered me the following example of conspiracy craziness:

"Thus when the National Academy of Sciences refutes by careful experiment the one reason offered by the House Committee to question the Warren Report, we can simply conclude that the scientists are in on the conspiracy. Anyone who knows them personally knows that this is laughable."

[27] Chomsky had said that assassination conspiracy theorists are "in a realm where evidence doesn't mean a lot," because they can eliminate all counterevidence "simply by appeal to the assumption," that is, by assuming the counterevidence is part of the conspiracy.

[28] See previous, 1992.12.24.

[29] See 1992.12.24.

[30] I am referring to Arthur Schlesinger's review of *JFK* ("JFK: Truth and Fiction," *Wall Street Journal*, Jan. 10, 1992). Schlesinger reads Johnson's NSAM 273 as "reversing the Kennedy withdrawal policy." But to connect this with the assassination, as Stone and Garrison do, is "reckless, paranoid, really despicable fantasy."

[31] *Newsweek* Nov. 25, 1991. See also *Looking for the Enemy*, Ch. 3.9.

[32] Chomsky had said (Feb. 11, 1993) that what I called the "coup" theory of the assassination was supported by "no evidence at all, just faith in JFK's hidden mystical qualities." We were dealing here, he said, with "faith and doctrine, not reason." He characterized this as a

"millenarian movement" in his Z article.

[33] What Chomsky had called the "M-thesis" he had now re-named "Thesis I: the US should withdraw after victory was assured" (Feb. 11, 199e). This was "basic policy," he said, that "never changed" until after the 1968 Tet offensive. "Thesis IA" was "there was a plan to implement the policy stated in Thesis I. As NSAM 263 put it, the US should plan to withdraw 1000 men by the end of 1963 and the rest by the end of 1965 if this could be done 'without impairment of the war effort.'"

[34] Chomsky had said that "JFK more or less went along with the McNamara-Taylor recommendations" but was hesitant about committing himself to the 1000-man withdrawal, "since he thought the predictions might be too optimistic." He said JFK endorsed NSAM 263 and the McNamara-Taylor plan "with reservations."

[35] Chomsky insisted that the phrase "without impairment of the war effort" in McNamara-Taylor's Recommendation 3 was the "explicit" and "crucial condition [his emphasis] of NSAM 263 (contrary to your contention that it is merely an assumption, not a condition)."

The irony of this should not be missed. Here I was explaining the difference between an assumption and a condition to the world's most famous linguist!

[36] The quotation is from the McNamara-Taylor report (PP Gravel, Vol. 2, p. 757), the conclusion of the section entitled "Military Situation and Trends":

> Acknowledging the progress achieved to date, there still remains the question of when the final military victory can be attained. If, by victory, we mean the reduction of the insurgency to something little more than sporadic banditry in outlying districts, it is the view of the vast majority of military commanders consulted that success may be achieved in the I, II and II Corps area by the end of CY 1964. Victory in the IV Corps will take longer – at least well into 1965. These estimates necessarily assume that the political situation does not significantly impede the effort.

[37] Chomsky had repeated that Thesis I and IA were uncontroversially true and therefore of no interest. "I take it you reject Thesis II as well," he said, "in which case our entire correspondence is a total waste of time, since that is the only thesis with any interest at all."

A crucial part of the "uncontroversial" truth of Thesis I and IA, however, for Chomsky, was the "condition" of "victory," which I did not accept.

[38] Chomsky had said that JFK was "hesitant enough about the prospects [for withdrawal] that he dragged his feet in October-November 1963, not entirely convinced by the optimistic pronouncements of the military and McNamara." That was why "he insisted that the 1000-man withdrawal be left as their recommendation, not part of his proposal, so he wouldn't be stuck with it." The Oct. 2, 1963 statement read:

> Secretary McNamara and General Taylor reported their judgement that the major part of the U.S. military task can be completed by the end of 1965, although there may be a continuing requirement for a limited number of U.S. training personnel. They reported that by the end of this year, the U.S. program for training Vietnamese should have progressed to the point where 1,000 U.S. military personnel assigned to South Viet-Nam can be withdrawn (*Documents on American Foreign Relations 1963*, Council on Foreign Relations, New York: Harper & Row, 1964, p. 296).

[39] Chomsky had said that JFK "indicated his hesitations right through November, always distancing himself from the withdrawal plans publicly announced by the military, and refusing to commit himself to them."

[40] And not attributable, for example, to a document drafted by McGeorge Bundy and that we are supposed to assume JFK would have signed, i.e. either the draft of final version of NSAM 273.

[41] Chomsky had said I was evading the question he had asked about Schlesinger et al. Since they mentioned JFK's withdrawal plan only after Tet 1968, were they 1) "lying, pre-Tet," 2) had JFK kept it a secret from his closest advisers, or 3) were there in fact "no plans to withdraw without victory"? "A rational person," Chomsky said, "will, naturally, assume (3)." I, he said, was "continually evading the question by shifting from Thesis II to Thesis I (or the specific implementation of I, IA), which is too uninteresting to discuss."

[42] Chomsky had written that after the Diem coup, "it became clear that the optimistic projections were built on sand." Doubts mounted through November and "were aired among the top advisers" at the Nov. 20 Honolulu meeting, and in the draft 273, which "everyone ex-

pected" JFK to sign, "some modifications can be detected."

[43] Para. 2 of NSAM 273, in both the draft and the final version, reads:

> The objectives of the United States with respect to the withdrawal of U.S. military personnel remain as stated in the White House statement of October 2, 1963.

The point I was making – simple enough, one would think, but obviously not in this conversation – was that one only has to take this sentence at face value to establish the fact that the withdrawal policy was reversed at a later time (and therefore also after the assassination).

[44] As Chomsky had put it, "From late December it became clear that withdrawal could not be carried out 'without impairment of the war effort.'" Therefore, "the plan to implement withdrawal on condition of military victory had to be cancelled by early 1964." None of JFK's top advisers "had any criticism of LBJ for departing from JFK's position – the reason being, of course, that they sensed no departure."

[45] Chomsky had repeated his belief that the conspiracy I envisioned "must be huge" because there is "not a hint, not a phrase" in the "declassified record" indicating that anyone suspected "any high-level involvement in the assassination." Thus a conspiracy would have required either "astonishingly well-disciplined" internal discussions, or a complete sanitization and rewriting of the whole documentary history, involving historians, physicists, physicians and high-level officials since "not one word has leaked, even in private gossip, for 30 years." This would have been "a miraculous series of events, absolutely unprecedented in history or personal experience."

[46] This first (1993) "edition" of *Looking for the Enemy* was basically a photocopy reduced, printed and bound by a machine that I think was called an "offset printer." There were only 50 copies. I republished slightly revised versions in 2007 and 2008.

[47] I regret my tone in this letter, but Chomsky's was no less combative. Oddly, it seemed my letter to Newman that upset him most. He wrote (March 13, 1995):

> After having read your utterly convincing theory of Newman being an agent, programmed to write a book that could easily be dismissed in standard black propaganda style so as to conceal the real truth, maybe that's true of others too. There is someone who comes to mind. How

about fessing up, finally, before someone else notices it too. Or maybe that would be too dangerous: the CIA has its ways of dealing with traitors, as we know.

[48] See 2008.06.15.

[49] http://home.rmi.net/~jkelin/fp.html; now defunct and is also archived at http://educate-yourself.org/cn/morrisseybeefwith-chomsky2000.shtml

[50] https://www.veteranstoday.com/2019/01/27/vietnam-how-they-played-us/

[51] E.g., here is an interview from 2018: https://www.youtube.com/watch?v=5OMqHnoDEts&fbclid=IwAR3XNgou2tG1jXEamfUFYWRRXst-hH1HATAAzcNJdgYZcR3vYMOs9XA-VUA.

[52] See 1989.04.

[53] See 1992.92.

[54] https://www.amazon.com/False-Witness-Garrisons-Investiga-tion-Oliver/dp/0871318792/ref=sr_1_1?ie=UTF8&qid=1546270328&sr=8-1&keywords=False+Witness%3A+The+Real+Story+of+Jim+Garrison%27s+Investigation+and+Oliver+...

[55] https://www.freedommag.org/english/30thanni/page29a.htm

[56] https://classic.esquire.com/article/1991/11/1/the-shooting-of-jfk

[57] https://jfkjmn.com/about/

[58] 1994.10.20.

[59] 1994.11.05.

[60] https://en.wikipedia.org/wiki/CovertAction_Quarterly

[61] https://en.wikipedia.org/wiki/Lies_of_Our_Times

[62] 1992.02.

[63] https://chomsky.info/199209__/

[64] 1992.12.24.

[65] https://www.mtholyoke.edu/acad/intrel/pentagon2/pent5.htm

[66] https://history.state.gov/historicaldocuments/frus1961-63v04/d167

[67] https://jfkjmn.com/

[68]   https://www.amazon.com/gp/product/153047793X/ref=dbs_a_def_rwt_hsch_vapi_taft_p1_i2.

[69]   https://www.amazon.com/Death-Generation-Assassinations-Prolonged-Vietnam-dp-0195052862/dp/0195052862/ref=mt_hardcover?_encoding=UTF8&me=&qid=1547030929

[70] See 1993.09, 1994.05, 2000.09, and 2008.06.15. "Chomsky and Newman – the False Debate" is omitted here because it contains much of the same material in this chapter, but see http://911blogger.com/blog/220?page=1 and https://sites.google.com/site/michaeldavid-morrissey/essays/2008-06-15-chomsky-and-newman-the-false-debate.

[71] http://bostonreview.net/archives/BR28.5/galbraith.html#fnr7

[72] See 1992.06,18.

[73] https://www.mtholyoke.edu/acad/intrel/pentagon2/pent5.htm

[74] https://history.state.gov/historicaldocuments/frus1961-63v04/d179

[75] https://history.state.gov/historicaldocuments/frus1961-63v04/d194

[76] https://www.mtholyoke.edu/acad/intrel/pentagon2/pent5.htm

[77]   https://web.archive.org/web/20070703224833/http:/www.democracynow.org/article.pl?sid=07%2F07%2F02%2F1331255

[78] https://www.mtholyoke.edu/acad/intrel/pentagon2/pent5.htm

[79] https://history.state.gov/historicaldocuments/frus1961-63v04/d331

[80] https://archive.org/stream/pentagonpapersde04beac/pentagon-papersde04beac_djvu.txt

[81] https://history.state.gov/historicaldocuments/frus1961-63v04/d331

[82] https://www.mtholyoke.edu/acad/intrel/pentagon2/pent5.htm

[83] https://www.mtholyoke.edu/acad/intrel/pentagon2/pent5.htm

[84] See *Looking for the Enemy*, Ch. 2.

[85] https://en.wikipedia.org/wiki/1964_South_Vietnamese_coup

[86] https://chomsky.info/19670223/

[87] http://bostonreview.net/archives/BR28.5/galbraith.html

[88] 2008.06.15.

[89] https://jfkjmn.com/blog/jfk-and-vietnam-2nd-ed

[90] http://bostonreview.net/archives/BR28.6/letters.html

[91] http://bostonreview.net/archives/BR28.5/galbraith.html

[92] https://www.mtholyoke.edu/acad/intrel/pentagon2/pent5.htm

[93] https://www.thebalance.com/vietnam-war-facts-definition-costs-and-timeline-4154921

[94] See *Correspondence with Vincent Salandria* (2007).

[95] https://ratical.org/ratville/JFK/FalseMystery/LawyersDissentingView.html

[96] Archived at https://ratical.org/ratville/JFK/FalseMystery/ConfrontingMilitaryMadness.html.

[97] https://ratical.org/ratville/JFK/FalseMystery/ModelOfExplanation.html

[98] https://www.freedommag.org/english/30thanni/page29a.htm

[99] https://en.wikipedia.org/wiki/JFK_(film)

[100] https://www.mtholyoke.edu/acad/intrel/pentagon3/pent3.htm

[101] https://history.state.gov/historicaldocuments/frus1961-63v04/d331

[102] https://history.state.gov/historicaldocuments/frus1961-63v04/d331

[103] See 1989.04.

[104] "Butcher Shop," in *Looking for the Enemy*.

[105] https://en.wikipedia.org/wiki/Inoculation_theory

[106] https://en.wikipedia.org/wiki/Stephen_Leacock

[107] https://jfkjmn.com/

[108] *Deep Politics and the Death of JFK*, Univ. of California Press, 1993, pp. 299-300.

[109] https://ratical.org/ratville/JFK/FalseMystery/ModelOfExplanation.html

[110] Kindle edition, 2011, Ch. 4, pp. 414.

[111] Kindle edition, Ch. 6, p. 811.

[112] Kindle edition, Ch 6, p. 811.

[113] Kindle edition, Ch. 6, p. 827.

[114] https://en.wikipedia.org/wiki/Pogo_(comic_strip)#%22We_have_met_the_enemy_and_he_is_us.%22

[115] Kindle edition, Ch. 6, p. 846.

[116] https://www.opednews.com/articles/Stupidity-Theory-Re-visited-by-Michael-Morrissey-Chris-Hayes_Conspiracy_David-Ray-Griffin_Intelligence-181023-117.html

[117] https://www.opednews.com/articles/Fake-News-9-11-and-MSNBC-by-David-Ray-Griffin-911_Chris-Hayes_Rachel-Maddow-181020-903.html

[118] *In Retrospect*, Vintage Books, 1996.

[119] https://www.youtube.com/watch?v=50MqHnoDEts

[120] https://en.wikipedia.org/wiki/Political_positions_of_Noam_Chomsky#Views_on_9/11_conspiracy_theories

[121] https://truthout.org/articles/the-leading-terrorist-state/

[122] https://zcomm.org/zblogs/9-11-institutional-analysis-vs-conspiracy-theory-by-noam-chomsky/

[123] See *The Transparent Conspiracy*.

[124] https://ratical.org/ratville/JFK/FalseMystery/ModelOfExplanation.html

Lightning Source UK Ltd.
Milton Keynes UK
UKHW021709271022
411196UK00013B/1946